EDUCATIONAL AND PSYCHOLOGICAL PERSPECTIVES ON STRESS IN STUDENTS, TEACHERS, AND PARENTS

EDUCATIONAL AND PSYCHOLOGICAL PERSPECTIVES ON STRESS IN STUDENTS, TEACHERS, AND PARENTS

Beeman N. Phillips
The University of Texas at Austin

Clinical Psychology Publishing Co., Inc.
4 Conant Square
Brandon, Vermont 05733

Library of Congress Cataloguing-in-Publication Data

Phillips, Beeman N.
   Educational and psychological perspectives on stress in students,
teachers, and parents / Beeman N. Phillips.
      p.   cm.
   Includes bibliographical references (p.) and index.
   ISBN 0-88422-122-9
   1. Counseling in elementary education — United States. 2. Stress
in children — United States. 3. Stress (Psychology) — United States.
4. Teachers — United States — Job stress. 5. Stress management —
Study and teaching — United States. I. Title.
   LB1027.5.P523   1993
   372. 14'6—dc20   92-75446
                                                          CIP

Library of Congress Catalog Card Number: 92-75446
ISBN: 0-88422-122-9

 4 Conant Square
Brandon, Vermont 05733

Cover design: Sue Thomas

Printed in the United States of America.

CONTENTS

Preface vii

Chapter 1. Building Bridges Between Stress Research and School
Reform: An Overture 1

Chapter 2. Targeting Students with Stress-Related Problems for Special
Educational and Psychological Services 17

Chapter 3. Stress, Coping, and Adaptational Outcomes 37

Chapter 4. Stress Intervention in the Schools:
Some General Considerations 55

Chapter 5. Stress and Behavior Settings in Schools 75

Chapter 6. Developmental Aspects of Stress: The Transition
of Students from Childhood to Adolescence 93

Chapter 7. Stress in Special School Populations 111

Chapter 8. Stress of Families with Handicapped Children and
Adolescents 131

Chapter 9. Stress Factors Associated with Family, School, and
Community Violence 147

Chapter 10. What We Can Learn About Stress from
"Vulnerable but Invincible" Children and Adolescents . . . 167

Chapter 11. Stress of Teachers in the Public Schools 185

Chapter 12. Key Tasks Underlying Successful and Enduring
            Stress Interventions in the Schools 201

References   223

Indexes   257

PREFACE

The lives of children and adolescents have always been stressful. Stress is an inescapable part of existence. All kinds of events and experiences, positive as well as negative, can evoke stress. At the ordinary end of this spectrum are such experiences and events as getting into a fight, being punished, doing poorly on a test, being chosen captain of the team, receiving a coveted gift, visiting a favorite grandparent, or going on one's first date. At the more severe end is the stress caused by the death of a parent, having a chronic illness, being developmentally disabled, being the victim of child abuse and neglect, and repeating a grade level.

Stress is nevertheless a phenomenon that is not easily defined. Biologists define stress as an independent variable, social scientists construe stress as an intervening variable, and clinicians and other helping professionals regard stress as a dependent variable or as part of a syndrome. Stress has also come to be viewed in public health as an umbrella term to characterize the manner in which maladaptive life-style choices yield a harvest of ill health.

Moreover, the stress of children and adolescents was not one of yesterday's "hot" topics. Although volumes on the subject of adult stress proliferated in the 1960s and 1970s, it was not until the 1980s that child and adolescent stress began to evoke widespread professional and research interest.

Despite this increased interest in child and adolescent stress, scientific progress has been slow, perhaps because the topic is so complex. Some advances may also have been swallowed up in the quagmire of varying definitions of stress. Another factor may be that too few well-trained investigators devoted themselves to the research problems. Stress-related research also needs to be interdisciplinary in nature.

It should not be surprising, therefore, that as I undertook the task of exploring this area I became more conscious of its vast size and undisciplined nature and the vagueness of existing maps. In fact, the literature on child and adolescent stress is in many ways like the great Okefenokee Swamp in Georgia. Attractive from a distance and especially from the air, it lures the unwary into quagmires and uncharted byways. Still, there are islands of solid ground, and exploration of them can become compelling, even addictive. Nevertheless, like many explorers, after this heady experience, I remain enchanted, although not eager to make the same trip again.

PURPOSE OF THIS BOOK

This book deals with the *other crisis* in American schools (the low achievement of students is the crisis getting most of the attention). America's students are under increasingly high levels of stress, and understanding and preventing its negative consequences is an important mission of the school of the future. This is necessary because the debilitative stress of students, teachers, and parents is a substantial obstacle to school reform and improvement.

Of course, stress alone is not a sufficient cause of the problems of America's students. To produce stress-linked learning and behavior problems, other factors such as school and family conditions and individual vulnerabilities and inadequate coping skills must also be present. Stress also represents a particular kind of relationship between the individual and the environment, and it therefore is necessary to identify the variables that underlie the relationship.

Efforts to help troubled children and adolescents should also focus on their troubled teachers and parents. One characteristic of school reforms proposed in the 1980s was the rediscovery of the teacher. Although many commission reports and national studies criticized the teaching profession, they did recognize that teachers were an essential part of the solution, and steps have been taken to help teachers improve their performance and effectiveness. Nevertheless, a high level of teacher stress persists, and its negative consequences for students, their parents, and for teachers themselves can be enormous.

It also makes sense for schools to do what they can to strengthen families. One of the lessons learned from past school reform efforts is that even the best schools cannot compensate for failure in the home. This means, among other things, that schools need to help parents develop adaptive ways of coping with family stresses related to their children's education.

OVERVIEW OF THE CONTENTS

There now are a substantial number of articles and some books on the stress of children and adolescents, but my sense is that this book differs from other books in several important ways. First, it deals with one of the pivotal issues of school reform — combating the debilitative stress and emotional illiteracy of students. Second, it frames the problem in terms of the child, the school, the family, and the community and thus widens the focus from solutions involving just the student to solutions that involve teachers, school administrators, school psychologists, other school and community professionals, parents, and policy makers. Third, this book provides multiple educational and psychological perspectives on the issues and problems of stress, stress reactions, and adaptational outcomes. Fourth, it addresses conceptual as well as practical issues and presents principles and argues for actions that hold real promise for helping students, their parents, and teachers to better cope with stress and its negative consequences. Fifth, it covers a breadth of school-related stress topics and supplies information on a wide range of stress interventions that can be used in the schools. Sixth, this book gives extra consideration to the unusual stresses and vulnerabilities of a number of different school sub-populations. Seventh, and perhaps most important, this book integrates information from a vast and widely dispersed research and professional literature. In the process of preparing scholarly chapters that have academic and practical utility, nearly 600 references were utilized.

Chapters 1 and 2 review past school reforms and show why an emphasis on stress relief for students, teachers, and parents is needed in future school reforms. Starting points for obtaining information on stressful events and experiences of students, teachers, and parents are put into focus, and opportunities for nurturing students' psychosocial well-being along with their intellectual growth are described. The challenges of creating contexts in which students, teachers, and parents can feel efficacious also are delineated. Chapters 3 and 4 look at the nature of stress, coping, and adaptational outcomes and examine general strategies and tactics for providing stress interventions in the schools. Lazarus' theory of stress and coping is discussed, as is expansion of the educational contract between the school and home to include the community. In Chapter 5, the focus is on the role of stress in different behavior settings. Special sections on homework (which involves the school and the home) and extracurricular settings are included. Chapter 6 reviews stress within a developmental framework. The transition of students from childhood to adolescence is emphasized, and the "goodness of fit" concept is elaborated. Chapter 7 takes a close look at stress in special school populations, including the handicapped, the overprivileged child, teenage mothers, and gay youth; in addition, it discusses acculturative stress. Chapter 8 addresses the stress of families with handicapped children and gives added attention to the stresses of parental involvement in special education. Chapter 9 focuses on violence in the family, school, and community as a stressor in the lives of children and adolescents. In Chapter 10, what we can learn from children and adolescents who overcome great adversity is discussed. It is further suggested that what happens to children and adolescents is partly in their genes. Chapter 11 examines the stress of teachers, including sources and consequences, and looks at solutions to teacher stress. Finally, Chapter 12 is a discussion of key tasks underlying successful and enduring stress intervention in the schools. The implications of an emerging paradigm shift in school reform also are considered.

This book is based on the research and professional literature that has accumulated over the years, especially in the past decade. It also is based on my own considerable research on school-related stress. This book is intended for school and applied educational psychologists, school counselors, and special educators; for professionals in other community agencies who work with children, adolescents, parents, and teachers; and for school administrators and other policy makers. It also should be of interest to educational and psychological researchers, and the book can be used as a text in graduate courses where stress is a major topic.

ACKNOWLEDGMENTS

In the preparation of this book, I received financial support, in the form of a Faculty Research Assignment for the 1991–92 academic year, from the University Research Institute at the University of Texas. My deep appreciation goes to the Institute and the University for making the extensive library work, which was vital to the writing of this book, possible.

I'd also like to thank several past and present graduate students. Russell Adams, Edward Gotts, Keith McNeil, Roy Martin, and Joel Meyers contributed in important ways to my earlier work on stress. I'm also grateful to Leigh Scott, Bradd Falkenberg, and Shungliang Tsai who, in conjunction with work on potential dissertation topics, prepared papers that benefited portions of Chapters 5, 8, and 11 of the book. All of them, and Annette Noorzad and Joy Bohmfalk, members of the departmental staff who taught me, as a first timer, everything I know about using the computer as a word processor, have my very deep gratitude.

In addition, I wish to thank Jack Bardon, University of North Carolina at Greensboro, Charles Spielberger, University of South Florida, and Wayne Holtzman, President, Hogg Foundation for Mental Health, for their strong support of my request for the Faculty Research Assignment that made this book possible. Thanks also to Gerald Fuller, President, CPPC, for his help in the early stages of the publication process and to Jane Todorski, a talented editor, who, through meticulous attention to things that matter, helped to make the book better. My wife, Sarah, also contributed in important ways. She understood when I was preoccupied, read and commented on an early draft, and encouraged me along the way. To her I say a heartfelt thank-you.

1 BUILDING BRIDGES BETWEEN STRESS RESEARCH AND SCHOOL REFORM: AN OVERTURE

One of the most difficult tasks in describing, explaining, and optimizing development of children and adolescents is trying to get a conceptual and operational handle on stress factors that influence development. Everyone from the most casual observer to the sophisticated scholar knows that there are myriad influences on the growing child and adolescent. There is the direct effect of mother, the age-old influence, as well as the direct and indirect effects of father, the family member attracting increasing attention during the last two decades. There are siblings as well as other relatives and peers who can affect the child's and adolescent's development. There are influences on the caregivers themselves, such as stresses in the work-place and on the pocketbook, and interactions in the community. And what about schools and schooling, neighborhoods and social class, and the pervasive influence of culture and the sometimes highly significant effect of public policy and industrial practices? Psychologists would add, of course, that we must also consider how the child or adolescent contributes to and even determines, in some cases, the nature of his or her environment. They would also remind us to consider the interaction between each of these influences, and to take into account that as the child or adolescent gets older, he or she changes and the effects of and interactions between all of these developmental influences also change.

DEFINITIONS OF SCHOOLING

How one defines schooling has an effect on one's expectations for what schools should do about stress. Those who think of schooling as narrowly defined will suggest a very different agenda for stress interventions in the schools than would those whose vision of schooling extends to all the influences and related stresses that affect young people, including peer relationships, families and neighborhoods, the mass media, and a host of other life factors. That is, there are different ways of framing the problem of stress and the role of schools in helping children and adolescents cope with it that depend on how one defines the purpose and nature of schooling.

Cremin's Views

For example, Cremin (1988) believes that we are asking too much of our schools. In describing the relationship between schools and society, he advances a definition of education that, in his view, would relieve the schools of the burden of unrealistic expectations. As a central thesis, Cremin argued that education is not synonymous with schooling and that debates about school reform must recognize the range of educational institutions in this country, and that these debates should be shaped as much by ideas as by social and political forces.

In his grand vision of American education, the public schools are freed from the excessive responsibilities we routinely place on them. But challenging the belief that public schools have the power to reshape society does not represent his loss of faith in the power of schooling. He does mean, however, that public school staff and officials should reject the blandishments of political and economic leaders who try to use the schools to solve whatever social and economic problems beset American society. In essence, he argued, we must rethink the importance of the public schools in the vast matrix of educational institutions that includes cultural centers, the mass media, and corporations. In doing so, he confronted what may be the most important school reform questions today: Is education the best solution for major social and economic problems? And should the schools be the primary institution for carrying out these educational solutions? Ultimately, he argued, we must support and encourage the public schools in those areas in which they can make a difference that really counts.

Views That Ask More of Schools

Despite Cremin's concerns about asking too much of our schools, no American institution presently generates greater expectations than our public schools. We look to the schools to solve almost every imaginable social problem and have demanded that schools lead us to a more just and equal society, restore our nation's preeminence in the world economy, reduce teenage drug addiction and pregnancies, and combat the spread of AIDS.

Comer (1980, 1986) is among those who acknowledge the significance of nonschool aspects of the lives of young people. He not only has made the case for better school–family collaborative relationships but has put his ideas into practice in several inner-city schools. One can conclude from his reports on his work that when parents are actively involved in the educational process, children and adolescents do better in school. Alternatively, problems within the family frequently place students under significant stress which, in turn, interferes with their school performance. Comer also has pointed out that, despite evidence supporting the critical link between school and family, as well as the considerable overlap of school and home socialization roles, genuine collaboration between these social systems is infrequent.

Others have envisioned an even more expanded role for schools in meeting the diverse needs of children and adolescents. Phillips (1990, especially Chapter 2), for example, has advocated a comprehensive model of schooling where "schools are centers of activity for the whole community and are open to children, parents, and other members of the community for a wide variety of activities" (p. 47). The collaborative interagency approach to providing services to students and their families that is described by Payzant (1992) is another example. His report outlines the results of a 3-year pilot project which had as its goals the delivery of combined, comprehensive services to an elementary school serving disadvantaged students and their families. In the process, the project developed a strategy for interagency collaboration and change. Although it is too early to tell what the outcomes of this project will be, the author reports some potentially important insights about the collaborative process when the institutionalization of long-term systemic changes in school–community relationships is a major goal. One other example is the Hogg Foundation for Mental Health *School of the Future* project (Holtzman, 1992). The Foundation has committed a large sum of money to demonstrate the effectiveness of the *School of the Future* concept in four different communities. Under this concept, which has been the stimulus for a variety of other school innovations, an integrated array of human services, both treatment and prevention, are provided, using the school as the locus for their delivery. Essential features of this conception of schooling include: (1) the integration of a broad spectrum of human services in the schools, (2) involvement of parents and teachers in program activities, and (3) involvement of both the public and the private sector.

Based on the belief that serious social and economic conditions defeat the advancement of schooling among young Americans, other advocates of school reform have argued that educational initiatives must include a focus on how the government might lessen the effects of poverty, family instability, and other debilitative societal factors on children and adolescents. For example, Boyer (1991) reports "that the family may be a more imperiled institution than the school and that many of education's failures relate to problems that precede schooling, even birth itself" (p. 3). Expressing a similar line of thought, Jaeger (1992) examined international studies which show that American students typically score well below students of similar age and grade levels in other industrialized nations and found that the amount of time students are exposed to instruction and a variety of classroom instruction factors predicted only *trivial* amounts of between-nation variance, whereas societal factors (such as economic support, family structure and stability) were *major* sources of national difference in performance.

The role of societal factors also is emphasized by Hodgkinson (1991), who pointed out that "one-third of preschool children are destined for school failure because of poverty, neglect, sickness, handicapping conditions, and lack of adult protection and nurturance" (p. 10). In the same vein, Kozol (1991) emphasizes the financial plight of inner-city schools and says that there are places in America where schools are destroying the prospects of children for lack of funds. Hewlett (1991) has also said that neglecting children is costly, and that prevention and early intervention are cheaper in the long run. In essence, these authors issue a call for broad-ranging action on behalf of children and youth.

DIFFERENT WAYS TO FRAME PROBLEMS OF CHILDREN AND ADOLESCENTS AT RISK FOR SCHOOL FAILURE

In heeding this call to action, one also becomes sensitive to the different ways that the problems of children and adolescents at risk for school failure can be framed. In one view, students who perform poorly in school lack ability, motivation, or character and thus are responsible for their poor performance. In another, families that are poor, lack education, and don't teach their children proper behavior fail to prepare their children for school, and this is why the children do poorly. But there are two alternative views represented in the literature on school failure. One is that students fail because the culture of the school ignores or degrades their cultural and community backgrounds and neglects the strengths that these children bring to school. The other is that school programs are seldom adapted to students' backgrounds and diverse abilities and interests.

Of these two sets of views, the more common explanation for school failure locates the problem in the students or in their families, and when the problems are attributed to deficits in children or families, the solutions include early education, compensatory education, longer school days, higher standards, and a variety of training and family support programs for parents. However, framing the problem in terms of the child, family, *and* the school and community widens the focus from solutions involving only the child and family to solutions in which teachers, administrators, other school professionals, and leaders in the community assume responsibility for also altering their views and practices to accommodate differences among students.

SCHOOL REFORM

The education scene churned with words and deeds during the 1980s. Carried by the brisk winds that blew across the education landscape, school reform seemed to move in every direction at once, although no shared vision and sense of community emerged. A great many reports about school reform were published, however, and there were many piecemeal reforms put in place.

Reports of Commissions and Study Groups

In this decade of discussion, there was an outpouring of public comment about the state of schools and schooling that saturated the American consciousness. In 1983, *A Nation at Risk*, prepared by the National Commission on Excellence in Education (1983), set an alarmist tone about the state of public schooling in this country, based primarily on comparisons of achievement of American students with those in other countries. Although sponsored by the U.S. Department of Education, the national commission was broadly representative of groups with an interest in schools and schooling.

Other reports soon followed. One was *Action for Excellence*, produced in 1984 by a task force appointed by the Education Commission of the States, which spelled out reform initiatives that states should take (Task Force on Education for Economic Growth, 1984). Another was the 1985 report on *Investing in Our Children* by the Committee for Economic Development (1985), which focused on the business community's priorities for the schools, although it also paid considerable attention to early childhood education. Still another report, *A Nation Prepared: Teachers for the 21st Century*, produced by a Carnegie task force in 1986, focused on teachers and conditions of teaching (Carnegie Task Force on Teaching as a Profession, 1986).

The myriad social problems and issues that affect special populations of students also have been addressed in group reports. One 1985 Education Commission of the States report, *Reconnecting Youth,* dealt with at-risk students (Business Advisory Commission, 1985). Another that was released in 1989, *Turning Points: Preparing American Youth for the 21st Century,* had a more general emphasis on the plight of poor and minority youth (Task Force on Education of Young Adolescents, 1989). This report dealt with eight essential principles for transforming the education of young adolescents that cut across subject-matter boundaries. In a similar vein, a broad perspective on needed reforms in science education is provided in *Science for All Americans*, a 1989 report by Project 2061 (American Association for the Advancement of Science, 1989).

The "forgotten half" of America's youth is the focus of a Grant Foundation report released in 1988 that is titled *Non-College Youth in America* (Commission on Work, Family, and Citizenship, 1988a). It calls attention to the 20 million Americans between the ages of 16 and 24 who are not likely to embark on a college education, and offers 10 recommendations to better serve the educational and other needs of these young people. In particular, it explores ways in which a range of community institutions, acting in concert with the schools, can better serve these American youth.

The crumbling infrastructure of the public schools has also been the focus of group reports. Capital funding for new school construction and for renovation is a rapidly growing problem. One of the most articulate warnings of this need came in 1989 when the Education Writers Association released a report titled *Wolves at the Schoolhouse Door* (Education Writers Association, 1989). This report estimated that school districts need $84 billion immediately for new construction and the renovation of old buildings and another $41 billion to take care of deferred maintenance and repairs. This report gave special emphasis to the needs of rural districts, even though urban school districts are in equally bad, if not worse, shape (see, e.g., Piccigallo, 1989).

Overall, the reports during the 1980s that came from commissions and study groups have relied on exhortations about the need to improve the public schools. Advocacy, in which equity is viewed as a lingering and neglected issue, has been stressed in other reports. And some have looked at reforms from the point of view of the school and the classroom. But one cumulative effect of such reports was a clearer recognition of an expanded national interest in improved schooling.

Actions, Actions, Actions

The visibility of the education reform movement in the 1980s is also indicated by the many actions that occurred. Starting with the premise that learning can be legislated (Wise, 1979), the first wave of activity emanated from the statehouse, as governors and legislators swept into action. According to Darling-Hammond and Berry (1988), there were 700 pieces of legislation enacted from 1983 to 1985 alone. The focus of these statutes was first on efficiency, next on teacher-proofing the curriculum, and then a return to the basics. In essence, they stipulated what should be taught, when it should be taught, and by whom it should be taught.

In the view of many, this mass of regulations imposed by the states usurped the authority that appropriately belongs to teachers, parents, and local communities. Teachers, in particular, felt overwhelmed by these mandates. Their morale declined and they were overburdened with paperwork and nonteaching duties (Boyer, 1988). With so much negative reaction to this top-down wave of legislation and regulation, a second bottom-up wave of school reform was ushered in. In it, reformers began to look to local schools, to teachers, and to community leaders to lead the educational improvement effort.

Examples of this second wave of reform include: School-site management (see, e.g., Clune & Witte, 1990), choice plans (see, e.g., Raywid,
1989), accountability for outcomes (see, e.g., Finn, 1990), the effective
schools model (see, e.g., Bancroft & Lezotte, 1985), partnerships or
collaborative relationships between business and the public schools (see,
e.g., Kearns & Doyle, 1988), school-sponsored programs featuring direct
participation of students in the community (see, e.g., Conrad & Hedin,
1991), computer technology and integrated instructional systems (see,
e.g., Collins, 1991), and early child care and education (see, e.g., National
Governors' Association, 1987).

Other reform efforts have been based on principles or values. For
example, the Coalition of Essential Schools (see, e.g., Houston, 1989)
stresses nine core principles to which the more than 100 participating
schools subscribe. Among these principles are the following: helping
adolescents use their minds well, establishing school goals that apply to
all students, personalized learning, and helping students achieve mastery
of a limited number of essential skills and areas of knowledge. Overall,
the Coalition regards redefinition of the school's mission as central to its
efforts.

The "Success for All" program is another example (see, e.g., Madden,
Slavin, Karweit, Dolan, & Wasik, 1990). Some of the important elements
of this model are: reading tutors, a reading program that includes regroup-
ing of students so that all are at the same level of reading performance,
8-week reading assignments, balanced and developmentally appropriate
preschool and kindergarten learning experiences, a family support team
resting on the basic tenet that parents are an essential part of the formula
for success, a program facilitator, extensive teacher training, an advisory
committee, and service to special education students in the regular classroom whenever possible. Preliminary evaluation of outcomes has demonstrated the importance of having additional resources in urban schools, and
the importance of using them in a coordinated way, although money does
matter and the costs of success are high.

In other reform efforts that have focused on urban schools, especially
the high school level, the aim has been to redesign the graded school
which, according to Oakes (1985) and others, is primarily responsible for
the academic failure of students in urban schools. There are certain features of these schools, programs, and classrooms that are important mark-
ers of these efforts to improve schooling (see, e.g., Carnegie Foundation
for the Advancement of Teaching, 1988). For example, such programs are

small, with small class sizes that allow more enduring face-to-face contact and personalized instruction. Teachers also volunteer for these programs and share a strong commitment to educating at-risk students. In addition, teaching is flexible, and working with small groups and individual students is common. Few, if any, distinctions are made among students. Tests are used only to match students with appropriate material, and passing and failing are viewed only as personal benchmarks. Students also are linked with a wide array of community social services. Overall, the aim in these schools is for the school, program, or classroom to become an extended family, where a sense of belonging is developed.

Family–school relationships have been the primary emphasis of other urban school reform activities (see, e.g., Comer, 1986). The premise of this parent participation model is that parents can play a major role in creating a desirable context for teaching and learning. A key element in Comer's projects is the school management team which includes parents as well as the principal, teachers, and support staff. With this as the key, a master plan is created that includes building-level objectives, goals, and strategies in the areas of school climate, academics, and staff development. Over time, parents are called upon to participate in all three areas, although such participation tends to fall mainly in the area of school climate. In essence, the parent participation model is designed to preserve and nurture critical elements of the interaction of parents with teachers and administrators.

A Summing Up

To sum up, schools in this country are at a critical juncture. There are parts of the educational and political spectrum that seem bent on working to narrow the vision of schools, whereas other parts are seeking to expand the role of schools. Nevertheless, both American society and America's schools have changed and are changing. There is widespread realization of the need to realign curriculum and instruction with the needs of society and with research. Teacher educators are rethinking how they educate teachers. Site-based management of schools has empowered many school systems to make significant changes. Inflation-adjusted funding for public schools also nearly doubled in the 1980s, and more resources are available from business and foundations than ever before. And increasing numbers of politicians and policy makers have made schools a top priority.

There also are indications that another wave of school reform began in the early 1990s. Educators and policy makers, community and businesss leaders, and school psychologists and other school professionals have recognized that piecemeal reform of schools did not work, and that schools cannot solve the educational, social, and political problems they face by themselves. To solve these problems, the vision for public education must be clarified, and school reform must be fundamental, structural, and all-encompassing.

STRESS AND THE SCHOOLS

In a larger sense, therefore, the reforms of the 1980s were a warm-up exercise for the school reforms of the 1990s. Thus, the good news is that by the end of the 1980s the entire school community finally joined hands to clarify further the role of the schools, and to make schools more effective for the young. The bad news, though, is that the concept of stress has not been very evident in past school reforms. In essence, in response to the question, "Where is the concept of stress in school reform?" one would be forced to conclude, after review of a great many school reform efforts, that the answer is, "Mostly nowhere."

This leads, of course, to the question of "Why?" Why has stress and its debilitative consequences not been an important consideration in past school reforms? The answer seems to be that, in our zealous pursuit of higher school achievement, we have somehow lost track of the emotions of children and adolescents and the affective aspects of school learning and behavior. Instead of looking at students in breadth and depth, we have pursued a narrow vision of schooling, one in which cognitive outcomes have become more important than adaptational outcomes. As a result, education and psychology journals and books are filled with reports decribing educational programs and manipulations of variables of little significance to the stress-filled lives of students and teachers. It is not surprising that the yield has been low, and as a result it has become fashionable to doubt the ability of schools to improve educational outcomes. Somehow we have come to the position of denying everyday experience of children and adolescents and accepting cognitively oriented school experience as the main reality in their lives, no matter the absurdities to which it leads school reform.

In a nutshell, while lagging test scores have troubled educators and have been the stimulus for school reform, a new kind of deficit, in many ways equally alarming, has become all too apparent: illiteracy about stress and emotion. America's children and adolescents seem desperately in need of lessons in coping with stress and emotion. The signs of this deficiency can be read, for example, in the number of teen-age suicides, homicides, and pregnancies in the past decade. Children and adolescents need preventive measures and curricular interventions that help them to cope with the stress in their lives and to handle their emotions.

It also can be argued that past school reforms have been a major source of new stress rather than a source of stress relief for children and adolescents. Somehow, schools must balance the stress associated with challenge and motivation with the stress associated with pressure to achieve success and avoid failure. In recent years, this balance has been threatened as schools have been under increasing pressure to place a stronger emphasis on the academic achievement of students. The pressure has been visible in widely published concerns about declining SAT scores, poor performance on high school placement/preparation tests, and the low ranking of the United States in comparisons of the achievement of American students with students in other countries (National Commission on Excellence in Education, 1983).

At the same time, there has been a growing concern that well-meaning efforts to prepare students better academically may be excessively stress inducing and in some ways misdirected (Commission on Work, Family, and Citizenship, 1988b; Rutter, 1983a). Although some students are no doubt benefiting, others are becoming psychological casualties, as reflected in statistics concerning school failure, substance abuse, delinquency, suicide, irresponsible sexual behavior, and dropout among adolescents (London, 1987). Paradoxically, the strong academic demands of the present educational climate could result in few increases in learning and instead exacerbate current stress-related problems and lead to further alienation among students (Eisner, 1988; Goodlad & Oakes, 1988). If this happened, one consequence could be that the effects of disabling stress, which is estimated to be severely impacting 30% of our school-age children and adolescents (Forman & O'Malley, 1984), would grow.

At this stage in the school reform movement, therefore, it is important that we give concerns about stress the highest priority. This not only means that we must give more consideration to factors in school reform that may be contributing to higher levels of stress in students, teachers, and parents. It, more importantly, also means that the ways in which stress from all sources influences the well-being of students, teachers, and parents must be analyzed, and that steps must be taken, on the basis of available research and other information on stress, to ameliorate its deleterious effects.

In this general formulation of the problem, personal competence and psychological well-being are viewed as a direct function of individual abilities and environmental resources and protective factors, and as an inverse function of individual disabilities and environmental stressors and risk factors. Presented as an equation, this formulation means that: personal competence, psychological well-being = (individual abilities + self-esteem + coping skills + social and other support systems + other protective factors) / (individual disabilities + social and other environmental stressors + other risk factors). This equation represents an interactionist view of factors leading to optimal development, in that individual factors moderate the effects of environmental stress. While accepting this general orientation, it also is important to include a broader macrolevel perspective. A person-oriented model may not be sufficiently sensitive to the situational and developmental status of individuals, with one result being that it may not give a proper emphasis to the modifiability of environmental stressors and resources.

STRESS RELIEF IN FUTURE SCHOOL REFORM: OVERVIEW OF THE CHALLENGE

School improvement efforts that involve stress relief for children and adolescents would include doing three kinds of things. The first is that one would develop lists including individuals and groups of children and adolescents who are likely to be at risk for stress and who should have the watchful eye of teachers and the personnel of psychological services programs. In identifying which children and adolescents are at risk, there are two stress principles to take into account. The first is that the greater the threat of loss or the actual loss to which children and adolescents are exposed, the greater their level of risk; and the other is that the fewer coping resources children and adolescents have, the more likely they will be overwhelmed by the losses or threats of losses encountered. This two-axis model is straightforward and based, first and foremost, on objective stressors and actual resources at the child's or adolescent's disposal. Risk factors, of course, do not necessarily lead to psychological or psychosomatic consequences. Indeed, a relatively low rate of serious problems should be expected for even the highest risk groups. Also, it is important to emphasize that stressors outside the school environment may piggyback on school stressors, creating school problems for children and adolescents that would not otherwise occur. In addition, children and adolescents are less likely than adults to speak about their problems or even to know they are having them. Their stress-related difficulties may be primarily based on their school experience or may only secondarily emerge in their school work. Children and adolescents are also vulnerable because they have had less experience coping with stressful situations. Lack of prior experience may lead them to exaggerate their problems and prevent them from seeing light at the end of the tunnel.

The monitoring of stress reactions is the second thing that would need to be done. As to those that can be monitored in the schools, there are a number of common stress reactions, including: guilt about actions; excessive drinking or drug use (by adolescents); uncontrolled or frequent crying and other extreme reactions to stressful events that would normally be handled more calmly; sleep problems (too much or too little); depression, anxiety, and anger; stress-related physical illness (e.g., headaches, gastrointestinal disorders, upper and lower back pain, poor stamina or resistance); difficulty concentrating or excessive ruminating; uncharacteristic social isolation; blunting of emotions; and suicidal thoughts or plans. In addition, children's and adolescents' discipline and academic problems and a number of characteristic symptoms of family stress should be monitored, including: family conflict that does not come to resolution; any signs of verbal or physical violence; family members isolating themselves from one another; extreme dependency and clinging; and making one or more children scapegoats for the family's difficulties. It is important to keep in mind, however, that many of these symptoms will be experienced in mild forms and should not raise cause for much concern if they are not prolonged. Most children and adolescents experience some rough times, but most concerns and problems should be resolvable with ongoing family, school, and social support resources. The problem for a child or adolescent becomes critical when symptoms are persistent or severe.

The third thing that would be done would be to develop preventive and remedial educational and psychological services for students experiencing high levels of stress. Guidelines by which such service programs can provide guidance and other benefits to children and adolescents who are at risk for debilitative stress can be loosely divided into individual, educational, family, and social coping efforts. However, it is important to understand that the individual, educational, and social spheres interact. Social support, for example, is not just delivered to those in need, but is based, in part, on both the recipient's social skills and the social skills of their potential supporters. Similarly, children's and adolescents' coping efforts are aided or impeded by the school, family, and social milieux. For example, teachers and parents can provide support that aids children's and adolescents' perceptions of their ability to master the demands of schooling. How effectively efforts of teachers and parents are used by children and adolescents is also moderated by the presence or absence of the personal resources of children and adolescents. It also is important to recognize that guidelines for coping with stress need to be adjusted on the basis of such resources.

OPTIMAL DEVELOPMENT OF CHILDREN AND ADOLESCENTS: THE ULTIMATE GOAL OF SCHOOL REFORM

One can also make the point that allocation of energies and resources in our schools must go increasingly to building wellness and life-time competence rather than just struggling to contain the school failures of children and adolescents. From this perspective, the challenge is to identify factors or conditions that advance or restrict optimal development, and to use such information to reshape schools and schooling in ways that promote educational, mental, and physical health. The factors and conditions that define well-being, and the relative strength of forces that promote it, differ, of course, for different groups of children and adolescents. There also is every reason to expect that complex and divergent solutions will be required, solutions calibrated to the particular characteristics of diverse targeted groups.

In this connection, one can argue, on the basis of the wellness model presented by Mills and his colleagues (Mills, Dunham, & Alpert, 1988), that there are inherent capabilities and higher levels of functioning within all children and adolescents that can be accessed if they are placed in supportive school and other environments in which external circumstances that reinforce their negative ways of thinking and behaving are removed. For Mills and his colleagues, higher levels of functioning include developing a more mature and responsible outlook, functioning with common sense, and having a natural interest in learning. Once they are in positive school and other environments and have positive interactions with significant others, children and adolescents who are seemingly unwilling to learn socially desirable knowledge and skills are "freed up" to function at more educationally and mentally healthy levels of perception, feeling, and behavior. According to Mills and his colleagues, such positive school and other environments must include adult caring and interest; validation of children's and adolescents' worth and significance; and opportunities to build genuine relationships, see authentic models, and experience mentoring in an atmosphere of mutual caring and support.

Harter (1989) further argues that socioemotional support from significant others is an essential factor in a climate that promotes positive growth and change in children and adolescents. Socioemotional support also is essential for the development of strong perceptions and skills because it cultivates the positive sense of self-worth required for such growth and change. Glenn and Nelson (1988) make the further point that children and adolescents exposed to a climate of socioemotional support experience being understood, accepted, and affirmed. In other words, in a socioemotionally supportive environment, children and adolescents: are listened to, not just heard, and taken seriously; their beliefs, thoughts, and feelings are respected; and they are genuinely needed and recognized as having value and worth. According to Nelson (1987), a socially supportive environment is also important to children and adolescents because it leads to a sense of belonging and significance, a fundamental goal of all behavior.

In the perspective of these authors, it also is assumed or taken for granted that schools represent a potentially powerful, but not yet well-harnessed, force for advancing the educational, mental, and physical wellness of children and adolescents. At an obvious level, the child's and adolescent's school experiences provide the knowledge and skills needed to master essential life tasks. Less directly, these school experiences also shape children's and adolescents' competence and efficacy views and, with these, a sense of control over their fate. School experiences can also serve as critical factors in advancing prosocial behavior and reducing stress-related misbehavior and delinquency. However, anyone who is committed to improving schools, and who tries to effect fundamental changes in schooling, should read Sarason (1990). He offers some useful advice and shows how innovative educators can respond to the challenges of school reform in turbulent times. In his commonsense approach to restructuring, combined with a strategic planner's vision, Sarason also reminds us that the fundamental reality of school reform is that power shapes schools and schooling, and that those who would restructure this institution must understand and use that authority well.

CONCLUDING COMMENTS

This chapter has provided an overview of the school reform movement and has shown that successive waves of school reform have not effectively addressed the increasingly serious stress problems of students, their parents, and teachers. The problem, in part, is that policy makers and educators still seem to be in an era of transition, without answers to the two most important questions: Should reform advocates redouble their efforts — taking on social problems and putting social prevention issues on an equal level with reading, math, and science — in order to build the school system of the future? Or should they concede defeat, look for a return to a more minimal vision of public schooling, and go back to the school system that used to be?

There are limits, of course, to the role that schools can play in dealing with debilitative stress and related emotional problems. But some important things can be done that will help students cope better with stress and its maladaptive outcomes, and that also will directly impact student learning and behavior and lead to general improvement in student achievement. The potentially powerful role of the schools in ameliorating, preventing, and overcoming the negative consequences of stress is discussed in the chapters ahead.

2 TARGETING STUDENTS WITH STRESS-RELATED PROBLEMS FOR SPECIAL EDUCATIONAL AND PSYCHOLOGICAL SERVICES

In past years, schools have primarily targeted handicapped and disadvantaged students for special educational services and benefits. But who are the "handicapped" and the "disadvantaged"? How do we understand their needs? And, most of all, what do we know about the link between their learning skills and behavioral tendencies and their "handicapped" or "disadvantaged" status? The answer, in part, is that we don't really know because, in identifying a particular group of students for special educational services, we have not taken into account that naming something is a far cry from explaining it. That is, our understanding of the educational problems of children and youth is minimally advanced by the common practice of dividing students into groups on the basis of some handicapping condition, such as learning disabilities, or some demographic characteristic, such as income or minority status, and then "explaining" their school success/failure by referring to their membership in one or another group. The fact that descriptors used to identify the "handicapped" or "disadvantaged" vary so widely also reveals some of the parallels between our varied conceptions of the problems of children and adolescents and the mixture of special services programs that more than two decades of educational efforts on behalf of such students have spawned.

PROBLEMS WITH PROGRAMS FOR HANDICAPPED CHILDREN AND ADOLESCENTS

The Education for All Handicapped Children Act (now the Individuals With Disabilities Education Act) is landmark legislation that has opened up the school doors for large numbers of children and adolescents who, before the original 1975 Act, were denied an appropriate education. But meeting the substantive as well as due process requirements of the law has been a difficult challenge. This is particularly true for children and adolescents with "invisible" handicaps, such as learning, behavioral, or emotional problems. Moreover, it is increasingly clear that there are large numbers of children and adolescents, including those experiencing debilitative stress, not covered by the mandate of the law for whom "education as usual" does not work. They, like their identified counterparts in special education programs, often need modifications in the educational curriculum and greater support services, including mental health services. In addition, the "right" children and adolescents may not always be the ones identified because whether or not a student is identified for special education programs has as much to do with local circumstances, attitudes, and resources as it does with a student's special needs.

PROBLEMS WITH PROGRAMS FOR THE DISADVANTAGED

Chapter 1 programs (formerly Title 1 of the Elementary and Secondary Education Act of 1965) illustrate some of the problems with the "disadvantaged" student approach. Although Chapter 1 is the primary mechanism for the federal funding of compensatory education for disadvantaged students, it does not represent a unified and coherent *treatment* program. Instead, it is better defined as a funding program rather than as an educational treatment (Carter, 1984).

Another problem is that studies of Chapter 1 effects show that its services are most effective with marginal students and least effective with the weakest students, for whom Chapter 1 programs are designed (see, e.g., Kennedy, Birman, & Demaline, 1986). Thus, over the years it has been necessary to bring the high expectations for Chapter 1 in line with actual results in order to maintain the popularity and stability of support for Chapter 1 as a vehicle for delivering added service to disadvantaged students.

Chapter 1 illustrates still another problem. Reauthorized by the Hawkins-Stafford School Improvements Amendments of 1988, its resources are distributed to districts and schools according to the percentage of students in poverty and are then distributed within schools according to students' actual performance. However, the required percentage of students in poverty is very low, so that more than 90 percent of school districts receive Chapter 1 funds, and one in every nine students receives Chapter 1 services (Kennedy, Jung, & Orland, 1986). This is why school districts serving middle-class communities often receive significant Chapter 1 resources, and why, according to these authors, 58 percent of the students who receive Chapter 1 services are not themselves from poor families. This broad targeting of Chapter 1 helps to maintain the political popularity of the program, but the use of the concept of disadvantage in this way is otherwise hard to justify, although there are alternative views of the situation (see, e.g., Pogrow, 1992, & Slavin, 1991).

IDENTIFYING AT-RISK STUDENTS

To identify the students we mean to help, it is important to identify the *problems* of children and adolescents as clearly as possible. A step in this direction, and an improvement over using handicapped or disadvantaged status for this purpose, is to identify students as "at risk." This heightens our focus on *behavior,* although as Ralph (1989) has pointed out, the terms handicapped, disadvantaged, and at risk are used interchangeably in the literature. However, when a distinction is made, handicapped is used to refer to students eligible for programs mandated by the Education for All Handicapped Children Act, whereas disadvantaged is used to refer to compensatory programs like Chapter 1. Ralph's suggestion that "at risk" is preferable and that it should refer to the behavior (rather than the handicapped or disadvantaged *status*) of students is a good one. After all, students who are *not* handicapped or disadvantaged regularly place themselves at risk through such behaviors as drug use and truancy (see, e.g., Mensch & Kandel, 1988; Meyers, Milne, Baker, & Ginsberg, 1987).

But what does it mean to say that a child or adolescent is "at risk"? Which children and adolescents are at risk? What are they like? One might begin with the assumption that children and adolescents are at risk if they are likely to fail in school or in life. For example, if a student is retained in grade or drops out of school, that student is at risk. Likewise, if an adolescent uses drugs, or has attempted suicide, that adolescent also is at risk. In essence, "at riskness" is a function of what bad things happen to a student, how often they happen, and what else happens in the student's immediate environment. In addition, if we think of at-risk-ness as existing on a continuum, then at-riskness increasingly shows up as one moves from the healthy or good end of the continuum to the unhealthy or bad end.

Utilizing this perspective, a major survey of students at risk, which involved more than 22,000 students in over 275 schools, including elementary, middle or junior high, and high schools, was conducted by Phi Delta Kappa (see Frymier, 1989). The school records of 100 fourth-graders, 100 seventh-graders, and 100 tenth-graders who were considered "typical" students by teachers and counselors in each of those schools were utilized. Standardized ways to collect information regarding students who might be at risk were developed via a 140-page *Manual of Instructions* that served as the basis of a 3-day training session for researchers who participated in data collection at each school. For each student, teachers and counselors obtained information on 45 factors that previous research had indicated are related to risk and on 13 instructional strategies that might have been used with the students. Data also were obtained through structured interviews with the principals, and all teachers completed a 116-item survey about at-risk students and about school practices.

Briefly summarizing some of their findings on these 45 risk factors, 3 percent of the students used drugs at least once in the past year, although the percentage rose to 9 percent at the high school level. Three percent of all students, and 7 percent of high school students, lived with family members who used drugs in the past year. One percent even sold drugs during the past year, rising to 2 percent among high school students. One percent of all students, and 3 percent of high schools students, also had attempted suicide. Although the figures reflect mostly female students, 1 percent was involved (for high school students it was 2 percent) in a pregnancy in the past year, with 2 percent (and 3 percent in high school) having been physically or sexually abused. As the last example of their findings, 5 percent of all students, and 15 percent at the high school level, used alcohol in the past year.

PROBLEMS WITH SOME AT-RISK APPROACHES

Some problems also arise with the at-risk approach of identifying students in need of special educational and/or psychological services. To illustrate this point, being at risk is sometimes taken to mean "likely to drop out of high school," and dropping out is often thought to be the result of poor school performance. There is evidence, of course, that poor academic performance is a good predictor of who drops out (see, e.g., Hess & Greer, 1987), and if students drop out because of poor grades it would appear that if we improve their grades we will solve the dropout problem. In reference to this matter, Ralph and Salganik (1988) have closely examined data from the High School and Beyond study and have presented some sobering second thoughts about such a conclusion.

Among the things they noted is that very few students in American high schools receive below-average grades. Less than 15 percent of all high school students have overall grade point averages below C. In addition, two out of three dropouts across the country report making "mostly Cs" or better. Even among dropouts scoring in the bottom 25 percent in achievement test performance, 56 percent report making "mostly Cs" or better. To add some clarity to this apparently contradictory situation, one needs to realize that very few high school students report making "mostly Ds," and less than 9 percent of all dropouts report making "mostly Ds."

Looking at the data another way, four out of five high school sophomores stay on to graduate, regardless of their grade-point average or level of achievement test performance. In addition, at the lowest level of achievement test performance (measured in their sophomore year), minority students are *not* the most likely to drop out. Overall, 19 percent of all of these sophomores drop out, but only 16 percent of the African Americans and 17 percent of the Hispanics in this quartile group drop out, whereas 22 percent of the Whites in this bottom category drop out.

According to Ralph and Salganik (1988), these data suggest that being at risk of dropping out does not follow simple racial or ethnic lines. Although African Americans and Hispanics have the highest overall dropout rates, poor high school performance (as measured by grades and achievement tests) is *not* a major factor in their dropping out. Nor is it a major factor for Whites. Clearly, both minority and nonminority students drop out at all levels of high school performance, and at every level of high school performance only a small proportion drop out.

The problems of identifying students who are likely to drop out as "at risk" are further compounded when one looks at the condition of high school *graduates*. Representative data from the National Assessment of Education Progress studies show that African-American high school graduates attain literacy levels that are about the same as those of White 8th-graders (Kirsch & Jungeblut, 1986). Moreover, this gap in achievement continues across the years of postsecondary education. White high school graduates perform about as well as African-American graduates of 4-year colleges. Similar, though less pronounced, literacy differences also separate Hispanic from White high school graduates. One danger evident in this situation is that, in giving so much attention to students who are at risk of being high school dropouts, we might lose sight of students who are at risk of being graduates of high school in name only.

THE PROBLEMATIC NATURE OF THE SEARCH FOR AT-RISK STUDENTS IN THE SCHOOLS

A related, and equally important problem, is that teachers, school psychologists, and other school professionals don't know who their at-risk students are. An example of the nature of this problem is the Phi Delta Kappa survey of students at risk mentioned earlier (see Frymier, 1989). In this survey the data on all schools were aggregated, and the authors reported that nearly one third of these "typical" students were identified as having 6 or more of the 45 at-risk factors investigated. For the purposes of the study, the authors defined these students as being "seriously at risk." However, this one third figure probably is too low. Teachers and counselors sometimes did not have access to the necessary information. This figure, therefore, is likely to be a conservative estimate of the proportion of "typical" students in the public schools who are seriously at risk, and who may be experiencing high levels of stress.

This problem was greatest for certain kinds of at-risk factors. For example, teachers said they didn't know about: drug use for 22 percent of the students; drug use by family members in 32 percent of the cases; students' suicide attempts in 29 percent of the cases; students' use of alcohol in 24 percent of the cases; students' involvement in pregnancies in 22 percent of the cases; and physical and sexual abuse in 26 percent of the cases.

In addition, in 50 percent of the cases teachers didn't know the father's level of education, and 45 percent didn't know the mother's level of education. In 25 percent of the cases they did not know the father's occupation, and in 19 percent of the cases they didn't know the mother's occupation. In 37 percent of the cases teachers didn't know whether a parent had lost his or her job; in 28 percent they didn't know whether a divorce or separation had occurred; in 27 percent of the cases they didn't know whether a student's parent had died; and in 35 percent of the cases they didn't know whether a student's parents had had a major change in health status during the past year. In 17 percent of the cases teachers didn't know a student well enough to estimate the student's sense of self-esteem.

There probably are several reasons for this lack of information. Some teachers and principals were reluctant to share confidential information. Many schools also maintain records on students in ways that prevent teachers from having ready access to information about students. Schools also typically don't collect information on out-of-school factors that involve at-riskness. Some teachers also consider such information as detrimental because it is sometimes used to label and stereotype students. Some critics even go so far as to argue that teachers should not know anything about a student's background and home situation.

There are, of course, teachers and other professionals who disagree with that position. They argue that one cannot help a student about whom one knows very little. One needs to know, for example, whether a student who needs help comes from a single-parent family, whether a parent is an alcoholic, and so on. Although this is an old issue, it emerges full-blown in any systematic effort to provide stress interventions for at-risk students, or to help them in other ways.

STRESSORS AS RISK FACTORS

Children and adolescents are exposed to many kinds of stressors. There are stressors imposed by developmental transitions, such as the fearfulness of a child going off to school for the first time, the advance of a child from elementary school to junior high school, the onset of puberty, the adolescent experience with the all-powerful peer in-group, and the stress of graduation and entry into college or the work force. There are chronic stressors: poverty, mental and physical handicaps, chronic illness, and ongoing school failure. There are acute stressors such as the loss of a parent through death or divorce, accidents, illnesses, and rejection by a college of one's choice. And there are man-made and natural disasters such as floods, earthquakes, and war.

However, in considering stress as a risk factor, it becomes necessary to clarify some of the definitional uncertainties surrounding relevant concepts. The definition of *risk* is a starting point. This concept is applied, for example, in research with the children of affectively disordered parents. In a nonspecific sense, risk implies the identification of variables or factors in biology, family, person, and environment that heighten the probability of a negative outcome of stress experience (e.g., mental or physical disorder) for the child or adolescent. Risk factors can have immediate as well as long-term consequences. Elder (1974) has written extensively, for example, on the later effects of the Great Depression on the children of the 1930s, who as adults have now reached senior citizen status. Thus, the event and the trauma it induces can become risk factors both at the time the event occurs and potentially at a later period.

Another concept that needs brief discussion is that of stress. According to Garmezy and Masten (1990), definitions of *stress* typically implicate four factors:

(1) the presence of a manifest stimulus event; (2) the event is one capable of modifying the organism's physiological and psychological equilibrium; (3) the disequilibrium is reflected in a state of arousal marked by neurological, cognitive, and emotional consequences for the individual; (4) these changes, in turn, disrupt the adaptation of the individual. (pp. 462-463)

The third construct that needs definition is *coping* because the response to stress is an effort at resolution that is termed coping. Using the approach to coping of Lazarus and Folkman (1984), a determiner of the adequacy of the coping response to stress is an act of appraisal by the individual. Such an appraisal presumably involves matching the demands imposed by the stressful event with an evaluation of one's ability to meet them. If demand is perceived to exceed ability, the event will have disruptive consequences; if ability matches or exceeds demands, the event may serve as a growth experience. However, this generalization has limits because the outcome of some events is unrelated to ability, as when the denial of an opportunity or benefit is unrelated to ability.

Finally, there is another emerging side to the literature on stress, relatively new literature that focuses on the mastery and competence of children and adolescents under stress. This literature remains small by comparison, but it is compensatory to the emphasis on threat, disruption, and even despair in the stressful lives of children and adolescents. Until now, the traumatic event and its severe consequences have commanded our attention to an extent that normal development and efficacy under stress have not. These matters, as well as other aspects of stress, coping, and adaptational outcomes, are given detailed attention in later chapters, beginning with Chapter 3.

SCHOOL-RELATED STRESSORS

Children and adolescents have a lot of stressors in their lives, many of which are related to school. Elkind (1988) and Sears and Navin (1983), in their discussion of the stresses of schooling, identify a number of common school stressors, including: anxiety about going to school, bullies, changing schools, conflict with the teacher, competition for grades and other honors, difficulty with classmates, failing an exam, failing marks at school, failing to make an athletic team, giving oral reports or speeches in front of the class, lack of parental interest in achievements, learning disorders, not being able to complete homework assignments, older siblings setting bad family reputation, older siblings setting school expectations too high, parental pressure to achieve, peer teasing about dental braces, glasses, obesity, etc., special recognition for outstanding peformance (e.g., honor role), and worrying about tests.

It is not surprising, of course, that so many child and adolescent concerns relate to success and failure in school. In fact, Elias (1989) has argued that academic success is overemphasized in many schools, and that students who perform the best in the academic subjects, especially reading, science, and mathematics, are singled out for special opportunities that enrich and accelerate their academic prowess. But, as Lightfoot (1987) has pointed out, only a few students can achieve this kind of academic excellence, and pressures to be "the best" can result in a sense of failure and alienation for many students.

But schools stress children and adolescents in a variety of other ways that go beyond academics. For example, schools are much more a host to theft and violence than ever before, and coming to school and leaving school also are sources of stress for many students. On this matter, Rutter

(1983b) has reminded us that students' most elemental sense of safety is paramount to managing stress, and that physically unsafe schools can hamper learning in all areas. In addition, unsafe schools hurry students into attitudes of wariness and fear that can redirect major energies away from learning, and this, in turn, can become a cause of school failure (Elkind, 1988). Unfortunately, crime and violence in schools, which often touches all students, is one issue that has not been addressed by the school reform movement.

In addition, schools tend to stereotype and impose false expectations on students, and increasingly to teach them in environments that impede learning. Elkind (1988) made the point, for example, that schools label children "too quickly and too early for management rather than pedagogical reasons" (p.158). One result is that too many young children, especially those from bilingual homes and with a limited command of English, or who have limited vision or hearing, are misdiagnosed as learning disabled or retarded and relegated to special programs.

Elkind (1988) has enumerated still other ways that schools stress students. The classroom is the wrong size for many educational activities. It is too small for films and lectures, and too large for classroom discussions and projects. The classroom day involves hundreds of interactions and events, but rarely is a teacher activity continuous for more than a few minutes. One-on-one talks between teachers and students seldom exceed 30 seconds, and attention in class to each student averages only about 6 hours per year. This means that, in actuality, little of the individualizing that gets talked about happens. Management, disciplinary activities, busywork, waiting, leaving and arriving, and other diversions severely limit the time given to actual instruction in classrooms, with such diversions reducing gross instructional time to about 3 hours a day. In addition, to "cover the material," teachers need a response from students able and willing to give it, so they pay attention to about a third of the class, largely ignoring those who need instruction the most.

In commenting on such practices, Elkind (1988) made the point that rushing from one subject or activity to another, and never having a sense of completion, is stressful to many students. Such practices also stress students because they are so tedious, repetitious, and often meaningless, and because they can lead to boredom and feelings of unhappiness and of being trapped. For these and other reasons, schools all too often have added to rather than subtracted from the stress experienced by children and adolescents.

The schools also reflect broader societal and parental demands, although responses to these demands usually are short-lived and incompletely institutionalized. This happens, in part, because the changes that are to be made in the schools fall largely upon teachers to carry out and students to absorb. In response to the increasing pressures of present school reforms, both teachers and students have begun to show more stress and need for stress management interventions, although Forman and O'Malley (1984) question whether the stress they are being called on to manage is necessary, appropriate, or desirable. To add to these difficulties, such stress is often seen as the problem only of students and teachers rather than as a problem that has components at both the person and environment levels (Elias, 1991).

STUDENT PERCEPTIONS OF STRESSORS IN THE CLASSROOM

However, we cannot determine the stress load of students just from the amount of objective stress in the school. Stress load is also determined by the student's subjective impressions of schools and schooling. Therefore, it also is important to look at the stresses of schooling from the student's perspective. This was done by Phillips in a study of student perceptions of achievement and social stressors in the classroom (see Phillips, 1978, pp. 35-44). The study involved 4th-graders in four elementary schools — one that was predominantly middle-class Anglo, another that was predominantly lower-class Anglo, a third that was predominantly lower-class African-American, and one that was predominantly lower-class Hispanic.

Perceptions of Achievement-Related Stressors

As to perceptions of achievement stressors, nearly three fourths of the children said that they often wish that the teacher would slow down so that they could better understand what she is saying. In view of the reliance on verbal communication in much of teaching, this was a significant source of achievement stress. As one might expect, this source of stress was strongest for Mexican-American students, who have a language barrier (and who usually have Anglo teachers), and weakest among middle-class Anglo students.

Almost the same proportion of students said that they work the hardest when they know that what they do will be compared with what others in class do. Although this is not surprising, it also is obvious that a great deal of stress is inherent in the competitiveness that underlies so much schoolwork. However, the fact that African-American students were the most likely, and Mexican-American students the least likely, to say that they worked hardest under competitive conditions is more problematic.

A majority of the children also said that it was hard for them to do as well as their teacher expected them to do, although middle-class Anglo children were less stressed in this way than other groups. Nevertheless, teacher expectations were a source of stress for almost 40 percent of this advantaged group. All subgroups also believed that smart children get privileges other children do not get. Almost two thirds said this, which helps to explain the importance of tests and test-like situations to children, and the stressfulness of taking both teacher-made and standardized tests.

Having a report card that met their parents' expectations was a problem for more than 60 percent of these children, with this stress being highest for the minority students. This fits well with studies which show that minority parents put strong pressure on their children for academic achievement, although these pressures often are not backed up by effective actions to translate these demands into success in school. Finally, a majority also said that if they made a mistake while reciting in class, there would be some children who would laugh at them. For this and other reasons, recitation is likely to be a potent source of stress for many children. It also is the one situation where middle-class Anglo children expressed a higher level of stress than other groups.

Other achievement situations that were perceived as stressful by less than a majority, but more than one fourth, of the children were: finding it hard to keep up with the rest of the class, believing that teachers sometimes give them a lower grade than they deserve, believing that those who do poorly on tests the teacher gives lose the approval of the teacher, and that they don't get as much approval from the teacher and other children in class as they would like.

Good grades, as well as the things that appear to be associated with good grades, is a theme that runs through these stressful school situations. However, Anglo students typically reported less stress in relation to such situations than African-American and Mexican-American students. Because these minorities usually do less well in school and make poorer grades, this appears to be a realistic difference.

Perceptions of Social Stressors

Phillips also reported results for student perceptions of social stressors in the classroom. One important overall finding was that social situations seemed to be less of a problem for these children than achievement situations, which is what one would expect because of the achievement orientation of elementary school. However, some specific social situations were widely perceived as stressful. For example, about half of the students indicated that they often feel that their classmates never want to do what they want to do, and that some children in class say things to hurt their feelings. In addition, more than a third of the students believed that most of the children in class never pay any attention to them, and that some children in class seem to get angry when they do better than they do. More than a third also said that they have been physically attacked by other children in class, that they are not as good in games like kickball as other students in class, that their classmates often make fun of them for the way they play in school games, that classmates sometimes make fun of the way they look and talk, and that the clothes they wear to school are not as nice as those most of the children wear.

As to racial-ethnic differences, more social situations were perceived as stressful by non-Anglo than Anglo students. For example, more non-Anglo children, especially African-Americans, said that they are physically attacked by other children. Mexican-American children, particularly, also said that classmates often make fun of the way they play in school games. Non-Anglos also were more likely to believe that the clothes they wear to school are not as nice as what most children wear.

There also was one social situation in which middle-class Anglo students showed more stress than all the other subgroups. This dealt with whether a student's mother brings cookies, helps at class parties, and does things like other students' mothers. This was a concern for more than 40 percent of these middle-class Anglo students, perhaps because of the generally greater school involvement of this group's parents. When the involvement of parents in school activities is highly valued, and some parents are heavily involved, whereas others are relatively less involved, children have a heightened awareness of and sensitivity to these differences, and some will feel at a special disadvantage.

It also is ironic that academic success itself was a source of social stress for many students, as indicated by their responses to the question, "Do some children in class seem to get angry when you do better than they do?" More than half of the African-American and Mexican-American students, and a third of the Anglo students, said that they create social stress for themselves whenever they are academically successful in school. As a consequence, one of the unintended effects of teachers who are the most dedicated to the encouragement of academic excellence may be that they create a "boomerang effect" on successful children that hits hardest at high-achieving minority students.

DETERMINATION OF STRESS LOAD ON CHILDREN AND ADOLESCENTS

Obtaining information on students who may be experiencing high levels of stress is a major challenge. Although inventories of major life events have been the most widely used, including checklists filled in by teachers, parents, or children and adolescents themselves, some researchers have investigated daily hassles and other experiences of daily living appraised as salient and harmful or threatening to well-being. In the first approach, the emphasis is on objective assessment of stressful events, whereas the emphasis in the second approach is on the individual's subjective assessment of his or her stressful encounters. There is an attempt in both approaches, of course, to integrate information from the environment with information from the person. This is necessary because there always is a connection between the reality of a stressful event and the person's appraisal of that event. However, giving a heavy weight to the objective situation is appropriate where the objective situation is extremely powerful and unambiguous (as in the death of a student's parent), although the subjective approach is more appropriate for the assessment of day-to-day situations that are often ambiguous and not particularly powerful (as when a student is moved to a different class). As an additional consideration, the objective nature of the stressor is, in general, less significant for a variety of outcomes than the individual's perceptions of the stressor.

One prime example of an instrument for charting a student's stress level is provided by Chandler (1985a, b). His Stress Response Scale (SRS), which represents a systematic and research-based approach to the assessment of stress in children and adolescents, has been used in a number of studies (e.g., Chandler, Million, & Shermis, 1985; Chandler & Shermis, 1986; Hutton, Roberts, Walker, & Zuniga, 1987; Shermis, Rudin, & Chandler, 1992). The SRS is interpreted as a measure of the impact of stress on the child's or adolescent's behavioral adjustment, whereas the five subscales (Acting Out, Passive-Aggressive, Overactive, Dependent, and Repressed) are seen as possible behavioral patterns a child or adolescent might adopt in an effort to respond to stress. The rating scale is typically completed by a parent or teacher, usually for children and adolescents referred for psychological study.

Another approach to measuring stress in children and adolescents is provided by Elkind (1988). This scale gives an estimate of the impact of various life events and changes that students find stressful. The scale can best be used by teachers with students in their own classes. In consultation with a teacher, counselor, or school psychologist, the scale can also be used by parents with their own children. To provide a normative and interpretive perspective, Elkind further pointed out that students who score below 150 are about average with respect to stress load. For students who score between 150 and 300 there is a better than average chance that they will show some symptoms of stress, and for those scoring above 300 there is a strong likelihood of serious changes in school learning and behavior and in mental and/or physical health.

Scales that focus only on major life events have also been used in a variety of investigations. For example, in a study of adolescents, Dornbusch and others (Dornbusch, Mont-Reynaud, Ritter, Chen, & Steinberg, 1991) used a major life events scale, derived from the Cornell Medical Index, that asked the question, "Have any of the following things happened to you in the past 12 months?" The things asked about were (pp. 113-114):

I broke up with my boyfriend or girlfriend; I began dating or going steady with someone; a brother or sister left home; I did not get into a club or sport I really wanted to be involved in; there was a change in the amount of money my family has; one of my close friends died or became seriously ill; one of my grandparents died; my mother began working; I was suspended from school; I became involved in some new religious activities; one of my parents became seriously ill or was hospitalized; I moved to a new school district; one of my parents changed jobs; I thought that I (or my girlfriend) was pregnant; one of my parents lost his or her job; a new baby was born in our family; my parents were divorced or separated; one of my parents remarried; my mother or father died; and I became seriously ill or was hospitalized.

In using this scale, the number of events reported by each student was used by the authors to form a stressful events score. Each event was thus given an equal weight.

It is important to note, however, that the pool of events used in such measures is limited by the omission of daily events, which research with children and adolescents is beginning to show are predictive of psychological and physical dysfunction (see, e.g., Banez & Compas, 1990). In essence, what is needed in the measurement of stress is a broadening of emphasis from major events, to persistent conditions and daily hassles and disappointments. One example of this approach is the scale for adolescents that has been developed by Compas and his colleagues (Compas, Davis, Forsythe, & Wagner, 1987). This *Adolescent Perceived Events Scale* has different age versions, including one for early adolescence (ages 11–14), middle adolescence (ages 15–17), and late adolescence (ages 18–20). In the early adolescence version, respondents go down a list of 164 events and indicate whether the event happened to them in the past 3 months. If it has happened to them, they are instructed to rank the desirability of the event. The events also are classified as major or daily stressors, and separate positive and negative event scores can be calculated for major and daily events. The two versions for older adolescents have similar directions, although respondents also are asked to rate the impact and frequency of the event.

Measures focusing on major life events also typically include only a few events that occur in school itself, mainly failing tests or courses, not being promoted, getting suspended, or going to a new school. Missing from such life events inventories are insults, not having required books, fighting, not being able to complete an assignment, and a host of other annoying and troublesome school-related concerns. In short, there are special benefits in having scales that specifically focus on the physical, social, and academic stressors that contribute to the stress of children and adolescents in school. A recent example of this school-centered approach is provided by Grannis (1992). His measure of stressor events (Things that happen in school, THIS) includes 20 stressor events, as follows (p. 10):

There was a lot of cursing in class; someone tried to copy my work when I didn't want them to; someone hit me or kicked or pushed me; I couldn't get an answer to a question I asked; people in the hall were bothering the classroom; someone made fun of something I said in class; people in the classroom wouldn't get quiet;

I was warned that I might not pass a subject or pass to the next grade; I or one of my friends was moved to a different class; someone shouted or screamed at me; someone tried to pressure me to cut class; I felt unsafe in the school; I could not finish my work in class; somebody treated me like I always do wrong; I didn't have a pen or paper or my book to do my work in class; I did worse on a test than I should have; someone was picking on me in the hall; there was a change of teachers in one or more of my classes; people were throwing things and fighting in the lunchroom; someone took something from me.

In responding to THIS, students answered two questions about each event: (a) If this happens to you in school, how do or would you feel about it (very good, good, makes no difference, upset, very upset); and (b) How often did this happen during the past week, or since the beginning of last week (hardly ever, sometimes, often).

An alternative approach to identifying students who might be experiencing high levels of stress is found in scales that measure behavioral deviance. In one such effort, adolescent deviance, a negatively evaluated set of behaviors in the eyes of society, was measured by Dornbusch and his associates (Dornbusch et al., 1991) with responses to the question, "Since the beginning of the school year in September, how often have you done each of these things?" The behaviors to which students responded included (pp. 115-116):

copied homework or a class assignment from somebody else; smoked cigarettes (other than marijuana) or used chewing tobacco; bought beer or liquor yourself or gave someone money to buy it for you; used a phony I.D.; cheated on a class test; took something of value from another person; ran away from home; used alcohol excessively or been drunk; came to class late; smoked marijuana; used a drug other than marijuana (for example, "uppers" or cocaine); got in trouble with the police; carried a weapon to school; got into a physical fight at school; and purposely damaged school property.

Other inventories and scales that have been used with children and adolescents are described in later chapters. In addition, Compas (1987a,

b) reviews a number of stress-measuring instruments and makes suggestions about ways they might be improved.

Measurement of Family Stressors

The family can be an important source of stress in the lives of children and adolescents. For this reason, measures of family stress are critical in identifying students who are experiencing high levels of stress. A widely used instrument that assesses family stressors is the Family Inventory of Life Events and Changes (FILE) (McCubbin, Patterson, & Wilson, 1987). It was designed to assess the accumulation of normative and nonnormative life events experienced by a family during the course of 1 year. Based on family systems theory and family stress theory, the FILE is a 71-item self-report instrument consisting of nine subscales: Intra-family Strains, Marital Strains, Pregnancy and Childbearing Strains, Finance and Business Strains, Work–Family Transitions and Strains, Illness and Family Care Strains, Losses, Transitions "In and Out," and Legal Strains. Family members are asked to respond by checking whether or not each event has occurred within the past year. National norms were based upon approximately 980 couples (1,960 individuals) across the family life cycle ranging from young married couples to retired couples.

Instruments with an emphasis on the assessment of a broader range of family needs and priorities also are available. Fifteen currently available, published and unpublished, instruments that assess these characteristics of families are reviewed and evaluated by McGrew, Gilman, and Johnson (1992). Of special note, one needs category, the emotional/mental health category, which includes items related to coping with stress and dealing with emotions and feelings, is covered by all 15 scales. In general, the authors concluded that empirical evidence in support of the psychometric characteristics of the scales was limited, and that these instruments, while useful in identifying the needs and priorities of families, should be cautiously used in the assessment of change in individual families.

Measurement of Macro-Level Stressors

When psychologists, researchers, and educators refer to environmental stressors in the lives of children and adolescents they usually mean life events that are subjectively cited as "stressful," such as death of a parent or a chronic illness (Cohen, 1988). Less well studied and more difficult to determine are the pathways by which more molar environmental events (e.g., economic policies, unemployment, urbanization, and housing patterns) influence health and psychological well-being of children and adolescents. Nevertheless, there is evidence that molar economic factors influence the development of stress and psychological symptoms (Dooley, Catalano, & Serxner, 1987; Kessler, House, & Turner, 1987), although the link is probably indirect, mediated by such factors as loss of social support and esteem. Measures of such variables are, of course, most often in the form of composite indicators (as in the measurement of social class), or in the form of quantitative indices (as in determinations of poverty). Some examples of these indicators of stress are provided in later chapters, especially Chapters 7 and 9.

CONCLUDING COMMENTS

Past school reforms have emphasized demographic variables in identifying students for special educational and psychological services. But more behavior-specific approaches to identifying students need to be developed and applied, and in this chapter there is an emphasis on the importance of stressful events and experiences in the lives of children and adolescents. A contextual formulation of stress and coping also is advocated as a framework for the development and implementation of stress intervention programs in the schools. This chapter also emphasizes that integrating the analysis of stress and coping processes and the analysis of demographic variables, so as to achieve the most understanding of factors that influence educational outcomes, is a major challenge of school reform.

In determining the level, impact, and significance of stress, it also is important to keep in mind that the objective world of the school, family, and neighborhood may be easy to describe physically, but not so easy to describe from the point of view of the subjective meanings it carries for children, adolescents, teachers, and parents. As an analogy, the physical properties of gold are not in doubt or contested, but the symbolic meaning of gold as money, or as reflecting other values, constitutes its subjective significance. In the same way, it is not only the physical properties of the school, family, and neighborhood environment that count in the stress process, but also their subjective meanings to students, teachers, and parents. In fact, the objective environment, physically speaking, may sometimes be irrelevant in the measurement and understanding of stress.

3   STRESS, COPING, AND ADAPTATIONAL OUTCOMES

There are two basic approaches to stress, the biological or physiological and the psychological or psychosocial. In the biological approach, stress is viewed as an individual's response to an event. For example, Walter Cannon considered stress as "a response to threat that was directly related to survival and adaptation" (Fleming, Baum, & Singer, 1984, p. 939). In Cannon's theory, stress and its emergency response prepared the individual to cope with danger. Recognition of danger was followed by adrenal gland activity and sympathetic arousal in which the individual could more easily fight or flee from the danger. Selye (1980) also took a biological perspective and defined stress as "the nonspecific result of any demand upon the body" (p. vii). To describe the effects of stress on the organism, he proposed a theory known as the General Adaptation Syndrome (GAS). The GAS consists of three stages: an alarm reaction, resistance, and exhaustion. According to Fleming et al. (1984), Selye's theory implies that the damage produced by stressors accumulates over time; that these effects are involved in serious pathology when they overwhelm the person's ability to cope; and that stress may be additive. Overall, this perspective focuses on the effects of the environment on an individual's physiological and endocrinal responses, and, consequently, psychological aspects of the individual are neglected.

In contrast, those who view stress from a psychological perspective take both environmental factors and the individual's psychological reactions into account. For example, Lazarus and Folkman (1984) view stress in terms of the interaction between an individual's cognitive-mediational processes and stressful situations. In addition, the individual's response to a stressor is related to how the stressor is appraised, and how the individual appraises his or her ability to cope with the stressful event. For them, stress is defined as "a particular relationship between the person and the environment that is appraised by the person as taxing or exceeding his or her resources and endangering his or her well-being" (p. 19).

As a whole, the biological or physiological perspective is an appropriate approach to understanding and dealing with the physical or medical aspects of stress. However, the psychological or psychosocial perspective takes into account both psychological and physical factors in stress and thus is more comprehensive, especially for examining the relationship between stress and coping.

DEFINITIONS OF STRESS

The term *stress* has been defined in various ways (see, e.g., Fleming et al., 1984; Matteson, 1987). However, most definitions fall into three categories: (a) stimulus definitions, (b) response definitions, and (c) stimulus-response interaction (or relational) definitions.

In a stimulus definition, stress is defined as the force or stimulus acting on the individual that causes the individual discomfort or strain (Matteson & Ivancevich, 1982). This approach tends to focus on events in the environment such as natural disasters, illness, or noxious conditions. Further, the stimulus definition assumes that certain situations are normatively stressful and that individual differences in the evaluation of events are secondary. But the degree and quality of stress reactions may differ markedly in a situation even when the loss is the same. Thus this approach does not represent the complexity of the situation well.

As for the response definition, it is most commonly utilized in the biological and medical areas. Selye's work is a good example of this approach. In this approach, stress is viewed as a state called a "strain," with the stimulus being the stressor (Matteson & Ivancevich, 1982). According to Matteson and Ivancevich, stress is a response to stressor conditions in our environment. However, one problem with defining stress by the response is that we then have no way of identifying prospectively what will be the stressor, and what will not. For example, we cannot conclude that a student's failure on a test will likely cause stress until the student makes some specific response such as becoming angry or crying (Lazarus & Folkman, 1984). We must wait for the response to occur. Furthermore, many responses can be taken to indicate stress when they actually may not reflect stress. For example, the heart rate of a person who is jogging will rise sharply even when he or she is psychologically relaxed. In other words, it is difficult to determine whether a response reflects psychological stress without reference to the stimulus.

The third definition, the stimulus–response interaction (or relational) definition, is based on the belief that there is no clearcut way to predict psychological stress as a reaction without reference to the characteristics of the person. Thus, Lazarus and Folkman (1984) suggested that it is more appropriate to view psychological stress as a relationship between the person and the environment. According to Matteson (1987), the stimulus–response interaction definition also offers the most realistic view of the dynamic nature of stress.

In short, stimulus and response definitions of stress have limited utility because a stimulus is defined as stressful only in terms of a stress response. More adequate rules also are needed in specifying the conditions under which some stimuli, and not others, are stressors. The stimulus–response interactional or relational definition of stress, which is also called the "transactional" view of stress, seems to be more comprehensive than the other two definitions.

STRESS VERSUS ANXIETY AND BURNOUT

There is a tendency among psychologists and educators concerned with stress to use the term *stress* as a synonym for anxiety and burnout. However, many psychologists have argued against this equivalency. For example, May (1983) has pointed out that anxiety cannot adequately substitute for stress. Phillips and Lee (1980) made the further point that anxiety is "only one of the reactions that can occur to stressful situations" (p. 93). In using stress as a synonym for anxiety we cannot adequately distinguish between the different emotions that often are reactions to stress. For example, prolonged anger may cause stress as much as prolonged fear. As May pointed out, anxiety is a subjective, objectless experience, whereas stress has an objective reference. Also, anxiety is an emotion, whereas stress is not an emotion but a threat to which the individual may react with emotion.

The relation between stress and burnout also is much discussed (see, e.g., Dunham, 1984; Farber, 1984, 1991). There is argument that stress and burnout are related, but there are different views of the nature of this relationship. According to Cherniss (1980), burnout is a process that begins with stress and is a coping response used in situations characterized by uncontrollable stress. For D'Arienzo, Moracco, and Krajewski (1982), burnout is the ultimate effect of continued stress. Others (e.g., Farber, 1991) think of burnout as a unique type of stress reaction experienced by people (e.g., teachers and school psychologists) whose work requires extensive contact with other people. For still others (e.g., Matteson, 1987), burnout is best viewed as a subset of stress reactions. In substance, it seems appropriate to adopt the position that stress and burnout, though related, are not equivalent terms.

THE CONCEPT OF COPING

The concept of coping has long been used informally, as well as formally, in the areas of psychology in which adaptation or adjustment have been emphasized. However, as with stress, coping has been defined in various ways. One of these approaches to coping is heavily influenced by Darwinian thought, in which the survival function of coping is emphasized. In this approach, according to Lazarus and Folkman (1984), coping is often defined as "acts that control aversive environmental conditions, thereby lowering psychophysiological disturbance" (p. 118). That is, coping consists of learned behavioral responses that are successful in lowering arousal by neutralizing a dangerous or noxious condition. However, Lazarus and Folkman take the position that this model of coping is "simplistic and lacking in the cognitive-emotional richness and complexity that is an integral part of human functioning" (p. 118). In other words, with an emphasis on the unidimensional concept of drive or arousal, little can be learned about coping strategies that are so important in human affairs, such as cognitive coping strategies and defensive reactions.

Psychologists interested in personality, and psychoanalytically oriented psychologists, have long been concerned with various forms of adjustment. For them, coping typically is defined as realistic and flexible thoughts and acts that solve problems confronting the individual and thereby reduce stress (e.g., Lazarus & Folkman, 1984; Edwards, 1988). Coping is viewed as the highest level of adjustment and most advanced and mature ego process, which is contrasted with more primitive means, such as repression, displacement, and denial of reality. In this approach, coping focuses on "ways of perceiving and thinking about the person's relationship with the environment" (Lazarus & Folkman, 1984, p. 118).

Although this adjustment approach is noteworthy for its rich, vivid descriptions of coping processes, Edwards (1988) and also Lazarus and Folkman (1984) have identified two major drawbacks. One is that this approach suggests that contact with reality is a necessary condition for successful coping when, in some cases, the denial of reality is an effective means of coping. For example, denial may help reduce stress when the student is overwhelmed by a stressful situation or appraises the situation as uncontrollable. There also is research which indicates that, while nonavoidant coping strategies are superior in the long run, avoidant coping strategies may be more effective in the short run (Suls & Fletcher, 1985).

The second major drawback is that this approach typically defines coping in terms of successful adjustment. That is, coping refers to meeting the demands of a stressful situation successfully, whereas failure to meet these demands indicates a lack of coping. However, Lazarus and Folkman (1984) have emphasized that defining coping in terms of its outcome compounds these two variables and further prevents meaningful tests of relationships between coping and well-being.

Reactions to stress also are described by some psychologists in terms of a series of stages through which the individual passes, an approach that, according to Edwards (1988), is particularly common in research on reactions to life-threatening illness and injury. For example, Kubler-Ross (cited in Edwards, 1988) suggested that terminally ill patients pass through stages of denial, anger, bargaining, depression, and acceptance. Although the stage approach may tap the multidimensional and dynamic aspects of coping, this approach, as reviewed by Edwards, lacks empirical support. That is, coping behaviors do not often occur in a specific sequence; instead, individuals select from an array of potential coping strategies and implement strategies in a variety of sequences. Those who adopt this approach also do not specify the factors that influence stage duration and transition or the complexity and variability of coping responses.

In still another approach to defining coping, a taxonomy is developed that classifies coping either according to the method used or according to the focus or target of coping efforts. A number of psychologists have suggested categorization schemes that distinguish between the foci or targets of coping efforts (e.g., Pearlin & Schooler, 1978; Moos & Billings, 1982; Lazarus & Folkman, 1984). The most common categorization scheme involves the following foci: (a) problem-focused coping, which involves attempts to manage or reduce stress by directly altering the situation or the individual's appraisal of the situation; and (b) emotion-focused coping, where attempts are made to regulate the emotional responses to stressful situations (see Lazarus & Folkman, 1984).

Aside from this two-focus coping categorization scheme, the approach of Billings and Moos (1981) is also widely utilized. They suggested three methods of coping: (a) active-cognitive, where the individual attempts to manage his or her appraisal of the stressful situation or event; (b) active-behavioral, which refers to overt behavioral attempts to deal directly with the situation or event; and (c) avoidance, where the individual avoids confronting the problem.

In addition, Lazarus and Folkman (1984) described four strategies of coping: (a) information search, (b) direct action, (c) intrapsychic modes, and (d) inhibition of action. These strategies are used either to mediate person–environment relationships in an instrumental or problem-solving mode or to control individual stress responses selectively in a palliative mode.

Although taxonomic approaches are useful for describing coping behaviors and include a comprehensive assessment of actual coping behaviors, Edwards (1988) pointed out several drawbacks. First, there is difficulty in distinguishing between coping methods and foci. Incomplete consideration of the determinants of coping methods and foci also is a problem. In addition, the mechanisms by which coping influences stress and well-being receive insufficient attention.

In sum, the approaches mentioned above all have provided a substantial contribution to our understanding of coping. They also, however, present a number of conceptual and methodological problems. Of all these efforts, Lazarus and his associates seem to have had the most success in improving upon the theoretical limitations of these approaches, and his theory of stress and coping is discussed in greater detail in the next section.

LAZARUS' THEORY OF STRESS AND COPING

Lazarus' theory (Lazarus & Folkman, 1984) emphasizes the person's appraisal of what is being experienced and the use of this information for coping and shaping the course of events. The processes of cognitive appraisal and coping are critical mediators of stressful person–environment relations and their immediate and long-range outcomes.

In this theory, cognitive appraisal is a process through which the person evaluates whether the situation in which he or she is involved is relevant to his or her well-being, and further evaluates what he or she can do about it. There also are two forms of cognitive appraisal — primary and secondary appraisal.

Primary appraisal refers to the cognitive process of evaluating the significance of a situation for one's well-being. Through the appraisal process the individual will come to one of three judgments about the situation, that it is irrelevant, benign-positive, or stressful. Only when the individual appraises the situation as entailing harm-loss, threat, or challenge can stress appraisal occur. Harm-loss refers to any kind of harm, loss, or damage that has been sustained. Threat refers to anticipated harm, loss, or damage. Challenge refers to the possibility for mastery, gain, or growth which are characterized by pleasurable emotions. In contrast, harm-loss and threat appraisals are frequently associated with negative emotions. Because challenge involves a judgment that the demands of a transaction can be met and overcome, the challenge appraisal can be expected to have a better outcome in a wide range of stressful situations. In addition, although challenge and threat are different in their cognitive component (the judgment of potential harm or loss versus mastery or gain), they are not necessarily mutually exclusive. An event can be appraised as being both threatening and challenging.

Secondary appraisal refers to a process of evaluating what, if anything, can be done to manage threatening or challenging situations. In addition to situational factors, the perceived capabilities of the person also are important determinants of whether stress will occur in a situation. On this point, the concept of secondary appraisal borrows from Bandura's theory of self-efficacy. Bandura (1986) proposed that one's behavior is determined not only by a general outcome expectancy (belief that behavior will lead to a desirable outcome) but also by a sense of self-efficacy (belief that one has the capability to bring about the outcome).

Lazarus and his colleagues have defined coping as a person's "constantly changing cognitive and behavioral efforts to manage specific external and/or internal demands that are appraised as taxing or exceeding the person's resources" (Lazarus & Folkman, 1984, p. 141). For them, coping is a dynamic process of adaptation and also a mediator of the outcomes of stress. In their view, process-oriented coping involves three main features. First, there is a concern with what the person actually thinks and does. Second, what the person actually does is examined within a specific context. Third, coping thoughts and acts will be changed as a stressful encounter unfolds. They further pointed out that "the dynamics and changes that characterize coping as a process are not random; they are a function of continuous appraisals and reappraisals of the shifting person–environment relationship" (p. 142). Furthermore, they suggested that coping is simply a person's efforts to manage stressful demands, and has nothing to do with outcome, which is why they believe that coping should be defined independently of outcome.

As mentioned above, Lazarus and Folkman also utilize a two-focus categorization scheme in their theory. One category is problem-focused coping (coping behavior directed at the situation), and the other is emotion-focused coping (managing emotional response). Along with these two types of coping, two major functions are recognized — regulating stressful emotion (emotion-focused coping) and altering the troubled person–environment relation (problem-focused coping).

RELATIONSHIP BETWEEN A THEORY OF STRESS AND A THEORY OF EMOTION

According to Lazarus (Lazarus, 1991a, b; Lazarus & Folkman, 1984), a theory of emotion has a lot in common with a theory of stress. Emotions are about person–environment relationships that involve harms (for the negative emotions) and benefits (for the positive emotions). That is, emotions involve transactional relationships. They are not generated by intrapsychic processes alone or solely by environmental factors but are products of encounters with the environment. There also are core person–environment relationship themes that elicit each of the main emotions. For example, being "slighted or demeaned" is the prototypic person–environment situation that elicits anger. Another example given by Lazarus is "experiencing irrevocable loss," which elicits sadness. Lazarus further believes that such core relational themes, and the emotions they elicit, are universals, being part of human experience across diverse cultures.

Motivation is another important component of his theory of emotion. It is included in two interrelated senses. It is a disposition variable, in the form of goal hierarchies that people bring to person–environment encounters, which determines the personal relevance of person–environment encounters. In addition, the activation of such dispositions depends on the demands, constraints, and resources presented by the environment. Motivation is thus a transactional as well as a dispositional factor inasmuch as it depends on the juxtaposition of a motive trait and a suitable environment.

The third important factor in emotion is cognition, which involves both the knowledge of and appraisal of what happens in person–environment encounters. In the words of Lazarus (1991b), "knowledge consists of situational and generalized beliefs about how things work" (p. 820) in the adaptational encounters of living, whereas "appraisal consists of an evaluation of the personal significance of what is happening in [a specific] encounter with the environment" (p. 820). For Lazarus, cognitive activity is intrinsic to emotion, and appraisal is necessary for an emotion to occur.

Both primary and secondary appraisal processes also are involved in emotion. Without the appraisal of a stake in the outcome of an encounter (primary appraisal), there is no potential for an emotion. If something is at stake, then its fate will result in a positive or negative emotion, depending on whether the encounter is appraised as beneficial (positive emotion) or harmful (negative emotion). In secondary appraisal, which concerns the options and prospects for coping, one may blame or credit oneself or another person for the harm or benefit, and this, in turn, determines whether there will be guilt, pride, shame, anger, or another emotion. As to options and prospects for coping, one consideration is whether there is the potential to influence the person–environment relationship for the better. Future expectations about how things will change are another consideration. This concerns whether there is the expectation that, because of effective or ineffective coping or other reasons, things will work out favorably or get worse.

Thus, Lazarus's theory of emotion has much in common with his theory of stress. Both are motivational-cognitive-relational theories; primary and secondary appraisal processes are central to both; and person–environment encounters are the source of both stress and emotion.

ADAPTATIONAL OUTCOMES

In its scientific and applied uses, there has been growing recognition that stress is an inevitable aspect of the human condition, and that how the individual copes with stress makes a big difference in adaptational outcomes. It also has become increasingly apparent that there are important individual differences in response to stress, and that this requires attention to the psychological processes that created such differences. In conjunction with this shift toward person factors, there were related concerns for environmental constraints and resources and the stressful demands of environmental transitions and social change. Stress, therefore, has become a concept that involves many variables and processes, although the sphere of its meaning lies in the relationship between the person and the environment. With this relationship focus, if we are to understand stress and its impact on human functioning, both the characteristics of the person and those of the environment need to be taken into account.

Looking at a broad range of stress phenomena and adaptational outcomes, one essential theme is the linkage of stress with illness and physical health. The point here is that threat appraisals and emotions are disturbers of bodily equilibrium and precursors of disease, and that the coping efforts stimulated by these threat appraisals and emotions produce effects on health in the long run. Stress also is related to the personal problems and psychological adjustment of individuals. In the causal chain of factors, there is a high level of stress that, when combined with inadequate methods of coping with this stress, may then lead in the long-term to developmental deviations and psychological impairment.

However, this does not mean that there is a one-to-one relationship between the outcome of any given encounter and its long-term counterpart. For example, dissatisfaction and negative affect in a single person–environment transaction say little or nothing about whether the individual is generally dissatisfied. Similarly, to know that a person has functioned effectively in specific kinds of encounters does not provide sufficient evidence of good overall functioning. As one example, the individual who can handle the environment of an inner-city ghetto may lack the understanding and resources for functioning well in a middle-class community context.

Another theme is that individuals are shaped by the social system, through multiple forms of influence, and because each person's experience and biological makeup are to some extent unique, they must act out both their social and individual destinies. Thus, there is some degree of mismatch between the individual and portions of the social system, so that there is a conflict among these relationships, which leads to stress. Aside from the many demands of a person's physical environment, such as crowding, noise, pollution, and crime, there are a host of demands that stem from the social environment, including those related to schools, the family, peer groups, and work. In addition to social demands created by the immediate social environment at any given moment, there also are internal demands founded in the socialization process that reflects the individual's developmental history. The social, as well as the physical environment, also is constantly changing and in a state of flux, thereby creating stress. At the same time, while the social system operates on the individual by creating demands, it also provides resources that the individual can and must use to survive and flourish. Social support, in the form of social networks and peer groups, is one important example of a social resource.

COPING AND ADAPTATIONAL OUTCOMES FOR CHILDREN AND ADOLESCENTS: SOME SPECIAL CONSIDERATIONS

Applying these general notions of coping and adaptational outcomes to the actions of children and adolescents requires considering some additional factors. First, the strong dependence of children and adolescents on adults emphasizes the need to give special consideration to social context in understanding their coping resources, styles, and efforts. Thus, adaptive coping cannot be characterized by a description of the child's skills and resources alone but instead lies more in the relation between the child and the environment than it does for adults. Second, basic features of cognitive and social development are likely to be more instrumental in what children and adolescents experience as stressful and how they cope. Important aspects of development include self-perceptions and self-efficacy beliefs, self-control or inhibitory mechanisms, attributions of cause, friendships, and parental relationships (Compas, 1987a). Thus, whereas coping during childhood and adolescence is affected by both personal and environmental factors, the degree to which coping is effective may depend, to a greater degree than for adults, on the goodness of fit between the child and the environment (see, e.g., Lerner, Baker, & Lerner, 1985).

Nature of Child and Adolescent Contexts

Despite early emphasis on ecological factors in behavior by Kurt Lewin and Roger Barker, the study of contexts has only recently become widely evident in research on children and adolescents. A strong emphasis in this direction came from Bronfenbrenner's (e.g., 1986) ecological analysis of the imbeddedness of individuals and families in a layered array of social systems, both proximal (e.g., children's schools) and more distal and molar (e.g., the economic milieu). This model has much in common with general systems theory (see, e.g., Gunnar & Thelen, 1989).

Social networks and support.

One example of the ecological analysis of contexts is the study of social networks. Work with mothers has provided considerable evidence showing that social support moderates the effects of stressful life circumstances. For example, social supports are associated with attachment security among preschoolers (Crittenden, 1985) and buffer the negative impact of infant irritability on maternal supportive caregiving (Crockenberg & McCluskey, 1986).

The social networks of children and adolescents are also receiving attention (e.g., Belle, 1989; Csikszentmihalyi & Larson, 1984). Children's networks expand across ages, with same-sex contacts accounting for the most frequent and extensive contacts. (See review by Hartup, 1983.) The evidence also shows that children's and adolescents' perceptions of the availability of social support are associated with positive psychosocial outcomes (Hoffman, Ushpiz, & Levy-Shiff, 1988). The availability of social support also protects against the stress of multiple changes during the transition to adolescence (Simmons & Blyth, 1987).

Overall, studies of social support as a resource for coping among children and adolescents indicate that there is a direct relation between social support and levels of psychological and physical problems, although this relationship varies with the gender, age, and socioeconomic status of children and adolescents, and with the number of supportive relationships, satisfaction with social support, and other aspects or dimensions of social support (Compas, 1987b). Studies of the interactive effects of social support, however, have been more mixed. For example, the combination of life events with social support does not consistently predict the level of mental and physical problems of children and adolescents.

Schools and school transitions.

Schools also have attracted increased attention because of the recognition that these institutions are major sources of socially imposed transitions (Higgins & Parsons, 1983), as well as primary vehicles for the educational and social agenda (see review by Minuchin & Shapiro, 1983).

Social relations in schools have received particular attention. Friend selection is affected by the structural and organizational characteristics of schools (Epstein, 1989). Also, under certain teaching methods and classroom organization, peers can and do significantly affect classroom learning (e.g., Damon & Phelps, 1989; Slavin, 1987).

Relations between family and school contexts have also begun to receive attention. School satisfaction has been shown to be a joint function of home–school authority congruence, and individual variables such as independence and internal locus of control (Epstein, 1983). Generally, the greater parents' involvement with schools and children's school-related tasks, the higher the school performance of their offspring (Stevenson & Baker, 1987). However, the critical dimensions of congruency/incongruency between home and school are yet to be fully identified.

Transitions from one school setting to another are especially significant. For example, the transition to junior high school has been studied by several investigators (e.g., Hirsch & Rapkin, 1987; Simmons & Blyth, 1987). This transition is particularly disruptive to psychosocial functioning and school achievement for girls, who are especially likely to be undergoing rapid pubertal maturation and beginning to date.

Niche-picking.

Of particular interest to work on stress and its effects are the implications of *niche-picking* — individual variation in responsiveness to, and selection of, specific aspects of the environment (see, e.g., Maccoby, 1988; Scarr & McCartney, 1983). The hypothesis that niche-picking intensifies as a function of age (Scarr & McCartney, 1983) points especially to the need for studies of stress processes in conjunction with the opportunities, constraints, and demands of schools and other salient contexts to which children and adolescents must adapt.

Macro-sociocultural factors.

Existing literature has focused largely on the stress in children's and adolescents' lives related to micro-social variables, such as parental relationships and supports. This is true for two reasons: parents are most significant in the child's life, and parents are the mediators of community stressors for their children. Both theory and conventional wisdom recognize the significant role of parents in protecting their children from trauma imposed by the outside world. Further, there are reasons to contend that the coping strength the child will have in order to deal with traumas imposed on the child by the outside world is, to a large degree, a function of relationships within the home. Nevertheless, children experience stress in response to events in the outside world, such as the experience of stress from poverty, catastrophe, and discrimination, that are independent of the parental response. Benedek (1985), for example, has shown that parental stability during a natural disaster or traumatic event such as war or crime cannot completely mitigate the impact of such events on their children.

However, not all macro-sociocultural factors that cause stress reactions in children and adolescents have been examined carefully. As one exception, Berry and Chiappelli (1985) have summarized the literature on the impact of unemployment on school-age children. It reduces family resources, the adequacy of family diet, and the amount of medical care, recreation, and clothing the family has. They suggested that the loss of things that facilitate peer acceptance, such as special types of clothing, games, and fad items, were a special source of stress for school-age children, especially adolescents.

Unfortunately, there are only a few studies that directly ask children and adolescents if they are concerned about parental unemployment. In one such study of 4th- through 6th-graders in urban and suburban schools, Pryor-Brown, Cowen, Hightower, and Lofyczewski (1986) included unemployment of parents in a study of stressful life events. Of the 22 events that were rated, parental unemployment was 11th in frequency. It also occurred more often among urban youngsters, and was rated more upsetting by them.

Unemployment, of course, is but a part of the larger picture of poverty, and one can document how being poor directly affects children. When parents either cannot or will not provide the consistent basic level of care needed for growth, children are damaged. Their physical and mental well-being may be harmed, and their sense of trust and security is threatened. Children sense the embarrassment of being poor among their peers and grow up with a diminished self-image.

Some implications of unemployment and the broader problems of poverty for interprofessional practice, which includes school and other professionals in the community, also need to be addressed. Interprofessional collaboration to identify and provide services in a coordinated manner is considered by many to be an ideal model for such activities. However, the model frequently breaks down as persons in the helping professions struggle in separate community service systems to ameliorate the many symptoms of poverty, and as agency policies become barriers to coordinated services. In this situation, the public schools are a potential locus for service. Because children attend (or should attend) school daily, school-based multiservice centers are suggested for the delivery of inter-professional services. The school is already recognized as an important socializing agent of society. It is also a nutrition and health center, with food programs, health education, and even medical clinics. The psychological services (including counseling and guidance) provided in the schools now are only a beginning for what could become family support centers in the schools. The school is an ideal setting because teachers and other school professionals are in a unique position to recognize the multiple problems of poverty in children. However, schools do not have the resources to provide all these services. Although schools have been consistently recognized as ideal settings for tackling problems like this, their budgets rarely are expanded to allow this role. A solution might be to bring other agency services into the school with financial support from outside the education budget.

Coping and Mastery of the Environment

It also is important to emphasize that we should not view the way children and adolescents cope with stress as inherently maladaptive and deleterious. Major stress, which is sometimes referred to as a crisis, causes some children and adolescents to draw upon adaptive resources they never thought they had. Such youth can gain strength from stress that can be used in subsequent crises. Children and adolescents who are protected from certain kinds of stress may be all the more vulnerable to stress later because they failed to learn coping skills that are needed for functioning effectively in schools and other areas of day-to-day life (see, e.g., Murphy & Moriarity, 1976). Thus the question is not whether stress is good or bad but rather how much and what kinds of stress children and adolescents experience and under what personal, school, family, and social conditions this stress is helpful or harmful.

A related point addressed by Lazarus and Folkman (1984) is that coping as a concept is sometimes equated with adaptational success. That is, coping is defined in ways that consider certain strategies inherently better or more useful than others, so that the best coping is that which changes the person–environment relationship for the better. This view of coping also is in keeping with American values regarding individualism, which lends support to the tendency to regard mastery over the environment as the coping ideal. In such a definition, coping is viewed as equivalent to solving problems by acting effectively to anticipate and prevent them.

The problem in applying this kind of thinking to children and adolescents is not that solving problems is undesirable, but that not all sources of stress in schools and in living are amenable to mastery or even fit within a problem-solving framework. Examples that involve children and adolescents include chronic illness and disease, violence, natural disasters, and the developmental disabilities of childhood and adolescence. Emphasizing problem solving and mastery also devalues other functions of coping, such as managing emotions and maintaining self-esteem and a positive outlook. For children and adolescents, coping processes aimed at tolerating difficulties, or at minimizing, accepting, or ignoring them, are just as important as problem-solving strategies that are aimed at mastering the environment. In essence, to make progress in understanding the relationship between coping and outcome, it is important to view coping as efforts to manage stressful situations regardless of outcome. Applied to children and adolescents, no coping strategy should be viewed as inherently better or worse than another. Instead, judgments as to the adaptiveness of a strategy for children and adolescents must be made contextually — e.g., in terms of conditions in their schools, the functionality of their families, and the characteristics of their neighborhoods and other environmental units and behavior settings.

CONCLUDING COMMENTS

This chapter described stress, appraisal, and coping processes and made the point that they take place continuously during waking life, and that they are largely evaluative processes which have a focus on meaning and significance. Stress occurs when some harm or loss is anticipated but has not yet taken place or when some damage to the individual has already been sustained. Appraisals of what is at stake in an enounter with the environment and coping options also interact with each other in shaping the degree of stress and the strength and quality of the emotional reaction. The chapter also emphasized that the quality of life of students, and what is usually meant by psychological and physical health, are tied up in the ways students evaluate and cope with stress.

Another task of this chapter was to spell out the mechanisms through which appraisal and coping affect adaptational outcomes. It was pointed out that stress is not inherently deleterious, and that coping should not be equated with adaptational success. Stress, in essence, is a struggle between opposing forces, i.e., the demands of the environment are always in some measure countered by the individual's coping resources and processes. Added attention was also given to the special condition of children and adolescents, and to factors involved in extrapolating coping and adaptational concepts and processes to them. There was the further emphasis that the school is not just a major source of stress; it must also be a means of adaptation to stress, and it must help to provide the vital resources that children and adolescents can and must draw upon to survive and flourish.

4 STRESS INTERVENTION IN THE SCHOOLS: SOME GENERAL CONSIDERATIONS

One premise put forward in Chapters 1, 2, and 3 (and which infuses later chapters) is that stress is an important feature of the learning and behavior problems of children and adolescents. A second is that schools ought to take more responsibility for helping students cope more effectively with stress. A third premise is that schools can offer interventions to students that will reduce their levels of stress and/or improve their coping skills and make a difference in how well they do in school. Stress intervention in the schools, in this third premise, means anything that is done by school professionals, especially school psychologists, counselors, and teachers, that is designed to prevent or ameliorate debilitating stress and coping inadequacies. For example, two kinds of intervention are included: counseling or therapy, which refers to interventions that involve working one-on-one with individual students or with small groups of students or parents; and stress management, which refers to formal programs for students in general or for special groups of students, parents, or teachers who share a common problem.

Another premise underlying this perspective on stress intervention in the schools is that of student–environment optimization. The optimization notion assumes that students strive to achieve "optimal" school, family, social, physical, and other environments or those that maximize the fulfillment of their needs and the accomplishment of their goals and plans. In actuality, however, students are often forced by situational constraints to accept undesirable conditions, or at best to achieve less than optimal improvement in their situation. In this connection, a distinction also needs to be drawn between optimization and adaptation. Adaptation refers to students' attempts (behavioral, cognitive, affective, and physiological) to cope with existing conditions, whereas optimization involves a more planful process whereby students not only adapt to the existing situation, but also opt to maintain or modify their milieux in accord with their goals.

A further premise is that stress alone is not a sufficient cause of any physiological, cognitive, affective, conative, or behavioral outcome. To produce stress-linked outcomes, other conditions such as vulnerabilities or inadequate coping processes must also be present. However, environmental and individual components of stress vary in importance. For example, when an event is extremely powerful and unambiguous with respect to the harms and threats it generates for students, we would expect that the environmental component would have a major impact and thus would have a leveling effect on student differences in stress appraisal and stress outcomes. In contrast, the individual component will exert more influence on the stress that students experience in daily hassles, leaving more room for individual differences in response to such situations and for the agendas of students to come into play.

WHO'S RESPONSIBLE FOR THE PROBLEM AND THE SOLUTION?

To clarify the conceptual foundations of the variety of approaches that can be used in planning interventions designed to help students manage stress, one needs to pose answers to two questions: (a) To what extent is the student considered responsible for the problem? (b) To what extent is the student held responsible for the solution? A model of helping and coping outlined by Brickman and his colleagues (Brickman et al., 1982) is one effort to bridge this gap between conceptual foundations and intervention planning activities. They described four different models of helping based on attributions of responsibility for creation of the problem and responsibility for a solution. Applied to students, the *moral model* holds that students are responsible for both creating their problems and finding solutions. In the *compensatory model*, students would not be responsible for their problems but would be responsible for the solutions. The *medical model* assumes that students are not responsible for either their problems or solutions. In their fourth model, the *enlightenment model*, students would not be responsible for solutions but would be responsible for their problems. These models can be held by teachers and other school personnel as well as by students, and the particular pattern of attribution of responsibility affects not only the way stress intervention services are provided in the schools, but also the way in which they are received by students. Therefore, the extent to which there is a mismatch between the school's model of helping and the recipient student's model of responsibility is the extent to which stress intervention programs will be less successful than they would otherwise be.

Support for each of these models will vary with the nature of the stress problems for which interventions are planned. For example, the moral model would have no support as the basis of interventions designed to help students deal with high stress caused by the death of a parent, although it might have more support in planning interventions aimed at stress problems arising out of drug abuse. Generally, both the medical and compensatory models would be preferable alternatives to the student-blaming orientation of the moral and enlightenment models. One serious limitation of the medical model, however, is that it suggests that students are not responsible for changing their stress-related maladaptive behavior. In contrast, the compensatory model assumes that students need to take an active, responsible role in the stress intervention process.

ANALYSIS OF HOW INTERVENTION WORKS: THE HOLLON AND BECK APPROACH

There are many intervention techniques that can be applied in the schools (see, e.g., D'Amato & Rothlisberg, 1992), although there is no simple principle by which to categorize them. However, Hollon and Beck (1979, 1986) developed a generic scheme for classifying interventions that makes as much sense as any of the others. They identified several types of intervention and, in each case, identified the theoretical rationale, strategies of treatment, and the specific procedures employed to produce changes. Hollon and Beck also have developed an analysis of how intervention works, for which they put forward four themes about how the process of intervention can change people. These four themes are: (a) feelings shape thought and action; (b) actions shape thought and feeling; (c) the environment shapes thought, feeling, and action; and (d) thoughts shape feeling and action. Although these are seemingly clear-cut formulations, they are merely heuristic aids for thinking about how intervention works. Distinctions between action, thought, and feelings are far from clear, and they also are interdependently and reciprocally related. However, they are useful as guides for examining interrelationships among the psychological processes in experiencing stress, and for coping with it.

Each of these themes also identifies one or more of the keys to stress intervention. As to the first, emotions are powerful determinants of a student's thought and action, in part as motivators of learning and behavior. But emotions also can interfere with cognitive or behavioral activities. When this happens, the intervention task would be to lower the level of counterproductive motivation so that its harmful effects can be eliminated.

In relation to the second theme, the key to stress intervention is to get the student to behave differently so that new, more effective coping patterns can be acquired. The groundwork here is that children and adolescents actively select and shape, rather than passively relate to, their environment.

Changing the student on the basis of the third theme involves changing his or her school, social, family, or physical environment. Although the application of this theme does not necessarily help to understand the cause of the student's problems, it does lead to an understanding of the environmental factors that maintain them. Under the auspices of this theme, we also confront the issue of whether maladaptation can be interpreted as a failure of the student or as a failure of the school, family, or community. But even with an emphasis on individual coping, some difficulties of children and adolescents can only be dealt with at the group or system level.

The last theme emphasizes the idea that how students act and feel depends on the way they think. In applying this theme, the central task is to change the way encounters significant to their well-being are appraised. The goal here is to make appraisal processes more conscious, rational, and deliberative.

TRANSACTION AND PROCESS IN STRESS INTERVENTION IN THE SCHOOLS

With these general themes as a framework, we now have the beginnings of a useful perspective within which to view stress interventions in the schools. However, the transactional views of Lazarus and Folkman (1984) are another important part of this perspective. Their position is that stress is neither in the environment nor in the person but a product of their interplay. Nevertheless, children, adolescents, and adults are not merely passive recipients of environmental demands. They actively select and shape the environments in their lives. Through this selectivity, and through cognitive processes such as appraisal, an organization of person and environment variables also emerges. However, children and adolescents are less capable of changing these environments than adults. The environments of children and adolescents also are to some extent given, although personal values, abilities, preferences, and other personal characteristics have a selective function.

Translated into the task of stress intervention with students, this means that we cannot focus solely on what is wrong with students but must consider the characteristics of students' environments and how they were selected. Thus stress interventions that are centered on changing these environments, where that is feasible, are just as appropriate as those designed to change the students. Schools and other contexts in which children and adolescents function, such as the family, also contain many regulations, demands, constraints, prohibitions on behavior, and resources with which the child and adolescent must deal and which also create important sources of stress.

Process, which refers to two properties of encounters, is another important aspect of Lazarus and Folkman's view of stress interventions. For them, coping through thoughts, feelings, and actions is contextual, changing from one type of encounter to another. In addition, stress and coping change as the encounter unfolds. Thus, person–environment transactions and coping processes are interwoven. For example, vulnerability to stress is a transactional variable in that it is not relevant under all environmental conditions but only under those that interact functionally with relevant person factors. That is, vulnerability is simultaneously an intraindividual and interindividual concept. It is intraindividual when the focus is on the pattern of stress within an individual, which means finding out which situations generate stress and which do not. On the other hand, it is interindividual when the person is compared with other people. Thus the concept of vulnerability can have special utility in relation to stress interventions in the schools (a point that is discussed in greater detail in Chapter 10). For example, when a student's pattern of vulnerability is compared with that of other students, it may become clear that this student reacts with stress in situations where most students do not.

The transaction and process model, when applied to stress interventions with children and adolescents, also has special developmental dimensions (which are explored in detail in Chapter 6). The developmental level of the child or adolescent is one important consideration. For example, cognitive appraisal processes, types of stressful events, and the role of parents as buffers against stress change across childhood and adolescence. Account also needs to be taken of the fact that the nature of the relationship between stress and mental and physical problems changes with age. There is the further need to realize that stress and psychological or physical symptoms in family members, particularly parents, may greatly affect and be affected by child and adolescent stress and disorder. In addition, we need to take reciprocal influence into account in planning interventions. For example, a child's or adolescent's loss of a parent through death or divorce may lead to depressed affect, and the behavior and emotions characteristic of depression may then influence the response of others, potentially increasing the frequency of negative interpersonal events for this child or adolescent.

ROLE OF COPING STYLES

There is substantial individual variability in responses of children and adolescents to stress. Thus, factors that make youngsters more or less vulnerable to stress need to be considered. Primary among these is the way children and adolescents cope with stress. That is, children and adolescents differ in the ways they try to deal with stress. For example, youngsters with a self-critical schema may be vulnerable to negative achievement events, whereas others with a dependent self-schema may be vulnerable to interpersonal loss events.

To get a handle on such differences, one can make use of the concept of coping style. Coping styles can be defined as methods of coping that characterize a child's or adolescent's reactions to stress either across different situations or over time within a given situation (Compas, 1987a). As one important example, children and adolescents attempt to cope with stress through the use of defense mechanisms. Defense mechanisms are automatic and unconscious, and they alter the perception of both internal and external reality. Defenses commonly used by children and adolescents, listed according to Hendren's (1990, pp. 257-258) progression from immature to mature levels of adaptive functioning, include:

> denial, projection, splitting (occurs when the child or adolescent unconsciously views people or events as being at one extreme or the other), acting out, regression, counterphobia (seeking out experiences that are consciously or unconsciously feared), identification, reaction formation, repression (unconscious) and suppression (conscious), displacement, isolation of affect (separating ideas or events from feelings associated with them), rationalization, intellectualization, sublimation, humor (used defensively to relieve anxiety caused by discrepancies between what one wishes for himself or herself and what actually happens), and altruism (seemingly unselfish interest in the welfare of others).

All defense mechanisms attempt to reduce stress, but immature defenses (relative to the age of the child or adolescent) often have greater long-term consequences and are more likely to be associated with psychopathology.

Temperament is another coping style factor that is important in children's and adolescents' reactions to stress. The tripartite classification of Thomas and Chess (1984) encompasses such dimensions as emotional flexibility, regularity, threshold of stimulus response, attention span or persistence level, prevailing mood, and intensity of reaction. These dimensions tend to cluster in patterns which they identify as three temperament types (i.e., the easy, the difficult, and the slow-to-warm-up temperament types), and these clusters give significant clues as to the role temperament will play in reaction to stress. A child or adolescent of easy temperament, for example, tends to be adaptable and positive in outlook, curious and persistent in explorations. A child or adolescent of difficult temperament is generally inflexible and easily alarmed by new stimuli, negative in outlook, and irregular and intense in reaction. The slow-to-warm-up child or adolescent, as the name suggests, displays slow adaptability, a certain reluctance to explore or confront new stimuli, and a low intensity of reaction. With these characteristics in mind, it is not difficult to see that children and adolescents of difficult or slow-to-warm-up temperament may be particularly affected by stressful experience. Given their level of adaptability, such children and adolescents may be particularly prone to physiologic disorders (e.g., reduced ability to regulate biological reactivity). In contrast, emotional flexibility and positive emotional outlook may be the most important temperamental factors governing a child's or adolescent's response to stress. Persistence, as a temperamental factor, may also enhance the child's or adolescent's ability to seek solutions or ameliorate the stress that is faced.

Other child and adolescent coping styles are described by Compas (1987a), including descriptions of (1) internal cognitive problem solving, (2) coping in achievement contexts, (3) the Type A behavior pattern, and (4) repression-sensitization coping responses. However, he acknowledges that there are few good measures of these coping styles that are useful with children and adolescents.

INCORPORATING STRESS IN DIAGNOSTIC FORMULATIONS AND INTERVENTION PLANS FOR CHILDREN WITH EMOTIONAL PROBLEMS: CHANDLER'S MODEL AS AN EXAMPLE

The effects of stressful life events on children and adolescents increasingly are being incorporated into diagnostic formulations and treatment plans. In the past, stressful events were most often seen as exacerbating preexisting conflicts and anxieties. Today, however, stress is looked on as a dynamic entity in its own right.

Chandler (1985b) illustrates this new incorporation of stress within discussions of the emotional problems of children and adolescents. He covers not only the sources of stress in children and adolescents but also their reactions to stress, ways of examining children and adolescents for stress, and strategies for helping them cope with stress.

In discussing the child's or adolescent's response to stress, Chandler uses a two-dimensional model of stress response, with passive-active as one axis and introversion-extraversion as the intersecting one. The resulting matrix gives rise to four basic stress response patterns: the repressed child or adolescent, the dependent child or adolescent, the passive-aggressive child or adolescent, and the impulsive child or adolescent. As the author suggests, the patterns are oversimplified, but they should be useful as a first step in arriving at a more differentiated diagnosis.

Another chapter examines stress in the child's or adolescent's life and provides an additional example of how stress is being incorporated into dynamic approaches to diagnosing and treating emotional problems of children and adolescents. The author does caution, however, that environmental factors need to be checked before assuming the problem is internal to the child or adolescent, and that physical/medical factors need to be considered before assuming that the problem is primarily psychological in nature. Chandler also provides a Life Events Inventory for assessing the number and types of stresses a child or adolescent is experiencing.

In his presentation concerning helping children and adolescents to cope, Chandler takes a broad, eclectic approach. He includes environmental manipulation, working with parents, parent education and training, counseling parents, child and adolescent behavior management, peer group counseling, and psychotherapy with children and adolescents. Chandler also provides in-depth discussions of the four response types mentioned earlier. He makes his descriptions concrete, with illustrative case studies, and provides additional examples of intervention strategies.

Clearly, the stress approach to emotional problems offers many treatment options for the school (or other) helping professional. It also is clear that Chandler's model, on the whole, is a good example of the stress approach to the emotional problems of children and teenagers.

SOME OTHER SOURCES OF GENERAL KNOWLEDGE AND SKILLS THAT ARE NEEDED AS A FOUNDATION FOR PLANNING STRESS INTERVENTIONS

To foster student growth in coping abilities, and to help students manage and eventually resolve stress problems, school-based helpers (i.e., school psychologists, counselors, social workers, nurses) also need a foundation of general intervention knowledge and skills. For example, conducting family interventions in the schools is an innovative idea, an idea whose arrival has been long overdue, according to Walsh and Giblin (1988). Among other things, their book highlights several interesting points about how family interventions can serve to strengthen the bridge between the school and the family. The volume edited by Bond and Wagner (1988), another good resource on family intervention, focuses on the need to help families cope with stressful life transitions, such as school entry and loss of a parent or spouse. Overall, skills training programs are highlighted, although some chapters review literature describing the nature of the problems that contemporary parents face (e.g., the need for quality child care, the problems associated with divorce and family violence, and the stresses that occur when there is a child with chronic physical illness in the family). One of the best chapters focuses on the development of programs for African-American parents.

In contrast to that family focus, the book by Rose and Edleson (1987) is a comprehensive and readable guide that is based on a unified multimethod approach using group techniques and procedures with children and adolescents with diverse problems in interpersonal, problem-solving, cognitive and affective coping, and self-management areas. Overall, its intervention approach is cognitive-behavioral in orientation.

A more general approach, aimed at helping at-risk students succeed in school, is provided by Kruger (1990) and Forman (1987). Both edited books provide practical intervention strategies that can be applied at the classroom or schoolwide level to a variety of problem areas. Each also was simultaneously published as a book and as a journal issue (in *Special Services in the Schools*, a continuing resource for practical ideas on school intervention).

In contrast, a case study approach to prescriptions for change is provided by D'Amato and Rothlisberg (1992). A unique feature of this edited book is that a very detailed case study of a single student is provided in Chapter 2. This case is then analyzed from a number of different psychological perspectives (e.g., behavioral, psychoanalytic, neurological, psychoeducational, ecological) in later chapters.

Turning to a more specific focus on stress, Meichenbaum's book (1985) on stress inoculation training presents an integrative conceptual scheme to help in understanding efforts to reduce and prevent stress reactions. He also provides a clinical guide to stress inoculation training.

Taking a more preventive orientation, the volume edited by Bond and Compas (1989) considers models and research that use the school as the context for the prevention of problematic learning, behavior, and emotions, and for the promotion of behavioral and psychological well-being. One important point that is made is that teachers are strong and underutilized resources for primary prevention efforts in schools. Related resources that would facilitate utilization of consultation with teachers in such prevention efforts include Kratochwill and Bergan (1990), Bergan and Kratochwill (1990), and Brown, Pryzwansky, and Schulte (1990). The first two provide detailed guidelines for the behavioral consultation process, whereas the third provides information on organizational entry, the consultant–consultee relationship, system influences, and other matters important to the development of consultation skills.

In overview, this sampling of intervention resource books represents a patchwork of conceptual and disciplinary orientations. Other key ideas they share are the value of promoting selective rather than universal interventions, the challenge of applying probabilistic research findings to the all-or-nothing decisions required by school intervention, and the notion that, in some cases, nonintervention or the policy of the ostrich might be the best policy of all.

OTHER ASPECTS OF STRESS INTERVENTION

There are a number of other considerations to take into account in a school-based perspective on stress intervention. One is that interventions dealing with stress are interrelated with interventions dealing with emotional problems. This is an important point because emotions, like stress, are products of how children and adolescents interpret the changing fates of their most important values and commitments. That is, emotions are products of how children and adolescents appraise what is happening to them. To paraphrase Freud, they are the royal road to understanding the most important agendas of the child or adolescent and how well he or she believes these agendas are being realized on a day-to-day basis.

The findings of research on adaptation level theory (Helson, 1948) also suggest that baseline conditions of a student's life will affect which transactions will be endorsed as positive or negative experiences. For example, this means that if a child or adolescent is living under negative life conditions and expectations, positive experiences will take on more salience than they would for a child or adolescent living under positive life conditions and expectations. Similarly, negative experiences will become more negative when they occur in the context of a child's or adolescent's positive conditions and expectations. Thus the stress experiences of a child or adolescent are not merely reflections of what has actually happened. They also depend on the baseline conditions of the child's or adolescent's life and how he or she appraises his or her experiences.

In thinking about stress interventions in the schools, it also is important to keep in mind that children and adolescents do not generally seek help for single or occasional episodes of stress, even though the episode may produce distress and impaired functioning on those occasions. Children especially, and many adolescents, also often fail to seek help even when stress, operating in an area central to their concerns, becomes overwhelming and seriously disruptive.

Cognitive appraisal and coping also are many-faceted processes that can go wrong in many different ways. The child or adolescent may tend to appraise threat where it is inappropriate and so experience counterproductive emotions and engage in unsuitable coping activity, or there may be a failure to appraise threat when it is appropriate. In these instances, the deficiency centers on primary appraisal and its determinants. The problem can also inhere in secondary appraisal, as when a child or adolescent appraises his or her coping resources unrealistically. For many children and adolescents the problem centers on coping itself, as when they are unable to relinquish problem-focused coping or are ineffective in emotion-focused coping. To frame a stress intervention strategy or direct it properly one has to pinpoint such appraisal or coping problems, even if only tentatively. Thus, in understanding and intervening with the student who is experiencing debilitating stress, there is considerable risk in ignoring his or her appraisal and coping processes and their determinants.

MACROINTERVENTIONS AS AN ALTERNATIVE TO MICROINTERVENTIONS

If one accepts the premise that macrointerventions (intended for general use with relatively large groups) can be used, in addition to microinterventions (intended for specialized use with individuals or small face-to-face groups), to reduce levels of stress and/or improve coping, then the differences between these two approaches provide another useful perspective from which to view stress intervention in the schools. That is, in contrast to one-on-one stress interventions for individual students or special groups of students, there would be other stress programs that are *not* tailored to the particular stress and coping problems of the individual or group. That is, there would be no attempt to pin down the particular vulnerabilities and coping deficiencies that get individual students into trouble. Instead, these programs would be created for students in general.

To appreciate the importance of the distinction between these two approaches one need only consider the well-documented principle that a particular approach will be effective only with certain kinds of people. As an application of this principle, group stress intervention programs may be most useful when coping failure is due to lack of knowledge, skill, or experience. An excellent example of such a program for children is Ladd and Mize's (1983) social skills training program. Although this program has value as an example of what is involved in problem-focused coping, a concern with the emotional factors that underlie maladaptation and impair rational problem-solving processes is missing. Furthermore, skills training emphases in stress interventions can also fail because of long-standing child or adolescent personal difficulties involving conflicts, hidden agendas, and fears originating early in life that have been continually reinforced and maintained by later patterns of experiences or from pervasive beliefs in one's inadequacies. The presence of these complicating factors may also have obstructed the learning of necessary social and coping skills. The burden of intervention then shifts from simple training or education to a more one-on-one type of intervention. Thus, we must be wary of the assumption that when coping has failed, all we need to do is to teach children and adolescents the necessary skills. Sometimes the very obstacle that has led to the coping deficiency in the first place will now obstruct the coping skills training.

As another application, some group intervention programs are designed to provide training in what we think and do when confronted with stressful encounters. The program developed and applied by Bramson (1981), which could be appropriate for teachers who have trouble dealing with other school professionals, a common source of stress in school work settings, is a case in point. In the program, six general steps are spelled out: assessing the situation; avoid wishing (unrealistically) that such people would change or simply go away; distancing oneself from the troubling behavior in order to understand it and even empathize with it; formulating a coping strategy that could change the unproductive pattern of interaction; implementing the plan by first practicing how to act or role-playing with a friend and then choosing an appropriate time for confrontation; and monitoring what is done to assess why it might not be working and ultimately to evaluate the possibilities for avoiding that person (assuming it is a relationship that could be eliminated).

Although the program represents an important attempt to grapple with stress problems, Bramson also attempts to carve out, as program benefits, a range of other outcomes. For example, he describes potential program benefits in relation to seven kinds of people whose behavior patterns are especially difficult to deal with, which is information that might be useful to teachers and other school professionals. Included among these seven categories are people who are indecisive, hostile-aggressive, negativistic, know-it-all, complaining, unresponsive, and overagreeable. As applications of the training provided in the program, he suggests stress-reducing ways to deal with each of these types of people. For example, the recommended strategy for dealing with indecisive people is to help them express their concerns or conflicts, provide them with support, and limit the alternatives offered to them. As a second example, the suggestion he gives for dealing with hostile-aggressive persons is to stand up to them without fighting, and to expect to feel anger but not to allow it to get out of control. As one last example, his advice in dealing with know-it-alls is to make factual rather than dogmatic statements, and even to accept a subordinate role to accomplish what needs to be done.

ROLE OF SCHOOL–FAMILY RELATIONSHIPS IN STRESS INTERVENTIONS

A transactional model says that stress is neither in the child or adolescent nor in the environment but a product of their interplay. Translated into the task of stress intervention in the schools, this means that we cannot focus solely on what is wrong with students, but must consider the characteristics of their school, family, and other environments. Intervention that is centered on changing these environments, when possible, is just as appropriate as intervention designed to change the student.

Among other things, this means that cooperative relationships between the school and family are essential. Supportive partnerships between families and their children's schools have been recognized both theoretically and empirically as capable of producing educational benefits for children and adolescents (Comer, 1986; Conoley, 1987; Goldring, 1990; Hoover-Dempsey & Brissie, 1987) and as necessary for parental commitment to needed changes in schools (Sarason, 1982). As open systems, families and schools share the responsibility for the education, socialization, and inculcation of cultural values in children and adolescents (Conoley, 1987; Epstein, 1986). Oftentimes, however, the relationship between parents and schools is one of polarization that is reflective of an unproductive power struggle (Sarason, 1982). This is especially true in situations where families have children and adolescents with handicaps (Margolis, Shapiro, & Brown, 1987). But the practices and effects of parent involvement in the educational process of their children and adolescents have been studied from the perspective of general education as well as from the perspective of federally mandated parent involvement in the special education process for children and adolescents with handicaps.

Parent involvement in the schools also has been characterized differently by different authors. In Goldring (1990), for example, three levels of parent involvement are identified that, ranging from low to high, include: (1) reception of information and provision of limited help at the school, (2) provision of assistance under the direction of the school staff, and (3) participation in educational policy-making decisions. On the basis of factor analyses of school principals' responses, Goldring (1990) also identified four roles of parents in the schools: educators, resource providers, partners in policy-making, and decision-makers. Epstein (1987) delineated five types of parent involvement: (1) basic obligations of parents to provide conditions at home conducive to learning, (2) basic obligations of schools to communicate with the home, (3) parents as volunteers at the school, (4) parental involvement in learning activities with the child or adolescent at home, and (5) parental participation in governance and advocacy groups. Parents as partners in the decision-making process as the highest level of involvement is common to each of these characterizations of school–family relationships.

Although there is a measure of agreement as to what constitutes parent involvement in the schools, few consistent findings have been reported regarding variables that affect parent involvement (Epstein & Becker, 1982; Hoover-Dempsey & Brissie, 1987). The most frequently studied variable has been the socioeconomic status of the school, and, in general, greater parent involvement has been associated with higher SES level (Goldring, 1990). Teacher characteristics also have been shown to influence parent involvement. Hoover-Dempsey and Brissie (1987) studied parent involvement in relation to organizational qualities of schools and determined that the most consistent predictors of school-based parent involvement were teacher self-efficacy and average family SES, with higher self-efficacy teachers and higher SES families contributing to higher parent involvement. From a survey of teachers at inner-city schools it was determined that teachers concurred regarding the importance of parent involvement for their own effectiveness and student success (Dauber & Epstein, 1989).

Other factors that affect parent involvement include school level, family characteristics, and grade level. For example, there is more involvement at the elementary than the middle school, with better educated parents also being more involved with their child's education both at home and at school (Dauber & Epstein, 1989). There also is less parent involvement in the upper elementary grades, which was attributed to parental perceptions of their incapability to help with more complex work and a lack of encouragement for parental involvement on the part of teachers (Epstein, 1986). Different types of involvement have also been associated with different family characteristics (e.g., family size was shown to be related to parent involvement at home but not at school, working outside the home was not a significant predictor of in-home involvement, but parents who work outside the home participated less at school, and marital status was not shown to have a significant effect on either at-home or at-school involvement; Dauber & Epstein, 1989).

Whether or not the teacher and the school provide opportunities for parent involvement also has been shown to be an important variable (Dauber & Epstein, 1989; Epstein, 1986). In fact, according to Dauber and Epstein, "the strongest and most consistent predictors of parent involvement at school and at home are the specific school programs and teacher practices that encourage and guide parent involvement" (p. 8). In a study of parental reactions to teachers' parent involvement practices, results revealed that 35 percent of the sample had not participated in a parent conference, whereas 70 percent had neither assisted the teacher in the classroom nor participated in fund-raising (Epstein, 1986). Although lack of involvement on the part of many parents was attributed to work outside the home, having small children at home, or other family responsibilities, 12 percent had not been asked to participate. Concerns regarding parent involvement that were gleaned from a large survey of teachers by Epstein and Becker (1982) included lack of time on the part of both parents and teachers, differential benefits expected for different subgroups of families, and problems with parental assistance experienced by teachers.

Although there are still many concerns about parent involvement in the schools, a subtle yet substantial shift seems to be occurring in how school–home relationships are framed. According to Powell (1991), less emphasis is being placed on how to involve parents in the schooling of their children, and there is more emphasis on the broader question of how schools can support families. There also is recognition that quality school–home collaboration involves two-way sharing, clear communication, mutually agreed upon goals, and shared planning and decision making (Seeley, 1989). We also know that most parents want their children to succeed. In a recent analysis of the situation by Davies (1991), it was suggested that school–home collaboration works best when: (1) school professionals and parents build new relationships; (2) there is effective and caring leadership; (3) there are many ways for parents to get involved; (4) there is communication among teachers, parents, *and* students; and (5) schools strive to remove personal and institutional barriers to participation and collaboration.

ROLE OF PARTNERSHIPS BETWEEN SCHOOLS AND SOCIAL SERVICE AGENCIES

However, the solution to the multiple problems of stress is not as simple as working cooperatively with parents and expanding stress programs in the schools. What also is needed is an overhaul of children's and adolescents' services in the community. This means bringing together public and private organizations to meet the stress-related needs of children and adolescents, their families, and the community. Schools also should constitute one of the centers of a coordinated network of services for children and adolescents.

There are a variety of problems with the present social services system. Some children and adolescents receive redundant services for overlapping problems. Youngsters with multiple problems are typically given a label (e.g., dropout, substance abuser, delinquent, teen parent) that oversimplifies the nature of the trouble and obstructs a real evaluation of what's going on and what needs to be done. As these youngsters move from one level of care to another, they move in and out of different department jurisdictions and encounter different groups of service providers.

Fragmentation also prevents social service professionals from seeing the cumulative impact of their interventions. Because problems are defined in the short term and are related to single issues, there is no "permanent record" of what happened over the long haul. That is, there is no joint assessment by the school psychologist, the welfare worker, the counselor, and the teacher. In addition, most of the resources are used for reacting to acute problems and emergencies, and prevention is usually neglected.

In our society, the school is the institution with the most sustained contact with children, adolescents, and their families. But most schools have no family and health services, and they lack information about and contact with other service providers who could help to address the stress problems and other needs of students. However, projects aimed at improving coordination and effectiveness of services for at-risk children and adolescents have been proliferating (National Association of State Boards of Education, 1989). There is an increasing realization that many crucial influences on the education of at-risk children and adolescents are outside the school's orbit. Only an alliance of school psychologists, teachers, and other school professionals; social service agencies; and parents can make a big difference for children and adolescents with multiple problems and dysfunctional families. Some schools have become "hubs" for integrated educational, psychological, and social services. They provide health care, child care, children's protective services, juvenile justice counseling, and parent education. They stay open from 7 a.m. to 7 p.m. and provide breakfast, snacks, recreation, child care, and a variety of psychological and social services. But these schools are rare, and there are few federal, state, or local policies to increase their number.

The urgent question, therefore, is "How can the present situation be changed?" Although no one can be certain, there are some general principles that can be useful. First is the idea that grouping a number of services in one place makes it easier to use all of them. Schools can be one hub, becoming a kind of "educational mall" that eventually would lead to new approaches to the construction of school buildings. However, if the decision is made to locate multiple services in the schools, the issue of who is "in charge" will need to be addressed. On this matter, Kirst (1991) argued that the parties involved should be regarded as coequals. He advocated collaboration in which schools and social service agencies would join to create improvements in services for children and adolescents that would be no single agency's (or the school's) responsibility. He made the further point that collaboration must be preceded by comprehensive community-wide planning that has broad citizen involvement. According to Schorr (1988), the process also needs to involve the line workers — teachers, school psychologists, other school professionals, social workers — from the start, and be reinforced by certain strategies that let workers know that no one agency can solve all the problems. These collaborative processes must also include a baseline assessment of the overall conditions of children and youth so that it will be possible to compile comprehensive assessments periodically to know whether collaborative efforts have made a difference.

However, Kirst (1991) sees these collaborative efforts as only a short-term solution to the fragmentation of services problem. For this reason, he advocates a number of long-term directions. One is for universities to design more interprofessional preparation programs to replace presently splintered preparation of professionals. He also believes that local governance structures need to be revamped, with more joint-powers arrangements as one outcome. Confidentiality requirements, especially in regard to the records of children and adolescents, need to be revised as well, so that information systems of various agencies can be merged. The need for school restructuring is also addressed, with restructuring that provides for more personal relationships between secondary school students and their teachers given special attention.

Despite all the promising developments, efforts to improve social services for children and adolescents are still in the trial-and-error stage. There are few proven strategies, and no single approach will fit all the complex and diverse local circumstances. At this point in time, therefore, the goal should be to devise some initial strategies and build on them. This is an effort, of course, that would facilitate the development and implementation of stress interventions in the schools.

CONCLUDING COMMENTS

There was a focus in this chapter on different approaches to stress intervention. It was emphasized that the range of choices gives rise to the need to think about how stress interventions might work and how stress interventions in the schools might be designed. In the process of making choices, it was further emphasized that there must be a focus not only on proximal factors (i.e., factors within the context of stress and coping) but also on distal factors (i.e., factors residing in the stress-permeated environments in which children and adolescents live). Thus, the challenge for school psychologists and other stress interventionists is to integrate the microanalysis of stress and coping processes with the macroanalysis of the characteristics of school, family, and other environments. Viewed in that light, it is evident that there is a need, in stress intervention efforts, to activate partnerships among school psychologists, teachers, other school professionals, parents, and community-based agency personnel. It also is evident that it is not just what the student does in the treatment setting that matters, but also that the intervention facilitates the complex process of finding new and more serviceable ways of coping in real-life situations.

5 STRESS AND BEHAVIOR SETTINGS IN SCHOOLS

By focusing on intrapersonal and interpersonal processes, educators and psychologists often overlook contextual influences on the behavior of children and adolescents. They also often fail to recognize the order and coherence that exist in the extrapersonal world. The immediate environment of children and adolescents is structured into readily identifiable sociophysical units, such as classrooms, playgrounds, grocery stores, churches and synagogues, shopping malls, and homes, all of which afford opportunities for and impose obligations on children and adolescents.

Fuller understanding of child and adolescent behavior in schools, and the role of stress in schooling, depends on our coupling the study of stress experienced by children and adolescents with the study of these environmental units or behavioral settings. However, such an undertaking is not as simple as it might appear. Some different laws and principles are needed. Moreover, children and adolescents must be thought of not only as relatively independent individual systems but also as relatively dependent components of the behavior setting systems they inhabit.

This ecological perspective was propounded by Barker (1968). His book is the standard reference for the methods and theories of behavior settings, and it has enjoyed the status of a classic almost since it first appeared. Over time, however, the book has become dated, although Barker's methodological and theoretical advances are reported in later publications (see, e.g., Barker & Schoggen, 1973). Among other things, this more recent volume, and Schoggen's (1989) revision and extension of Barker's classic, provide rules for identifying behavior settings and scales for describing various setting facets. Links of settings to community authority systems such as schools, and the degree to which settings are locally autonomous and are designed to benefit certain groups, such as children or adolescents, also are described. A taxonomy of setting types also is presented. Overall, behavior settings are portrayed as small-scale social systems that regulate their internal processes either by corrective feedback or by discharging inadequate components.

BEHAVIOR SETTINGS IN WHICH SCHOOLS?

It is an obvious fact that there are many kinds of schools that vary considerably in many dimensions. Take, for example, public and private schools. Nonpublic schools are both residential and day-schools. Some are religious schools related to local churches or synagogues or a religious hierarchy. Still other private schools are oriented toward a particular life-style (e.g., the military) or are college preparatory schools.

Another group of schools can be identified as serving the needs of special populations. There are special schools for children and adolescents with severe physical and emotional handicaps. There also are schools with special emphasis on certain cultural or linguistic issues. Further, one cannot lump schools in low-income urban settings with schools in more affluent suburbs or rural areas. Moreover, new types of schools (e.g., magnet schools) have been devised.

The purpose of this enumeration is to demonstrate the difficulty of summarizing behavior setting research on "the schools." For this reason, most of the generalizations in this chapter concern behavior settings in public schools.

BEHAVIOR SETTINGS VIEWED FROM A
DEVELOPMENTAL ECOLOGICAL PERSPECTIVE

One of Bronfenbrenner's (1979) more interesting ideas is that of developmental contexts and settings. He believes that typical analyses of environmental influences on development do little more than identify the environments from which students come. For example, studies regularly show that family background is an important factor in school achievement. But such studies tell us little about the processes involved, even where there is a focus on interpersonal factors, as in studies of parent–child relationships, because they lack generalizability across settings and contexts. In developing his general thesis, Bronfenbrenner has specified three properties of ecological environments that foster development, including;

1. *primary* developmental settings, where the child or adolescent engages in ongoing activity with or under the guidance of a person(s) knowledgeable in those activities, and with whom the child or adolescent has a positive relationship;
2. *secondary* developmental settings, where there are opportunities and resources to engage in these activities without the involvement and guidance of the aforementioned knowledgeable person(s); and
3. the developmental *potential* of settings, which depends on the extent to which third parties in such settings support or undermine the activities of those persons engaged in interaction with children and adolescents, and which increases as a function of supportive links between settings in the form of shared activities, communication, and information.

If these concepts are applied to behavior settings in the school, the classroom could be considered a key primary developmental context. On the other hand, many extracurricular activities fit the concept of a secondary developmental context. Furthermore, the extent to which a principal supports his or her teachers is illustrative of the role of third parties, and collaborative relationships between parents and school personnel exemplify supportive links.

To apply Bronfenbrenner's general thesis, the behavior settings in schools in which children and adolescents function are crucial to an understanding of stress. Although the classroom is a primary behavior setting, the classroom is linked to other school and nonschool settings, and the ways in which these behavior settings influence stress need exploration.

AGE-GRADED CLASSROOM SETTINGS

During the past decade, research on tracking, ability grouping, and other aspects of age-graded curricula and classrooms has indicated that such practices have a negative impact on the school opportunities and outcomes for many students, expecially low-income, minority, and low-achieving students (e.g., Gamoran & Berends, 1987; Slavin, 1990a). As a result, there are those who claim that the graded school is responsible for the academic failure, and much of the school-related stress, of those labeled "at risk." Cuban (1989) has argued, for example, that the age-graded school sorts out differences in order to preserve uniformity, and through the mechanisms of labeling and separate classes and programs makes it more difficult for at-risk students to succeed. In essentials, he asserted, it is an organization that is ill-equipped to provide stress relief for these students and to erase the effects of social and economic forces acting on the family and in the larger culture.

Although a comprehensive study of detracking and degrading has not yet been done, there are informal observations and reports from schools that have made efforts to detrack and degrade their classrooms, curricula, and teaching practices. Based on these accounts, which are interpreted from the perspective of their own educational philosophy, values, and beliefs, Oakes and Lipton (1992) paint a positive picture of the future of these efforts at far-reaching school reform. However, they do point out that the major lesson to be gained from these early efforts and accounts is that "a *culture of detracking* is more important than the specific alternative or implementation strategy chosen" (p. 449). This leads them to make a corollary assertion, which is that "each school must find its own way to create a *culture for detracking* that enables it to make sense of its own situation and create alternatives that fit" (p. 454). Ultimately, of course, detracking and degrading both the classroom structure and the curriculum of the schools will trigger many changes in other school behavior settings, with consequences for stress relief for students that can be enormous. However, the initial challenges of such profound changes could create additional stresses for students and school personnel, especially teachers.

BEHAVIOR SETTINGS WITHIN THE CLASSROOM

Teachers and students work together in a number of behavior settings within the classroom. That is, classroom activities occur in a number of differently structured minisettings, including seatwork, teacher-directed small groups, recitation, sharing time, and student-directed small groups. Each of these activity settings, in turn, has the potential for creating different amounts of stress for students (see, e.g., Phillips, Pitcher, Worsham, & Miller, 1980). For example, recitation places special demands on students. They must understand when to respond by raising their hands and when to respond chorally (Weade & Evertson, 1988). Occasionally, ambiguity in the teacher's initiation or evaluation of recitation makes the task even more difficult for students. Learning the norms of recitation also poses a difficult task for students who come from subcultures in which patterns of interaction are disparate from those required in recitation (Cazden, 1988). In addition, public evaluation is inherent in recitation, so that ability to participate appropriately and effectively may influence the status of students in the classroom, and their friendships (Morine-Dershimer, 1983). These are all circumstances that can, of course, be fertile sources of stress for some students.

As another example, seatwork is an individual enterprise where the ability to work independently and remain free of distractions is essential to success (Berliner, 1983). In seatwork, students must also use appropriate ways to obtain assistance from both the teacher and peers (Rizzo, 1989). Unfortunately, some students do not work well independently and are ineffective at soliciting help from the teacher and peers. Because this often means that individual tasks are not adequately completed, this therefore can be a source of much stress for some students.

Finally, the opportunity to work together in peer-directed small groups presents unique challenges to both teachers and students. Teachers must give up direct supervision of student behavior and performance and engage in supportive supervision. But many teachers are unfamiliar with this facilitative and consultative role, and are likely to feel uncomfortable with it, as well as stressed by it, at least in the initial stages of its use. Such groups also place special demands on students. For example, it is difficult for more passive students to assume a more active role (Lazarowitz, Baird, Hertz-Lazarowitz, & Jenkins, 1985). Some students also have difficulty providing coherent, complete explanations to their peers (Webb & Kenderski, 1984). Gender differences can also be a problem because of the higher social status of male students in many small group contexts (Lockheed & Harris, 1984). Overall, however, the purposes of student-directed small groups can be well served. They can have a positive impact on social relationships among students of different ability and achievement levels and racial-ethnic and socioeconomic backgrounds (Slavin, 1990b). One would also expect that, for low-achieving, minority, and handicapped students, the potential for high levels of achievement and social stress would be greatly reduced.

GIRLS AND BOYS IN SCHOOL: TOGETHER OR SEPARATE?

Riordan (1990) reviews the history of practices and debate concerning coeducation. He traces the pro and con arguments from ancient Greece to contemporary American theories and shows the inexorable trend toward mixed-sex schools. He argues that such schools are economically efficient, conform to modern egalitarian thinking, and provide more de jure equality of opportunity. But they can encourage sex bias against both boys and girls, allow less order and control, and provide less de facto opportunity for girls, creating potentially important sources of stress. With respect to the central purpose of schools — academic outcomes — students, especially girls, appear to do better in single-sex schools.

The author reports sophisticated analyses of a large national sample of high school students in 1982. One major finding is that boys', girls', and mixed-sex schools differ significantly in discipline and homework policies and in the socioeconomic and other familial characteristics of their students. Various analyses of academic and affective outcomes show small and inconsistent effects of coeducation for boys. Girls, however, appear to do consistently better in single-sex schools. In explaining the effects, it would appear that they are statistically attributable to curricula, course work, homework, and adolescent subculture.

Analyses were also made of long-range cognitive and affective outcomes, educational and occupational attainment, and attitudes toward the changing role of women in modern society among the high school class of 1972. Generally, the results again favored single-sex schools, especially with respect to educational attainment and occupational prestige.

Contrary to common assumptions and contemporary practice, the weight of the results suggested the superiority of single-sex institutions for girls and women with respect to the plurality of significant outcomes. Yet, the results were neither as large nor as consistent as one would like to set policy confidently.

STRESS IN DESEGREGATED SCHOOLS

According to Hanna (1988), desegregation of schools is generally assumed to be working satisfactorily if there is a mix of African-American and White students, no media reports of violence, sufficient allocation of resources to create magnetic effects, and if the desegregation starts with young children. She concluded, however, from her study of what had been

an all–African American school in an all–African American urban neighborhood that was turned into a 50 percent White–50 percent African-
American school using magnet procedures, that her findings challenged
that assumption. The central theme that emerged from her study was that
the main concern expressed by students was "meddling," the physical and
verbal harassment occurring among students that resulted in stress, fear,
and anxiety. Formal schooling in such circumstances often takes second
place to the challenges of coping with meddling. The unwanted behavior
(the meddling) that occurred in this school, and that Hanna believes now
occurs at many schools, would have been considered shocking 25 years
ago, but strict teachers and rigorous discipline of the past no longer
characterize the schools. Schools also have built-in pressures of comparison, embarrassment, shame, anxiety, and self-doubt that lead some
youngsters to behave in ways not conducive to academic success. In
desegregated schools, this behavior also tends to interfere with interracial and inter–social class friendship.

At first, Hanna assumed the problems were in communication. However, she later concluded that the students were communicating quite well
but that they did not like the messages. Although the emphasis in classrooms is on verbal communication, among children there is much communication on the nonverbal side, using body language and movement,
interpersonal space, physical intimidation, and fighting. Unfortunately,
adults (including teachers and other school professionals) do not pay much
attention to what occurs nonverbally among children whose senses of
sight, touch, movement, smell, and space are especially active and whose
language skills are unsophisticated. Children hesitate to talk openly at
home about their traumas in school because they sense that there would be
disbelief or confusion on the part of their parents. Even teachers and
principals may not know what is going on in their schools, because much
of the meddling goes on while the teacher is out of the room.

Much of what is going on in multiracial and multicultural schools is
pleasant, but many unpleasant incidents are occurring as well. For the most
part, school professionals have not been open in discussion of the
realities in desegregated schools. In some circles there even has been a
taboo against recognizing and discussing differences between racial-
ethnic groups and between middle-class and lower-socioeconomic
populations. For example, Hanna found that disruptive school behavior occurred disproportionately among lower-socioeconomic populations
(at this school most African-American students were low SES). On the

other hand, middle-class African-American students exhibited behavior similar to that of middle-class White students. Discussion of these matters can lead easily to stereotypes, which Hanna recognized. Still, it is necessary to recognize differences in roles of various behaviors by groups or classes, although it also is necessary to be aware of the great individual differences within groups or classes.

According to Hanna, the sources of meddling are to be found in the expressive style of the milieu in which children grow up. Some students gain status with peers through violent behavior. Others, when they feel humiliated in school, may react by abusing or humiliating others. The erosion of the status of teachers, and the children's rights movement, which have limited the ability of the school to deal with misbehavior, also were given credence by Hanna as part of the context for increased meddling.

Hanna also offered some good advice for teachers and other school personnel as well as parents. Some of the particulars are:

a. There need to be more "bridge-building" activities by parents;

b. More explicit talking and teaching about individual and group differences as part of the school curriculum is important;

c. More cooperative modes of grouping for instruction should be utilized;

d. Middle-class children need to be taught the skills of assertiveness and alliance behavior.

Undoubtedly, it would be a good thing for school professionals, parents, and community leaders to read this book (or comparable materials). After reading it, more of them would find it more difficult to be optimistic about the schools and multicultural and interracial relations in this country. However, they might also be better prepared for candid discussions about the problems and prospects for improvements, and at the same time be more realistic about the problems in urban schools and about the life of children and adolescents in our society.

DENSITY OF PHYSICAL SURROUNDINGS AS A STRESSOR

Much work on environmental stressors has involved density (e.g., Epstein, 1982). Fortunately, one trend in research on density has been an interest in the effects of high density on children. For example, Heft (1985) reviewed work on residential density (relating to both crowding and associated noise) and perceptual-cognitive development. He reported an inverse relationship between density and visual and auditory discrimination, object permanence, the development of schema, and language skills such as verbal imitation and reading. As another example, Aiello and others (Aiello, Thompson, & Baum, 1985) reviewed research on high density and children's social behavior and concluded that density in school and playground settings has been linked, in some circumstances, to decreased social involvement, more verbal and physical aggression, increased competition, and more fearful behavior. As one other example, Saegert (1981) studied children in New York City public housing and reported that number of persons per room was positively related to more frequent conflicts, more angry reactions to conflicts, and teachers' ratings of lower behavioral adjustment.

Spatial behavior in terms of personal space, territoriality, and privacy also has been widely investigated. Concerning distraction and privacy in the classroom, Ahrentzen and Evans (1984) interviewed 13 teachers and 65 students from five elementary schools reflecting a variety of classroom designs. They found that environmental factors causing distractions were particularly salient for teachers. The amount of structural wall space in classrooms (i. e., self-contained in contrast to open classrooms) was positively related to satisfaction with the classroom, reduced teacher distraction, and less restriction in potentially distracting classroom activities. At the same time, teachers were effective at managing their curriculum to prevent distracting other classes, and tended to like open-perimeter space, possibly because it facilitated mutual support among teachers. As Ahrentzen and Evans (1984) have pointed out, there is a general need for more empirical data on the educational effects of classroom design. In addition, specific research is needed on coping strategies used by teachers and students in response to environmental stressors in classrooms and other aspects of school buildings.

In addition, in contrast to what is known about development and the social environment, very little is known about the role of the physical environment in development. One key area for research is longitudinal analyses of how children and adolescents adapt to adverse environmental conditions. Process-oriented research is also needed on the behaviors through which children and adolescents develop environmental competencies, skills for coping with stress, and relative control over the environment. Analyses of the contextual conditions that interact with major developmental transitions and their impact on stress coping processes are also needed.

INTERRELATIONSHIPS BETWEEN SCHOOL AND HOME BEHAVIOR SETTINGS: STRESS ENGENDERED BY HOMEWORK

Homework, which is an important example of Bronfenbrenner's concept of supportive links, has moved to the forefront of many efforts at school reform. This has occurred because current concerns regarding the American school system have led to increased interest in understanding various influences on school learning, and one variable that has been linked with increased student achievement is homework (see reviews by Keith, 1987; Otto, 1985; Paschal, Weinstein, & Walberg, 1984; Cooper, 1989). In general, time spent on homework has important and positive effects on achievement, whether measured by grades or test scores, and long-term and cumulative academic gains have been associated with efficient homework programs for handicapped, gifted, at-risk, and low-achieving students. Other positive effects are also attributed to homework, including motivational and concentration skills that generalize to nonschool settings. However, homework also is a source of much stress, because it often is perceived as an intrusion on students' time and private activities. Some parents and educators also perceive homework as a sign of excessive pressure on students to achieve. In addition, homework compliance has been a continuing source of concern for teachers and parents alike, and students' poor motivation and avoidance of academic tasks outside of the school setting, and poor study habits and academic performance, are a source of continual conflict in many families (see, e.g., Anesko & O'Leary, 1982). For this reason, the increasing interest in home–school collaboration and cost/time concerns have placed increasing pressure on schools to become more sensitive to parental input and role in homework programs.

Because homework problems, and the related stress and conflict, are prevalent in the general student population, preventive and remedial interventions would be very useful. Although there is a relatively small body of research dealing with parent–child conflict over homework, targeting parents for interventions emphasizing homework problems would be a potentially helpful strategy. For example, Anesko and O'Leary (1982) evaluated the effectiveness of parent training to remediate homework problems of elementary school children. Group meetings were supplemented by readings and activities described in a parent manual. The treatment proved to be effective for parents having problems with their children's homework compliance.

Several commercially produced sets of materials also are available for parent training related to homework problems. Anesko and Levine (1987) have developed *Winning the Homework War*, which contains materials for assessment and treatment of homework difficulties. The assessment-of-homework checklist included in this program was well-researched (Anesko, Schoiock, Ramirez, & Levine, 1987), and many of the intervention techniques are based on best practices (e.g., daily homework record, setting appropriate goals, self-instructional training). These materials may be especially helpful to the teacher, school psychologist, or other school professional who consults with parents about homework problems.

Canter and Hausner (1987) market a parent training package, *Homework Without Tears*, that includes a homework organizer for the student and a manual for the teacher. The program emphasizes time scheduling, incentives, communication techniques, and commonsense tips. These materials also can be implemented in conjunction with assertive classroom techniques that many teachers use. However, the effectiveness of the program has not been well-studied.

Two other programs directed toward parents and teachers that include many examples of homework contracts, various types of homework assignments, study skills sheets, and other aids to facilitate homework completion are provided in publications by Kuepper (1987) and Hart and Rechif (1986). Although these materials have many virtues, their effectiveness has not been systematically evaluated.

Given that homework is assigned by the teacher but compliance is expected at home, integrated home–school intervention strategies would seem like a potentially more promising approach to homework problems. Consistency across parents and teachers is important to increase intervention effectiveness and enhance maintenance and generalization of outcomes. There is a need for well-articulated and easily replicated procedures that can be carried out by parents, teachers, and students. The role of the school psychologist in developing and implementing home–school programs is broad and may include training, direct intervention, and parent and teacher consultation.

One approach for this type of program would be a group-based parent training program that has an emphasis on parents designing their own individual programs. The basic design would center around a group training sequence led by a school psychologist or school counselor. It also would be advantageous if such training were based on a behavioral model which provides opportunities for parents to identify specific areas of concern (including areas of parent–child conflict), practice appropriate interventions specific to identified problem areas, and evaluate their efforts in a small group format. Another approach would be to develop a program that gives students the primary responsibility for managing the completion of homework. Such a program would rest on the premise that, ideally, students need to develop and exercise self-direction and motivation to complete academic work outside of school. Several options can be provided that would allow teachers to tailor the basic model to specific circumstances, student characteristics, and problem situations. The program also could include student/peer mediated intervention and take advantage of positive peer influences to reinforce homework proficiency.

In addition to their benefits in dealing with homework problems, integrated programs can have other benefits as well. Effective communication and cooperation between parents and teachers is essential to provide a good education for students. When parents are actively involved in school programs, students are more academically productive; there are fewer discipline problems; self-esteem and social skills are increased; and school attendance, study habits, and attitudes toward school are better (Becher, 1986). Parents involved with their children's learning also develop (a) more positive attitudes about schools and school staff, (b) more frequent and effective communication with the schools, and (c) improved parent–child relationships. Furthermore, teachers who are regularly and constructively involved with the parents of their students experiment more with teaching activities, become more involved with the curriculum and proficient in their instructional activities, and develop more student-oriented activities. In sum, the more clearly parents and teachers can collaborate in their work with children, the greater the probability for success of homework programs.

STRESS IN EXTRACURRICULAR SETTINGS: COMPETITIVE YOUTH SPORTS

The relationship between personal development and sports has received increased attention in the past decade. For example, a comprehensive examination of sport psychology is provided by Silva and Weinberg (1984). This edited volume contains an overview of the evolution of sport psychology, chapters that focus on personality and performance, and other chapters that address social-psychological issues as well as individuals' motivational concerns and how sport can play a role in the development and maintenance of physical and psychological well-being. However, one need not be a sport psychologist to understand that athletic competition and sports performance can be very stressful. Edited volumes by Jones and Hardy (1990) and Hackfort and Spielberger (1989), the book by Martens, Vealey, and Burton (1990), and the review article by Gould (1982), make that quite clear. It also is clear, according to Jones and Hardy, that "the sports environment provides a natural laboratory in which to study behavior in general and stress-related behavior in particular" (p. 12). In this sense, therefore, the study of competitive sports can be a source of practical lessons about the stress of life in general and the variety of ways that individuals can experience and negotiate that stress.

One could select a larger piece of the puzzle, of course, and as a case in point look at the psychology of sports, exercise, and fitness. It has been shown, for example, that children and adolescents who engage in regular physical exercise, which frequently includes organized sports as well as nonsports exercise, are less susceptible to the negative effects of life stress (Baum & Singer, 1982). These salutory effects also are not limited to physical health, but extend to the development of friendships (Bigelow, Lewko, & Salhani, 1989) and to the realm of emotional well-being as well (e.g., Brown & Lawton, 1986).

A specific issue related to this finding is whether there is a relationship between life stress and the frequency of injury in sports. Although most of the research has been conducted on contact sports, there seems to be a significant, though marginal, relationship between stressful life events and sports injury (Jones & Hardy, 1990). At this point, however, it would be inappropriate to use life stress measures as a screening device to assess "injury potential." Further research, particularly with school-aged youth, will be needed to determine if this relationship is consistent and strong enough to be of clinical use.

Another piece of the puzzle that needs close examination is the stress that is engendered by competitive youth sports, which is one of the extracurricular activities in which children and adolescents often engage. Based on surveys (e.g., Martens, 1988), a majority of boys and more than one third of girls ages 6 to 18 participate in organized in-school and/or out-of-school competitive sports. However, by 8th grade, which is typically the point at which school-sponsored sports begin, many adolescents drop out of competitive sports. Because of the large number of students involved in organized sport programs, and the competitive nature of such endeavors, there has been considerable interest in the effects of competitive sports on youth, the situational and intrapersonal mediators of competitive stress, the children and adolescents who are most vulnerable to that stress, and the sports that are the most and least stressful (see Gould, 1982; Martens et al., 1990; Jones & Hardy, 1990).

In terms of research efforts, the four-stage social evaluation of competition in sports model has been most influential (Martens et al., 1990). In the first stage, the Objective Competitive Situation (OCS), the young athlete is confronted with an evaluative situation and recognizes the objective factors in the sports environment that make up that competitive situation.

The second stage in the competitive process is the athlete's cognitive appraisal of the OCS, which is defined as the Subjective Competitive Situation (SCS). Various factors in the OCS, such as type of sport (individual or team, contact or noncontact) and the degree of success or failure, combine with different mediators in the SCS to influence how stressful the competitive situation is to the young athlete. Mediating factors in the SCS include self-esteem, performance expectations, achievement orientation, and so on.

The third stage involves the individual's response. Depending on his or her subjective evaluation of the situation, the individual decides to approach or avoid the OCS. If the individual decides to participate, then a response is made at the behavioral, physiological, and psychological levels.

The fourth stage of the competitive process is the consequences that originate from comparison of the individual's response to a standard. This comparison must occur in the presence of another person (or persons) who has knowledge of the standard and can evaluate the individual's performance according to this criterion. The standard can be one's own past performance, one's desired level of performance, or another's performance. Both positive and negative consequences accrue over time, of course, which make developmental considerations such as self-esteem, as well as individual differences, relevant.

As to factors in the OCS that contribute to higher levels of stress, Simon and Martens (1979) found that boys in individual sports (e.g., wrestling and gymnastics) had significantly higher levels of stress than those involved in team sports such as football. They also examined the influence of the degree of contact involved in sports and found that individual contact sports were the most, and team contact sports the least, stressful. Martens et al. (1990) also reported greater stress in individual sports than in team sports. However, even individual contact sports were less stressful than nonsport activities such as band solos.

The criticality of the game or match also determines precompetitive stress. Studies demonstrating this effect include those by Gould, Horn, and Spreeman (1983) with junior elite wrestlers, and by Feltz and Albrecht (1986) with young elite runners. A related factor, the time remaining before a game or match, also has been studied by several researchers (e.g., Weinberg & Genuchi, 1980; Gould et al., 1983). They found that stress increased as the time of the contest drew nearer.

The amount of stress that is experienced during competition is another consideration. For example, in two laboratory studies by Martens and Gill (1976) and Gill and Martens (1977), the stress of being ahead or behind the other team was assessed. Results indicated the obvious (i.e., being behind was more stress producing than being ahead).

Another frequently investigated mediator of competitive stress is the variable of success/failure. In a large-scale study involving male and female soccer players, Scanlon and Passer (1978a, b, 1979) found that the effect of losing was so strong that it overshadowed the effects of intrapersonal factors. Laboratory studies have demonstrated similar effects (see Gill & Gross, 1979; Scanlon, 1979; Caruso, Gill, Dzewaltowski, & McElroy, 1990). Members of winning teams also experienced greater satisfaction, greater perceived ability, and made internal attributions to their own effort and ability (in contrast to losers, who made external attributions to luck and task difficulty). Overall, the outcome of a game (i.e., winning or losing) is the most significant situational mediator of competitive stress in youth sports.

Various intrapersonal predictors of competitive stress also have been examined. For example, there is evidence for the strong role that self-efficacy plays in youth sport performance (Feltz, 1988). However, the predictor given the most attention has been the person's inclination to perceive competitive situations as threatening or nonthreatening. One important finding of studies reported by Martens and his colleagues (Martens et al., 1990) was that the effect of these generalized feelings and perceptions diminished from pre-, mid-, to postcompetition due to the influence of other significant situational and intrapersonal variables such as success/failure. Nevertheless, when other factors in the situation are taken into account the results are complex. For example, youngsters who perceive competitive situations as threatening expect to play less well, make more mistakes, lose more frequently, and receive more negative evaluations even though they do not perceive themselves as less athletically competent than other children. It would appear, therefore, that these students are preoccupied with worry about evaluation as well as performance (Martens, 1988; Rainey, Conklin, & Rainey, 1987).

Another important mediator of competitive stress is the achievement or competitive orientation of the young athlete. As discussed by Martin and Gill (1991), two competitive orientations are now accepted in the literature. One is an outcome orientation which refers to athletes who are most concerned with winning and performing better than their peers, whereas in the other, a performance orientation, there is an emphasis on doing well in relation to one's ability and improving on past performances. This second type of orientation is referred to as a mastery orientation by Roberts (1986), who further asserted that children and youth with a mastery orientation perceived and experienced less stress than children and youth concerned with competitive outcomes.

Age also has been looked at, although the findings have not been generally consistent (Gould, 1982). Although age differences in competitive stress have been found, the differences have been contradictory; and when intrapersonal and situational variables are taken into account, the effect of age alone becomes insignificant. To arrive at less equivocal conclusions, research utilizing longitudinal rather than cross-sectional designs will be necessary.

A related issue, because of the increased participation of girls in competitive sports, is the unique stress problems facing the female athlete. To deal with this situation, there is a need for more studies concerning sex-role conflict (see, e.g., Anthrop & Allison, 1983), the role of sex-role orientation in level of sport participation (see, e.g., Mateo, 1988), and socialization into athletics (see, e.g., Greendorfer, 1987).

The level of skill development of individuals involved in sports is another factor that is potentially important to the experience of competitive stress. Low-skilled, inexperienced athletes in college sports tend to have higher levels of competitive stress (see Martens et al., 1990), although, unfortunately, comparable studies using younger athletes are hard to find.

To sum up, youth sport research has dealt with a number of issues and provided some definitive answers, although many questions remain. For example, substantial inroads have been made in determining the situational and intrapersonal mediators of competitive stress. But researchers have relied almost exclusively on cross-sectional, between-groups designs. Though effective in revealing group differences, these designs fail to illuminate individual differences. In addition, Rowley (1987) has pointed out that the frequency, duration, and intensity of athletic involvement have not been taken into account. This rules out most developmental and etiological considerations that may be especially important in understanding age and gender differences in competitive stress. The multi-dimensional nature of competitive stress, the long-term as well short-term consequences of sport-related stress, and the effects that schools, parents, and coaches have on young athletes' competitive stress levels also need to be addressed. The reciprocal relationship between many intrapersonal and situational variables with competitive stress also needs to be acknowledged. Additional attention also needs to be devoted to (a) basic concepts in stress research, (b) the effects of stress on performance, (c) strategies for stress control, and (d) the importance of individual differences. What is required is a composite theory that indicates precisely how stress interacts with self-concept and other individual difference variables to influence both affective states and performance in competitive youth sports. Finally, progress in addressing these questions will not be achieved by approaching competitive youth sports from the simplistic point of view of how beneficial or detrimental, how good or bad such participation is. The issues are too complex. As Passer (1982) has put it, research must determine "when, for whom, and why participation in organized sports can be stressful" (p. 241).

CONCLUDING COMMENTS

Throughout this chapter, behavior settings are seen as a vital contributor to student–environment relationships, so that adaptive demands arising from different characteristics of school-related behavior settings are given special attention. The premise is that students orient to behavior settings in terms of existing information, goals, and expectations. That is, they function in behavior settings in ways designed to achieve their goals and maintain desired levels of satisfaction. Suggestions were made on how different behavior setting conditions, and students' responses to them, affect stress, coping, and adaptational outcomes. The point was also made that some school behavior settings can be a "natural laboratory" for the study of child and adolescent stress, and for the study of their performance under pressure. Concurrently, greater attention needs to be devoted to the mechanisms that might mediate the stress–competitive sports situations relationship.

6 DEVELOPMENTAL ASPECTS OF STRESS: THE TRANSITION OF STUDENTS FROM CHILDHOOD TO ADOLESCENCE

Over the past 50 years, the study of child and adolescent development has evolved in several significant ways. In the 1940s and 1950s, the field was primarily descriptive and normative. By the 1960s, however, the field was concerned both with the study of developmental processes and with theories that may explain the character of a given developmental change (Mussen, 1970). In the 1970s and throughout the 1980s, the concern with explanations was taken to a more abstract level. In this shift, scholars such as Reese and Overton (1970) and Riegel (1975) discussed philosophical models that were involved in the generation of distinct theories that provided explanations of developmental change. There also were discussions about connections among philosophy, theory, and core conceptual issues, e.g., the nature-nurture controversy (Lerner, 1986), and the issue of continuity-discontinuity of change (Baltes, 1987).

In addition, scholars demonstrated an interest in devising and assessing the usefulness of philosophical models that could provide new frames for developmental theory. This interest was associated with the evolution in the 1970s and 1980s of a concern with contextualism (Rosnow & Georgoudi, 1986) and with the formulation of what has been termed a "developmental contextual" approach to understanding developmental change (Butterworth & Bryant, 1990). Representing much of the scholarship about developmental theory, this approach to explanation involves the appraisal of change as it occurs at multiple, integrated levels of organization ranging from the biological through the psychological to the sociocultural. With this focus on developmental contextualism, there has been emerging interest in ideas involving the concepts of interactionism and transactionalism, and the range of developmental problems addressed has broadened. Increasing interest has been paid to development after infancy, with middle childhood (the elementary school years) and adolescence being the focus of considerable new conceptual and empirical work.

Interest has also increased in basic constructs and processes of development in connection with naturally occurring stressors. Once tied to the study of normative processes in the laboratory and special environments (e.g., nursery school classrooms and playgrounds), researchers are now addressing basic developmental processes across varied settings and tasks. Of particular note is the effort to link research and application and the emphasis on problems of policy.

STRESS AND DEVELOPMENTAL STAGES AND TASKS

In examining stress within this developmental contextual framework, it is necessary to keep in mind the child's and adolescent's developmental level (i.e., cognitive, social, and emotional competence) and the tasks that need to be negotiated at that level (e.g., separation in early childhood, entry into school, transition from childhood to adolescence). Together, the child's and adolescent's developmental competence and investment in related tasks will provide the lens through which certain events are viewed as stressful. At each developmental level, there are several tasks that need to be negotiated, and that remain important to the child and adolescent throughout development, although they diminish in importance in relation to new emerging developmental issues (Cicchetti & Schneider-Rosen, 1986). The child and adolescent also will be more vulnerable to stressors related to those areas in which developmental investment is greatest (Maccoby, 1988).

In early childhood, separation is one of the major developmental tasks to be negotiated (Cicchetti & Schneider-Rosen, 1986). Toddlers will view even brief separations from primary caregivers as particularly stressful because of the developmental importance of the attachment relationship at that age. Similarly, the birth of a sibling, which changes the nature of the parent–older child relationship, will constitute a significant challenge at this age. Thus, family stressors will be particularly salient for children at this time.

In middle childhood, the development of peer relations is a primary developmental task (Cicchetti & Schneider-Rosen, 1986). For this reason, peer conflicts will be viewed as particularly stressful because of their developmental salience. In addition, in middle childhood, children are developing a sense of self-efficacy, of right and wrong, and a sense of the psychological aspects of self and others. Empathy and perspective taking become more advanced and complex. This allows the child to compare himself or herself to others, and to be more greatly affected by evaluations from others. Thus, excessive peer rejection, unpopularity, school failure, or unrealistic expectations from parents and teachers would be particularly stressful at this time.

In adolescence, the major tasks involve developing identity and life goals, independence from family, and deepening intimate relationships within friendships and with the opposite sex (Compas & Wagner, 1991; Johnson, 1986). In addition, adolescents are developing new roles with new expectations, are changing rapidly physically (and often unevenly), and have a greater cognitive capacity (especially for abstract thinking). Adolescents also move from the relatively stable and protected environment of the elementary school to the constantly changing middle or junior high school. The timing of these changes becomes important, i.e., whether puberty changes coincide with school transition, and whether one student's puberty changes occur earlier or later than his or her peers' (Compas, 1987a, b). Thus, there are many opportunities for challenge and many areas vulnerable to stress (Hendren, 1990). However, among the most salient may be developing a sense of identity and long-term goals (e.g., getting a good job after graduation, or getting into college), establishing independence (e.g., dealing with parental overprotectiveness), and developing intimate relationships (e.g., losing a boyfriend or girlfriend, managing sexual intimacy).

STRESS AND DEVELOPMENTAL TRAJECTORIES

The child's and adolescent's capacity to cope with new challenges involved at successive phases of development plays a key role in whether outcomes are healthy or unhealthy. By "coping capacity" we mean the individual characteristics that the child or adolescent brings into a situation. Adaptation or the resulting coping performance is the interaction among coping capacity, availability of social resources, and extent of challenge in the situation. Adaptive coping or optimal development results from a good balance between the power of the child or adolescent and the power of the situation.

Although adaptation consists of many components, it also may be considered as the result of a child's or adolescent's developmental history. There is considerable evidence that certain factors can predict a course of better versus poorer adaptation and that certain earlier characteristics and experiences put children and adolescents on particular developmental trajectories. By "developmental trajectory" we are referring to a pattern of growth and to a path that a child or adolescent has traveled and is likely to travel in the future. It includes a child's or adolescent's developmental history and connotes some sense of direction and value (i.e., positive versus negative, growth or maturation versus retardation or regression, health versus illness). Adaptive efforts during childhood and adolescence also influence and perhaps constrain the likelihood of particular trajectories not just in terms of adaptive capacity but also in terms of life "choices" and patterns of adaptation in the roles and responsibilities expected of children when they become adolescents and of adolescents when they become young adults.

Taking a developmental perspective on stress, then, requires asking not only where stress comes from and how it affects behavior and adjustment but also asking where stress experiences eventually lead the child or adolescent. That is, what are the consequences of stress over time? This leads to the asking of three kinds of questions about the stress problems of children and adolescents. First, is there continuity of stress problems over time? Do stress symptoms persist or abate? Are there transformations in the nature and manifestations of stress? Second, what factors are related to the continuity or change in stress problems? Finally, what are the consequences of stress problems in other domains of functioning later in the lives of children and adolescents?

ROLE OF NONSHARED ENVIRONMENTS IN STRESS

One of the most striking findings of the behavioral genetics literature is that, for a variety of traits, most of the environmental variance is contributed by nonshared environmental influences (Scarr, 1992). What this means, in part, is that each child and adolescent constructs a reality from the opportunities and challenges posed by the environment, and this constructed reality, in turn, has considerable influence on variations in the cognitive, affective, and behavioral characteristics of children and adolescents. For example, behavioral genetic research has shown, for the range of environments sampled, that there is more variation *within* families than *between* families (see, e.g., Plomin, 1990).

Possible origins of this nonshared environmental influence are suggested by Dunn and Plomin (1990). Differential parental treatment is one possibility. In this connection, perceived parental treatments rather than treatments as they would appear objectively to an observer constitute a crucial factor. Another possibility is the unequal treatment of one sibling by another. One example provided by the authors is that disparities of siblings giving and receiving affection relate to sibling differences in self-esteem. Nonshared differences outside the family (e.g., in the school) may also be an important source of sibling differences. The role of chance in producing sibling differences also must be considered.

Practical applications of research on nonshared environments is another focus of their work. They note, for example, that there needs to be more research on environmental influences that differ between siblings. The microenvironment experienced by each child and adolescent rather than unitary family influences also needs more emphasis. Implications for social intervention also are addressed. Most social interventions are designed from a shared environment perspective (i.e., by intervening in families to make them better, the lives of children will be improved). However, from the nonshared environment perspective, the task of intervention is not to focus solely on what is wrong with the family, but also to consider the characteristics of the children in the family and the influence of their nonshared environments. Moreover, in extrapolating these ideas to stress, one might speculate that it is largely nonshared environments that act to make children and adolescents different from one another in the nature and amount of stress they experience, their reactions to it, and the outcomes that occur. For this reason, individual ways of evaluating the sources of stress and ways of coping, and individually tailored stress interventions, would be necessary. It also should be noted that nonshared environmental influences, because of their interactive nature, would be more difficult to manipulate and control, and thus less amenable to intervention efforts.

SPECIAL STRESSES ASSOCIATED WITH PUBERTY

Adolescence is a time of special stress, when a number of psychological, physical, and sociological influences are brought to bear, including: pubertal growth, hormonal changes, genetic vulnerabilities, heightened sexuality, changed relationship to parents, newly developed cognitive abilities, peer pressure, cultural and societal expectations, school changes, and family functions/dysfunctions. Adolescents negotiate these stresses with varying degrees of mastery. Although most do well, some, who have not developed successful coping skills, may suffer stress-related disorders such as depression, eating disorders, and substance abuse.

It is commonly believed that hormonal changes directly influence adolescent behavior, although only a few scientific studies have looked for this effect (Peterson, 1985). In one study (Nottelman et al., 1987), adjustment problems for late-maturing boys and girls between the ages of 9 and 14 were associated with high adrenal androgen (androstenedione) levels, a steroid particularly responsive to stress. The authors concluded that this relationship may reflect either endogenous hormone effects or the stresses of later maturation, such as adolescent self-comparisons with same-age peers. In another study of adolescent boys (Udry, Billy, Morris, Groff, & Madhwa, 1985), free testosterone was a strong predictor of sexual motivation and behavior. The authors suggested that this was a direct effect rather than an effect that worked through the social interpretation of the accompanying pubertal development. A direct relationship between hormone levels and the cognitive functioning of adolescents also has been demonstrated in a series of studies (Gordon, Corbin, & Lee, 1986).

Whereas hormones may influence adolescent adjustment directly, they also do so indirectly, through their effects on physical maturation and the subsequent reactions of the adolescent to these maturational changes, as well as the responses from other people to these changes. Some important mediating factors include general social norms regarding deviance in timing, and local norms regarding preferred appearance and gender (Peterson, 1985). In general, studies of the effects of the timing of maturation suggest that early maturation is more socially advantageous for boys, and middle or later maturation is advantageous socially for girls (Livson & Perkin, 1980). One possible consequence is that late-maturing boys and early-maturing girls will experience more stress than early-maturing boys and late-maturing girls, respectively.

The family of the adolescent also feels the stress of this developmental process. For example, potential stress is higher among parents of early adolescents than among parents of preadolescents or middle adolescents (Peterson, 1988). In this review, the author also suggests that parental conflict over the early adolescent's push for autonomy is the cause for this stress. Thus, these developmental changes during adolescence produce effects on parents that, in turn, produce another source of stress for the adolescent. Because parents under stress are less able to be supportive of their adolescent, there can be interactions between parents and adolescents that result in greater stress for all involved.

The parent–adolescent stress cycle initiated by puberty also has other ramifications. For example, Cohen and his colleagues (Cohen, Adler, Beck, & Irwin, 1986) surveyed parents' reactions to the onset of adolescence and found that first-born children were perceived more negatively and generated more negative feelings in their parents, and that older parents (39 and above) perceived fewer negative changes and experienced fewer negative and anxious feelings toward their children than did younger parents. This suggests older parents and later siblings benefit from increased parental experience, self-confidence, and knowledge and ability in coping with the autonomy struggles of adolescence.

Mothers and fathers also perceive the stress of having an adolescent somewhat differently (Silverberg & Steinberg, 1987). According to these authors, mothers, but not fathers, appear to be adversely affected by the intensity of the conflict they experience with their sons or daughters. These authors also found that social class is related to the amount of perceived conflict over adolescent autonomy struggles in families. Working-class fathers reported stronger concerns about autonomy struggles with their sons than white-collar and professional fathers. Blue-collar fathers also reported less life satisfaction with daughters who were emotionally autonomous. One reason for these differences may be that working-class fathers place greater value on conformity and obedience than on autonomy and independence for their adolescents (Kohn, 1977).

Interaction with social and cultural values is another factor in determining the stress and coping ability of the maturing adolescent. Values given to physical size, body shape, gender stereotypes, and stereotypes about early and late maturers influence the feelings of adolescents. Norms about expressions of sexuality, competition, and independence also vary in different societies, cultures, socioeconomic classes, and at various times. All of these must be considered in determining the nature and degree of stress faced by early-, middle-, and late-maturing adolescents.

ROLE OF LIFE STRESS IN THE PROBLEMS OF HIGH SCHOOL BOYS AND GIRLS

Colten, Gore, and Aseltine (1991) studied the stress process in the high school years using 13 different mental health problems that were classified into four domains: (1) *affect*, including depression, anxiety, hostility, and other emotional problems; (2) *body*, eating disorders and psychosomatic symptoms; (3) *substance use*, drinking problems and drug use; and (4) *role problems*, school behavior problems, delinquency, grades, dropping out, and sexual risk taking. In considering the role of life stress, they used items from measures of stressful life events that had previously been developed in research by others (e.g., Compas, Davis, & Forsythe, 1985; Newcomb, Huba, & Bentler, 1981). Events happening in the past year were divided into four groupings: (1) *events of self*, such as illness, assault, accident, work problems, and financial problems; (2) *relationship events*, including conflict with family and friends, and loss of friendship or romantic relationships; (3) *family events*, events happening to parents and siblings; and (4) *friend events*, events happening to friends. Each of the event groups was dichotomized into high and low stress groups, with the proportion in each high stress event group being: events of self, 28 percent; relationship events, 32 percent; family events, 28 percent; and friend events, 27 percent.

Considering each of the four domains of problems separately, they found that, among girls, high levels of stress in each of the arenas of events were associated with a high rate of problems in each of the four domains. These effects were consistently large, with from one and one-half to more than two times as many girls in the high stress group as in the low stress group having problems in each domain. The same pattern of relationships generally held for boys but was, as a whole, somewhat less powerful for boys than girls. The authors also found a strong correlation between the number of spheres of events in which an adolescent experiences high stress and the number of domains in which he or she has problems. Of those youth who had no areas of activity in which high stress was experienced in the past year, 41 percent of the boys and 50 percent of the girls had no problems in the domains. In contrast, among those exposed to high levels of stressors in three or four arenas of events, only 12 percent of the boys and 6 percent of the girls had no manifest problems. Their results make clear the very strong linkages between exposure to stress and multiple problems in adolescents. It also must be recognized, of course, that adolescents with multiple problems in turn manage to more often expose themselves to stressful events. In addition, such descriptive analyses are not designed to establish the direction of causality. Although research strongly supports the assumption that stressful life events have an impact on problem behavior, there are routes by which problem behaviors can increase an adolescent's exposure to further stressors. For example, heavy drinking could lead to relationship problems within the family, or an adolescent who is delinquent may be more likely to find or place himself or herself in the company of friends who have delinquency problems or who are acting out because of their own family problems.

STRESS AND NEGATIVE EMOTIONS

Negative emotions, theorists tell us, reflect breaches in the cultural and moral order — violations of "things that matter." In essence, they reflect a disjunction between the "ideal or desired world and actual world" (Lutz, 1988, p. 5), a disjunction between life as people expect and want it to be and life as it actually is. Thus, negative emotions occur when there is a discrepancy between what is valued and expected and what really happens (see, e.g., Roseman, 1984; Scherer, 1984). To put it another way, negative emotions indicate points of friction between these values and beliefs and the world as it is. In Piagetian terms, they reflect a state of disequilibrium between an internal representation of life and life as it is actually encountered. Early adolescence, for example, is a time when these internal representations are rapidly changing, fueled by cognitive development and an expanding domain of things that matter. In the process, old points of friction are replaced by new ones that reflect the emergence of a more penetrating set of values and concerns.

As one major consequence, between preadolescence and early adolescence there is a substantial increase in the experience of negative emotions.

Larson and Lampman-Petraitis (1989), for example, found that junior high school students had more occurrences of anger, worry, and hurt than did 5th- and 6th-graders. Furthermore, adolescents who report more negative states are more likely to be depressed, to do more poorly in school, and to have disturbed eating patterns (Larson, Raffaelli, Richards, Ham, & Jewell, 1990; Richards, Casper, & Larson, 1990). Findings such as these are important for two reasons: first, because negative emotions are manifestations of stress; and second, because, for some, these negative states may also be a precursor of severe psychological problems (e.g., delinquency, affective disorders, eating disorders, and suicidal behavior).

As to an explanation for adolescents' more frequent negative states, there is reason, of course, to believe that they are attributable, at least in part, to stressful events. For example, adolescents who experience more negative life events also experience a greater frequency of negative states. This does not necessarily mean, however, that negative events are the "cause" of the negative emotions, because research suggests that dysphoric states, in which individuals feel unhappy or unwell, may be as likely to cause negative events as the reverse (see, e.g., Cohen, Burt, & Bjorck, 1987). Thus although stressful events are related to the negative affect of adolescents, there are compounding factors.

DAILY EXPERIENCES THAT ELICIT NEGATIVE EMOTIONS

To understand the relationship between stress and negative emotions it also is important to identify what segments of the daily experience of children and adolescents generate negative emotion, and to determine whether there are age and sex differences in such relationships. Important information on this issue is provided by Larson and Asmussen (1991) in a study of almost 500 randomly selected 5th- to 9th-grade students from a working-class and middle-class suburb. Following the procedures of Csikszentmihalyi and Larson (1987), these students were signaled randomly during each 2-hour interval between 7:30 a.m. and 9:30 p.m. for 1 week. On receipt of the signal, they filled out a self-report form asking about their thoughts, activities, and emotional states at that point in time.

Among other things done in the study, they determined what segments of daily experience generated negative emotions, using the following eight categories to classify the types of explanations students gave for their negative emotions:

self, in which the emotion experienced is related to appearance, looks, and abilities;

school, the most common context for both boys and girls, accounting for over one-fourth of the negative states;

activity, including leisure pursuits, competitive games, and special outings;

media, i.e., books, television, and magazines, which accounted for few negative emotions;

material objects, such as machines and food;

family, including references to the family as a whole as well as to individual members, which was a significantly greater source of negative emotions for girls than boys;

friends, including emotions attributed to the peer group as well as friends of the same or opposite sex, which was more often a source of negative emotions for girls than boys;

others, including reference to a neighbor, the mail carrier, and people unknown to the student, as well as reference to the weather, time, etc.

In addition to findings included in the above listing of categories, for both boys and girls, they found a dramatic drop from preadolescence to adolescence in the frequency with which the activities category was identified as the context for negative states. For older boys, activities accounted for one third, and for older girls almost one half, fewer negative emotions. However, contrary to popular notions, the family was not a greater source of negative experience for adolescents as compared to preadolescents. Thus it is the friends category, not the family category, that expands as the category of more frequent negative emotions. For preadolescent boys, friends were rarely a source of negative emotions, but among the older boys this rate is more than double. There is a comparable age difference for girls. It is well known that friends increase in importance from childhood to adolescence (e.g., Steinberg & Silverberg, 1986), and it is not surprising, therefore, that more frequent experiences of negative emotion (such as anger, worry, hurt, distress, anxiety) are part of that change.

In addition, when the students' perceived causes for negative emotional states were grouped into attributions to the self (traits, actions, and performances), to the situation (activities, circumstances, and events), or to a social dynamic (affiliations, the feelings of others, social give and take, general social circumstances), there was a marked increase between the younger and older students in attributions of negative emotions to social dynamics. In contrast, there was no difference between the younger and older adolescents in attributions related to the self. Another important point is that, for the sample as a whole, situational factors were the perceived cause of about as many negative emotions as the other two categories combined. Also, if one looked at their findings in terms of implications for intervention, a general conclusion would be that, while increased social support or other network intervention may be effective with girls in reducing their stress, we need to be more cautious about assuming that such interventions will be as influential in buffering boys from stress.

STRESSFULNESS OF THE TRANSITION TO ADOLESCENCE

From research in foregoing sections, it would appear that the transition from childhood to adolescence is a particularly stressful time in an individual's life. This should not be surprising, of course, because many of the events occurring for most young adolescents are novel, perhaps threatening, and important. Indeed, the concentration of events occurring at this time might be one of the two aspects of this transition that makes it distinctive from other life transitions, the other being puberty (Brooks-Gunn & Warren, 1988). However, there is almost no research that has addressed the issue of distinctiveness in number and type of events the young adolescent faces, although studies cited in preceding sections, and in this section, provide good examples of the extant research. Also, limitations on the number of available coping responses are not known. It seems plausible, nevertheless, to believe that the prepubertal adolescent has few coping responses appropriate for events such as dating, moving to a large and less personal school, and making decisions about behaviors such as drinking, smoking, and sexual intercourse.

One approach for such research would be to focus on the interaction of different life events; another would be to look at the effects of number of life events occurring in a given period of time; and a third would test the effects of different features of life events (timing, novelty, number of events, number of events relative to one's peers, and type of event). In all three approaches, a distinction would need to be made between biological and social events because a striking feature of this transition is puberty and all that it entails.

In the research that has been done on the interaction of pubertal and social events, girls have been the focus of attention. In such research, there is the premise that certain social events are experienced differently by girls as a function of their pubertal development. Puberty acts as a social stimulus for others, altering how adults and peers respond to the girl as her body develops. Given the wide variability in physical development in young adolescents of any given age, studies have been able to tease apart effects of age and pubertal development. Controlling for age, examples include increased independence given to girls by their parents, interest by boys, and in some cases enhanced same-sex peer relationships (Brooks-Gunn & Warren, 1988; Simmons & Blyth, 1987). At the same time, girls' own experiences and interpretations of pubertal events influence how they respond to or interpret social events. As girls mature, they demand more independence from their parents (Simmons & Blyth, 1987), and some seek out girlfriends who are similar in pubertal maturation (Brooks-Gunn, Samelson, Warren, & Fox, 1986).

Further evidence of such interactions is found in studies looking at the context in which girls develop physically. In attempting to explain why early maturing girls are likely to engage in smoking and drinking sooner than later maturing girls, Magnusson and associates (Magnusson, Strattin, & Allen, 1985) found that the effect was due to many early maturers having older friends who presumably were engaging in such behaviors, which were normative for that older cohort. Other researchers report that early-maturing girls also have more difficulty moving to middle school in 6th grade than do their peers who are on-time or late maturers and who therefore are not in the midst of puberty during this school transition (e.g., Blyth, Simmons, & Zakin, 1985).

The cumulative effects of events is another important consideration for both boys and girls. For example, Simmons, Burgeson, and Reef (1988) have demonstrated the effects of sheer number of events on middle school children's well-being. In their analyses, the addition of life events increased the report of both academic and behavioral school problems and decreased self-esteem scores. The associations were primarily linear and were found for both boys and girls.

Another concern, at least from an adult perspective, is how parent–child interchanges are affected during the adolescent transition. Not only are such interactions believed to be transformed but they are thought to be rife with conflict. The transformations are portrayed as a change from unilateral authority to mutuality, from a more vertical to a somewhat more horizonal relationship (e.g., Hartup, 1989). In such studies, the measures that have been used to study parent–child interactions include time spent with parents, perceptions of relationships as less positive, indications of emotional distance, and yielding to parents in decision making. All four decrease from early to middle adolescence (Hill, 1988).

There also is research that has focused on conflict, which seems to be higher in early adolescence, although the frequency of conflict is similar in early and middle adolescence. For example, both parents and children agree that these conflicts are significant, although adolescents tend to see conflicts occurring more frequently than do parents (Smetana, 1989).

In studies of girls, these increases in conflict have been postulated to be due to self-definitional change, social cognitive alterations, direct biological changes, and psychodynamic processes (see Smetana, 1988; Hill, 1988). As to self-definitional changes, the underlying mechanism could be based on conflicted feelings that are elicited by pubertal change or a reorganization of self-definitions based on bodily changes and the social role alterations that accompany such bodily changes. For example, although almost all girls learn about pubertal changes, in particular menarche, from their mothers, they tend not to discuss their feelings with her, instead turning to girlfriends (Brooks-Gunn & Ruble, 1983). In some cases, girls even perceive their mothers as insensitive to their concerns about bodily changes (Brooks-Gunn & Zahaykevich, 1989).

Looking at the experiences of both boys and girls, Smetana (1988) has systematically presented a social cognitive perspective on conflict. She finds that teenagers and parents disagree as to the legitimacy of parental authority in many situations. Teenagers tend to classify more situations as involving personal choice, and parents classify more situations as involving social conventions. The greatest shift toward personal choice catergorizations by children occurs between 5th and 6th grade, and between 7th and 8th grade for teenagers.

Psychodynamic perspectives are the least studied of the available perspectives. Generally, this perspective predicts that young adolescent boys and girls will go through an initial aggressive and oppositional phase of interaction with their parents, before reverting to more passive modes of resistance to parental authority, such as indifference and denial. A few studies done with girls have found support for this thesis (Brooks-Gunn & Zahaykevich, 1989; Hill, 1988). Generally, mother–daughter conflicts are more pronounced than conflicts in other parent–child combinations (e.g., father–daughter). Why this is the case has not been studied extensively, although comparisons of observational studies of mothers with sons and daughters do highlight differences in interactions as a function of the sex of the pubertal child (Hill, 1988).

STRESS, SCHOOLING, AND CHILD AND ADOLESCENT DEVELOPMENT: IMPORTANCE OF "GOODNESS OF FIT"

The increases in academic difficulties and the decreases in academic motivation experienced by many adolescents on entering junior high school may be due to the poor fit between the developmental needs of young adolescents and the nature of the school environment (Paikoff & Collins, 1991). For both girls and boys, those who experience a greater number of life changes — change into junior high school, recent puberty change, early onset of dating behavior, geographical change, and changes in parents' marital status — are at greater risk (Simmons & Blyth, 1987). For girls, multiple life changes affect self-esteem, GPA, and extracurricular activities. For boys, multiple changes affect mainly GPA and extracurricular activities. Moreover, the cumulation of change has more negative effects than any one change in itself.

In examining change from elementary school to high school, Simmons and Blyth (1987) utilized a natural experiment in the Milwaukee public schools where some students attended the 12 grades in a 6-3-3 pattern and others attended in an 8-4 pattern. With this arrangement, they were able to compare transitions of the elementary to junior high school variety with those of the eight-grade elementary school to the 4-year high school variety. They also were able to compare students who had double transitions (those in the 6-3-3 pattern) with those who had only one transition. A stratified random sample of over 600 White students were followed for five school grades (grades 6 to 10 inclusive) if they stayed in the Milwaukee schools. The specific lines of development they examined were the students' self-image, their sociopsychological adjustment, and their school performance and extracurricular activities.

Overall, student changes on average did not involve widespread negative effects. But the timing of change (i.e., whether the student was developmentally ready, whether the student was on time or off time with respect to peers, and whether the student was "top dog" or "bottom dog" in terms of relative grade level position in the school) did determine the negative effects that did occur.

The authors suggest that this research supports the development of middle schools to cover either grades 5-6-7 or grades 6-7-8. These modifications would be made in part to adapt to the fact that puberty seems to occur earlier than it used to. The use of middle schools, however, guarantees that girls will experience pubertal change when they are in the large and impersonal context of the middle school. Also, having a middle school does not reduce the number of times students are "bottom dogs." Furthermore, with the 5-6-7 pattern, boys may be subjected to more stress than has been true in the past, because their pubertal change would then coincide with school change.

To sum up, the crux of the matter is that stress, schooling, and the development of students are interrelated, and that one way of viewing these interrelationships is in terms of the concept of "goodness of fit" between the student and his or her school environment. According to this concept, many of the problems of students result from a poor fit between the student's developmental characteristics and the characteristics of the school environment, especially school tasks and demands and parental expectations and behavior. Stress is one important consequence, of course, of this poor fit.

The goodness-of-fit paradigm also has broad applicability in terms of stress intervention because it implies that both the developmental characteristics of students and the challenges of the school environment can be determined, and then utilized in two ways: in identifying students for whom there is a poor fit and who therefore are likely to be experiencing high levels of stress; and, for students so identified, to plan and implement appropriate stress interventions.

CONCLUDING COMMENTS

This chapter examined developmental aspects of stress. The chapter's underlying theme is that much can be learned about stress, coping, and adaptation when we examine interrelationships between the biological, cognitive, and affective changes and developmental sequences which occur in children and adolescents and the demands of their social, school, family, and cultural environments. Adolescents, in particular, are challenged to achieve a wide range of developmental tasks. For instance, they are expected to master more difficult and abstract academic curricula; to establish emotional and psychological independence from adults, while maintaining a respect and appreciation for adult values and authority; and to form positive and healthy relationships with peers, especially opposite sex peers. In short, adolescence is a period of enormous change in which children, in making the transition into adolescence, experience new demands to coordinate a diverse set of intellectual and social objectives in positive and complementary ways.

In this chapter, it was argued that the ability to adapt to these changing demands may be understood more clearly by exploring the ways in which stress and coping influence this transition from childhood to adolescence. Especially noteworthy is the emphasis on how stress and coping interact with family, school, peer, and other social contexts to jointly influence development. The complementary and, in some respects, unique role of the school was given special attention. The need for school policies and programs designed to prevent, ameliorate, or overcome debilitative stress originating in developmental aspects of the transition from childhood to adolescence was also maintained.

7 STRESS IN SPECIAL SCHOOL POPULATIONS

Researchers have made progress in studying the various stressors, stress reactions, and mediators of stress in children and adolescents. Seifer and Sameroff (1987) point out that researchers also have begun to look at special groups of children and adolescents who are at risk for stress. These groups include: children and adolescents with mental or physical handicaps; children and adolescents whose parents are suffering from depression, schizophrenia, or other mental disorders; children and adolescents from economically deprived, minority, or overprivileged backgrounds; children and adolescents who have lost a parent; lesbian or gay youth and teenage mothers; and so on.

STRESS IN SPECIAL SCHOOL POPULATIONS: AN OVERVIEW

One common theme in the research literature on stressors and their correlates is that persons of lower socioeconomic status are exposed to more stressors and consequently manifest more symptoms of distress (Garmezy & Rutter, 1983). Moreover, it has been suggested that chronic stress, such as poverty, is more likely than other stressful events to be tied to psychological impairment (Kagan, 1982). Research has found that poverty is associated with depression, poor school functioning, and behavior disorders (Gibbs, 1986; Myers & King, 1983). The data by Dornbusch and associates (Dornbusch et al., 1991) also showed that stressful events are more common among lower-class youths, where social class was determined by parental education level, although stressful events did not have a greater impact on adolescents in the lower parental education groups. In addition, studies indicate that the relation between stressful events and health impairment is strongest in the lower class (Dohrenwend & Dohrenwend, 1974; Kessler & Cleary, 1980).

Previous studies have indicated that children in single-parent households experience more stressful events and show greater sensitivity to them (McAdoo, 1986; Pearlin & Johnson, 1977; Weintraub & Wolf, 1983). Dornbusch and associates (1991) also found a higher frequency of stressful events among adolescents in all alternative forms of family structure than was found in two–natural parent households. When they looked at associations between stressful events and health symptoms, high school grades, and deviance for adolescents in different types of families, they noted that the relations were always in the same direction, with stressful events associated with negative behavioral outcomes. But they did report an interesting set of findings: although adolescents from two–natural parent households reported fewer stressful events, there was a tendency for stress experienced by these adolescents to have a greater negative impact than for adolescents in other types of households.

Much previous research also indicates that disadvantaged minorities experience more stress and evidence more symptoms of stress (Dohrenwend & Dohrenwend, 1974; Kessler & Neighbors, 1986; Neff, 1985). Dornbusch and associates (1991) likewise provide some support for this perspective. Non-Hispanic White adolescents reported fewer stressful events and health symptoms than most minorities. Yet Asian Americans, in contrast to African Americans and Hispanics, reported fewer major events and fewer health symptoms than all other groups. Asian Americans also showed higher grades and lower deviance. They also found a general relation between stressful events and negative outcomes in each ethnic group. In this connection, Dornbusch and associates (1991) pointed out that the impact of stressors in the personal domain, in contrast to stressors in the familial and school domains, was particularly strong. They interpreted this differential effect in terms of the greater salience of these more personal experiences during adolescent development (i.e., there is a lack of differentiation among status groups in the association between stress and outcomes because many of these personal events cut across groups and may be highly significant to all adolescents).

In another line of research, Pryor-Brown, Powell, and Earls (1989) have shown that urban adolescents experience a greater number of events and more highly stressful ones than suburban youth. Other reports show that youth from some ethnic groups encounter certain types of life events more often than do others (Newcomb et al., 1981). This supports the view that there are ethnic-specific sources of stress (Lewis, Siegel, & Lewis, 1984), and that culture can both cause and moderate stress effects (Mirowsky & Ross, 1980).

Gender also is an important factor in stress differences and outcomes. In their study of stress differences among adolescent school populations, Dornbusch and associates (1991) found that girls reported more mental and physical symptoms than boys. They also found clear stress and outcome patterns in comparisons of adolescent ethnic groups. Asian Americans of both sexes reported fewer stressful events, fewer physical symptoms, lower deviance, and higher grades compared to non-Hispanic Whites. However, for psychological symptoms, only female Asian Americans showed a significantly lower incidence. Among African American adolescents, both males and females reported more stressful events, fewer psychological symptoms, lower grades, and lower deviance than did non-Hispanic Whites. Hispanics reported more stressful events, fewer psychological and physical symptoms, and lower grades. Only Hispanic females reported a lower rate of deviance.

When Dornbusch and associates (1991) divided their sample into low-stress and high-stress subgroups, they found, among both males and females, that those adolescents in each ethnic, parental-education, family-structure, and age group who reported more stressful events also had more negative outcomes. Psychological symptoms and physical symptoms were more frequent, grades were lower, and reported deviance was greater for those who reported experiencing more stressful events. Overall, it also appeared that stressful events have about the same association with negative outcomes for both sexes. They also concluded that stressful events affected each of the outcomes studied, even when a battery of status variables was controlled.

STRESS OF HANDICAPPED CHILDREN AND ADOLESCENTS

Children and adolescents who are at risk because of their developmental disabilities have seldom been included in the study of stress. This population not only may experience more stress, but they also have fewer resources for dealing with stress than average children and adolescents. To add to their at-riskness, these children and adolescents not only perceive themselves as handicapped, they also are aware that others see them that way, and are aware of their differences and the rejection they generate at school and from family and peers (e.g., Wayment & Zetlin, 1989). One consequence is that they are more depressed and anxious than non-handicapped children and adolescents (e.g., Cullinan & Epstein, 1984). For these and other reasons, it is reasonable to believe that handicapped children and adolescents are at substantial risk of experiencing higher than average levels of stress in school and other life contexts.

School Stress

Although there are many stressors that could affect handicapped children and adolescents within schools, the focus here will be on school policies and practices and the environmental stressors they create for handicapped students. Because of the federal mandate to educate disabled students in the least restrictive environment, many handicapped students are mainstreamed into regular education classrooms. One result of this policy is that children and adolescents with disabilities have come to be viewed as a stressor, both to the teachers in regular education classrooms and to administrators in the school district. To add to the problems of handicapped students, they are often viewed as the most difficult to educate because of the questions raised about how much integration should take place and at what age. Unfortunately, policies of many school districts also produce unpredictable transitions, inconsistent learning environments, and social isolation for these students. Thus, the teachers are stressed, and, in turn, these students are stressed both indirectly (as a result of the additional stress of the teacher) and directly (through the number and types of school situations and classroom changes these students must adjust to on a daily basis).

As to the source of additional stress for teachers, many mainstreamed students are moved from one class to another, spending minimal parts of the day or week in regular classrooms. Thus, they are never fully integrated into the normal routine of these classrooms. A result is that many regular classroom teachers are uncomfortable with mainstreaming and see handicapped students as an impediment to teaching and to behavior management in the classroom. One consequence of this situation is that teachers see these students as disturbing and disapprove of their placement in regular classrooms (Horne, 1983), and another is that they show more negative affect to these students (Siperstein & Goding, 1985). In addition to research showing that teachers perceive the handicapped student as an extra source of stress and respond with negative attitudes and affect, there also is research showing that handicapped children are aware of these negative teacher expectancies and attitudes and are negatively affected by them (Brophy, 1983). Thus, these students are not only a source of stress to those around them in the schools, they also are reciprocally stressed by these circumstances.

The school policies that determine the placement and level of integration of these students are another source of stress, because many of these integration policies are dictated by convenience rather than these students' needs. For example, some handicapped students are integrated one year but not the next, and such a move back into a segregated classroom after being integrated can have a variety of consequences, one being that such students experience a sense of failure. In such moves, students also are sometimes integrated with students younger than themselves, and at other times integrated with older students. In addition, handicapped students who are placed in regular classrooms tend to become socially isolated because they are generally rejected or ignored by their nonhandicapped peers (Bak & Siperstein, 1987).

In overview, it is evident that handicapped students' school environments are often full of unpredictable, uncontrollable, and sometimes questionable transitions, which are factors that can lead to perceptions of threat and symptoms of distress in these students. As evidence that this is likely to occur, research on nonhandicapped students shows that even regular, predictable school transitions can be stressful (e.g., Felner, Primavera, & Cauce, 1981). In essence, there is good reason to believe that the combination of nonnormative transitions (when transitions for handicapped students are compared with those for other students) and teachers' negative responses toward handicapped students in the regular classroom place handicapped students at substantial risk for high levels of stress.

Family Stress

Researchers have been concerned about stress in families with handicapped children, and some have focused on the impact of these children on their families, an impact that seems to be mostly negative (e.g., Miller & Keirn, 1978; Friedrich & Friedrich, 1981; Crnic, Friedrich, & Greenberg, 1983). From such research, we know that parents of handicapped children tend to show greater depression, more preoccupation with the handicapped child, less marital satisfaction, less of a sense of maternal competence (mothers), lower self-esteem, less interpersonal satisfaction, and more problems with impulse control and aggression. Furthermore, research shows that the stress presented by raising a handicapped child is chronic, with periods of greater and lesser stress as the child grows into young adulthood. Some of the periods of heightened stress occur when parents first learn that their child is disabled and when developmental milestones are late or not attained. The financial strain, disruption of family routines, social stigma, and limitations on social outlets that often plague parents raising a disabled child are other important sources of additional stress.

However, one may also contend that the stressful family climate created by the presence of a handicapped child may, in turn, become a stressor for the handicapped child. For example, there is a growing body of research that points to a reciprocal relationship between handicapped children and their home environments (e.g., Nihira, Mink, & Meyers, 1985). There also is evidence indicating that the most detrimental kinds of stressors in childhood are those that are chronic and that involve the family, such as marital discord, parental rejection, and maternal depression or psychiatric disorder (Garmezy, 1983; Wallerstein, 1983). Further, these stressors affect children of all ages, even preschoolers who may be too young to comprehend the meaning or nature of stress. It seems safe to assume, therefore, that if the families of handicapped children experience higher levels of stress, the handicapped child also will experience more stress.

Peer Stress

Handicapped children and adolescents are often rejected and socially isolated by nonhandicapped peers. In one recent study, for example, Wayment and Zetlin (1989) found that the stressors most frequently mentioned by handicapped adolescents were conflict with others (e.g., with peers) and social injustices (e.g., being teased). Peer rejection and social isolation can be devastating to a child's self-concept, adjustment, and developing social skills, and this in turn can further isolate him or her. As one result of this higher rate of rejection, handicapped children experience greater loneliness than their nonhandicapped peers (e.g., Luftig, 1988).

Further, when given the choice, they choose to be with other handicapped children, which further isolates them from their nonhandicapped peers. Thus, handicapped children show that they are aware of this rejection and they no doubt experience considerable stress in relation to it.

The stress created by school integration and segregation policies also contributes to and magnifies the stress within their peer network. The lack of stability created by integration policies is compounded by other policies that segregate handicapped students in ways that contribute to problems with peers. For example, although handicapped students tend to form friendships with other handicapped students, these friendships may be compromised by such integration policies and lack of school environmental stability. Further, neglect and rejection from nonhandicapped peers, which start at an early age, become a chronic source of stress for handicapped students.

In sum, handicapped children face many stressors — at school, in the home, and in relation to peers. Some of these stressors arise from the child's disabilities, some arise out of the stress created in other people because of the child's disabilities, whereas others arise from school policies and social stigmas over which the child has little influence. Although handicapped students appear to be aware of these stressors, and research indicates that they are negatively impacted by them, there appear to be no studies in which this impact has been directly examined.

Resources for Dealing with Stress

One factor that may serve to compound the challenges that handicapped students face in the school, family, and with peers is their coping style. Children with handicaps often exhibit inflexibility, emotional simplicity, and external locus of control, and tend to give up rather than persevere in achievement situations in which they may fail, and to use more passive and emotion-focused coping strategies than nonhandicapped children (e.g., Wayment & Zetlin, 1989). In general, handicapped students also tend to show a more passive response to new situations and in interactions with nonhandicapped peers. Because achievement and peer interaction situations tend to require more active, problem-focused coping strategies, it is reasonable to believe that, in general, the coping strategies typically used by handicapped students may not be effective in mediating many of the stresses they face.

Another factor that may interfere with the handicapped student's ability to deal with stress is a limited network of social support. Research with nonhandicapped children has shown that social networks and social supports are effective buffers against stress, and are important to development, adjustment, and psychological health (e.g., Hartup, 1989; O'Grady & Metz, 1987). Although there are few studies of social networks and social supports for handicapped children and adolescents, studies by Wayment and Zetlin (1989), Siperstein and Bak (1989), and Bak and Siperstein (1987) have thrown some light on the situation. Focusing on friendships inside and outside the classroom, they found that handicapped adolescents named a wide range of people as important, including parents and other adults in the school and community, and frequently formed friendships with other handicapped peers (although girls more often turned to adults for help whereas boys turned to peers). However, they did not examine whether these relationships were a source of support for these adolescents. Little also is known about the role of these relationships in mediating stress.

INTERACTION OF FAMILIES AND CHILDREN FROM DIFFERENT CULTURES: ACCULTURATIVE STRESS

The concept of acculturation can be used to refer to changes that families and their children undergo when they come into contact with another culture (see Berry, Kim, Minde, & Mok, 1987). Such acculturation entails changes in behavior, values, attitudes, and identity. In understanding the general acculturative situation it is necessary to adopt a cross-cultural perspective, rather than simply treating acculturating groups as minority groups. It also is necessary to recognize that many acculturation phenomena do not reside solely in acculturating groups but arise as a result of the interaction of such groups. There is the further need to realize that families and their children enter into, deal with, and react to acculturative situations in different ways.

There also is the need to take into account that a student's or parent's style in perceiving situations greatly influences coping abilities in dealing with new situations. As Lazarus and Folkman (1984) have noted, the kind of appraisal made of a situation will in part also determine if a situation is seen as a threat or a challenge. They also pointed out that an appraisal of threat will be accompanied by emotions such as fear, anxiety, and anger, whereas a challenge appraisal will produce such positive emotions as eagerness, excitement, and exhilaration. Lazarus and Folkman further noted that, "Challenge, as opposed to threat, has implications for adaptation. For example, people who are disposed or encouraged by their circumstances to feel challenged probably have advantages over easily threatened people in morale, quality of functioning, and somatic health" (p. 34). That this is the case has been demonstrated by Scheier and Carver (1992) who, in their review of the literature on optimism and health, showed that variables such as hopefulness, general expectancies, and optimism are linked with successful coping.

Within this general perspective, one can propose that acculturative stress accounts for some of the outcomes that have been observed for acculturating families and their children in American schools. The concept of acculturative stress refers to stressors having their source in the process of acculturation that often results in various kinds of stress behaviors, including feelings of marginality and alienation, identity confusion, depression, anxiety, and heightened psychosomatic symptoms (Berry & Kim, 1988). Stressors may result from the varying experiences of acculturation, although acculturative changes may lead to positive as well as negative stressors. In particular, parents' and their children's appraisal of acculturation experiences and their coping skills in dealing with stressors can affect the level of acculturative stress experienced. The mode of acculturation also is an important factor (Berry et al., 1987). Those who feel marginalized or who seek to remain separate tend to be highly stressed. In contrast, assimilation leads to intermediate levels of stress, and for those who pursue integration there is minimal stress.

Other moderating variables — such as the nature of the larger society, the type of acculturating group, and the demographic, social, and psychological characteristics of the family, the parents and their children — also influence the amount of stress generated (Berry, 1989). For example, not all children and their parents deal with acculturative pressures in the same way, leading to highly variable stress outcomes. As another example, the sense of cognitive control that an individual has over the acculturation process seems to play a role; those who perceive the changes as opportunities that they can manage may have better educational and other outcomes than those who feel overwhelmed by them.

As a concrete example of the acculturation process and related stress, and its significance for schooling, Suarez-Orozco (1989) portrays the experiences and achievement patterns of Central American students who recently immigrated to the United States. The subjects of the study were

50 students (30 boys and 20 girls) enrolled in two inner-city public high schools on the West Coast. Most of these students worked part-time or full-time to help support themselves and their families.

The author spent a year working in the schools while collecting data for the study. In addition to being observed, the students were given the Thematic Apperception Test (TAT) to uncover any recurrent themes in their stories that could help in understanding their motivation to succeed in the United States.

Through the author's observations and interactions with students, parents, and relatives, it was found that, in spite of traumatic experiences in their prior homeland and in their present neighborhood, these adolescents showed a great desire to succeed. This discovery led the author to try to understand what influenced their success.

Based on the author's observations and results of the TAT, there were certain dominant themes that came to the fore. One was parental sacrifice. as the dominant factor in the students' motivation to succeed. A need for reciprocity and nurturing those who sacrifice was another. The other two major themes were: guilt as a psychological burden, and a desire to "become somebody" as a vehicle to nurture loved ones. From these themes, it seemed clear that the need to "become somebody" was central to these students' desire to succeed.

The frame of reference from which these students try to achieve this goal also is described by the author. This frame of reference includes the perception that opportunity overshadows hardships and the view that their experiences of crime, deprivation, and depression in the inner city are no worse than the disruption and violence they left behind. It also includes the sense that their own values do not have to change in order for them to succeed and, in addition, an instrumental attitude toward the host society that allows them to accommodate to life in the inner city without giving up their shared code of behavior. In essence, these students engage in a strategy which might be called "accommodation without assimilation" (Gibson, 1987).

Looking at their experiences, it seems clear that these students feel their hard work and study will bring success, although success is not defined in terms of independence and competition but from a perspective of caring. For them, schooling in this country is more accessible and fair, although not as rigorous and disciplined as it is in their native countries.

To sum up, in the lives of these students from Central America, "becoming somebody" fulfills instrumental as well as expressive functions. In an instrumental manner, achievement leads to status mobility and wealth. From an expressive perspective, achievement is a manner of showing love, care, and closeness. It also makes the sacrifices of their parents worthwhile.

It also is clear that acculturation is a normal part of the adjustment process, so that, in considering acculturation from this broader perspective, a preventative strategy would be a desirable approach for schools to use, especially with immigrant children and their families. For such prevention-oriented school programs, there are a variety of procedures, such as social skills training (Furnham & Bochner, 1986), intercultural communication competence (Imahori & Lanigan, 1989), and social-cognitive techniques that emphasize self-concept (Zaharna, 1987) that would be useful. Such programs would be concrete tools for dealing with the acculturation problems of both students and their parents.

AFRICAN-AMERICAN MIDDLE-CLASS FAMILIES

It has been common in discussions of the family to identify African-American family life with lower-income culture but to view the prototypical middle-income family as White (Staples, 1978). One attempt to rectify this situation has been provided by Coner-Edwards and Spurlock (1988), who provided a collection of papers on a wide range of social and psychological topics that relate to the African-American middle-income family. They included sections on: work and stress, male-female relationships, parenting, educational issues, health and illness, and therapeutic intervention. One of their goals was to educate professionals, including teachers and other school professionals, concerning the stressors faced by African-American middle-class families and the implications of these stressors for psychological well-being. In particular, they offered positive approaches for the assessment and treatment of middle-class African-American families.

From a family–school relationship perspective, one important source of stress that was identified and discussed is the way the new middle class handles racial status. In differentiating the "old middle class" from the "new middle class," a contrast that sounds very much like the distinction between the aristocracy and nouveau riche, the new African-American middle class is described as having a sense of importance in the fact of their "Blackness" but also as showing identity confusion and an inability to be comfortable with either African Americans or Whites.

Two other noteworthy topics discussed in this book are the psychoso-cial issues and special stresses in families coping with the problems and conflicted racial identity faced by African-American middle-income chil-dren in many integrated school settings. However, because of the paucity of research on normal processes in African-American families of any social class, it is difficult to know how the findings reported by Coner-Ed-wards and Spurlock on these topics are applicable to the African-American middle class as contrasted with lower income African Americans, other middle-class groups, or other socially marginal groups.

ASIAN-AMERICAN FAMILIES

The scholastic success of Asian-American students is well recognized (e.g., Divoky, 1988). Despite their hardships, and with little knowledge of English, children and adolescents of refugee families from Asia also excel in academic achievement, even when they attend school in low-income, metropolitan areas (e.g., Caplan, Choy, & Whitmore, 1992). As Divoky noted, their success has in fact created a new stereotype: the "model minority" in education. But this success has, in some cases, come at a high price. Because of their high performance and overrepresentation in many elite universities, a pattern of discrimination may have emerged in some institutions. Their cultural values and family patterns also are a two-edged sword, with tension between parental expectations and educational values and their children's and adolescents' desire to be more like their non-Asian-American peers. They also are a diverse group, and not all are superior students with no school problems (Yao, 1985, 1987).

Asian-American immigrant students who speak little or no English present a special problem. Accurate assessment and placement in the schools is one issue. For refugees from Southeast Asia, the trauma of their experiences, and the sometimes resulting post-traumatic stress syn-drome, represent an additional challenge. Without effective stress in-tervention programs and other psychological assistance, even the best students may become severely depressed and come apart. The hurdles they face sometimes also cause them to leave school early, creating a bad dropout problem.

The stereotype of Asian-American students as polite and hard working brings additional problems (Yao, 1985, 1987). Teachers expect more of them academically and, by assuming them to be self-sufficient, can over-look a lot of these students' personal, social, and family problems. Because teachers expect docility and passivity from Asian students, when these students do act up, teachers treat them more harshly than they would treat African Americans or Hispanics. A belief in the stereotype of the good Asian student can also generate hostility from other students, which can lead to verbal and physical abuse.

Driven by their families to pursue academic success, some Asian-American students lack the extracurricular interests that make for well-rounded students. Some parents also hold such high ideals for their children that they overlook or deny mental, physical, or social limitations. Also, their parents, respectful of authority, are slow to challenge the system, which creates the need for special strategies in working with and involving Asian-American parents in the school. To deal positively with the stressful experiences of these students and their parents, there is a need for teachers, school psychologists, and other school personnel to understand the social, cultural, and personality traits that make these students and their parents unique.

STRESSFUL LIFE EVENTS OF GAY YOUTH

In one of the major studies of gay youth, Rotheram-Borus, Rosario, and Koopman (1991) looked at stresses in the lives of gay males recruited in New York. Most of the youth were African American or Hispanic. To assess the stresses that these 12- to 18-year-olds experienced, they used a life events checklist that focuses on the occurrence of desirable and undesirable life events and also asks youth to evaluate the impact of each event, although it does not assess daily hassles. The instrument consists of 62 items that monitor events over a period of 3 months. In their report they focused primarily on events that had a negative impact.

Their results showed that minority gay youths experience a great deal of stress, with rates about four times as high as rates reported for other populations of adolescents. For example, friends and romantic relationships were important stressors, and about one fifth of the gays had ended a romantic relationship in the last 3 months. In addition, a large percentage had lost friendships, had friends who died or were injured, as well as had friends with drug problems.

The most striking results, however, were those concerning victimization. Over a period of 3 months, about 20 percent had been physically assaulted, another 20 percent had been sexually assaulted or raped, and still another 20 percent had been robbed or burglarized. In addition, 20 percent had been in trouble with the police, but had not been arrested, whereas more than 10 percent had been arrested, 20 percent had been jailed, and another 10 percent had been convicted of a crime. Other personal stressors involved substance abuse behaviors, with 17 percent reporting a drug or alcohol abuse problem.

Gay youths also have unique sources of stress related to issues of being discovered or disclosing to family and friends, reactions by others to their homosexuality, and chronic stress associated with their homosexuality. For example, Remafedi (1987) found that more than 40 percent of gay male youth had lost a friend over their homosexuality, and, in a study of young gay male suicide attempters and nonattempters, Schneider, Farberow, and Kruks (1989) found that recent attempters, unlike nonattempters, rated rejection by others as important to them, and that they were more dependent on those who rejected them. Gay youths also are at greater risk for abuse by their families (Martin & Hetrick, 1988) and often experience verbal abuse and physical assault by classmates (Remafedi, 1987).

Overall, it is clear that gays must cope with issues of survival, as well as attempting to resolve problematic home and living conditions, and that they have to come to terms with their sexuality, seek friendships with others who share their orientation, and cope with anticipated and actual responses of family and others to their sexual orientation. Given their high rates of stressful life events, it also is clear that these youths need help in coping with life stressors, although these youth also need to be convinced that there is need for intervention. It also is critical for these youths to reduce their risk behavior. One useful approach would be behaviorally based preventive programs like that implemented by Schinke, Schilling, Palleja, and Zayas (1987), which demonstrated effectiveness in reducing high-risk sexual and drug behavior and in managing stress. Most importantly, schools need to become more aware of the plight of these adolescents and take more responsibility for finding out about their special stresses and helping them deal with them.

TEENAGE MOTHERS

Each year, more than one million teenage girls in the United States become pregnant (National Research Council, 1987). Of these, more than 400,000 get abortions, and 500,000 others (the majority of whom are unmarried) give birth. This is a very serious problem because disciplinary, academic, and other school problems tend to increase for pregnant teenagers, and because many pregnant teenagers drop out of school. Adolescent pregnancy also creates a developmental crisis, compounding the stresses of two normative stages and endangering the successful resolution of either one.

The problem of teenage pregnancy also is enormously complex. Most laypersons, and many educators, understand the problem of teen pregnancy as an increase in the number of children having children. In fact, although the overall rates of teen pregnancy have risen, the availability of abortion has actually lowered the teen-age birthrate. Teen pregnancies are a problem not only because they result in births but because they demonstrate that sexual intercourse is beginning at ever-younger ages, and because these pregnancies so frequently result from apparent disregard of available contraception. They also are a problem because those pregnancies that are carried to term usually result in children kept and raised by their young, unmarried mother, and because teen pregnancy may have adverse effects on the health of the adolescent and/or infant.

The question society poses to researchers is, Why are so many teenagers acting in a way that seems, at least to most adults, to be so irrational and counter to their own best interests? By and large, researchers have been unable to answer this question. Nevertheless, there is a large body of data about adolescent sexual behavior, although what has emerged from these data are primarily descriptions rather than explanations (see, e.g., Lancaster & Hamberg, 1986). We know a great deal about what social factors (demographic, economic, as well as psychological) are related to pregnancy in adolescence, but this knowledge has not led to a coherent model of adolescent sexual and contraceptive behavior. Increasingly, it seems that the causes of adolescent pregnancy involve more than social factors, and include biological and cultural forces that interact with social factors in a complex chain of causation that can be modeled only when both sets of factors are integrated.

As to what can be done about the special stresses and other problems surrounding teenage pregnancy, the National Research Council report concluded that programs and policies designed to address adolescent pregnancy should make pregnancy prevention their highest priority. Although a specific role for schools is not addressed, many of the approaches suggested can be, or are already being, carried out in many schools (see, e.g., Education Research Group, 1987; Children's Defense Fund, 1986). The problem is extreme, however, and coordinated school and community, as well as governmental and societal efforts, are needed. Such efforts are addressed by Brooks-Gunn and Furstenberg (1989) and Furstenberg, Brooks-Gunn, and Chase-Landsdale (1989), and the evidence they present supports the importance of increasing the availability of services to adolescents and the need for more integrated school and community services.

STRESS OF OVERPRIVILEGED
CHILDREN AND ADOLESCENTS

To gain a better understanding of the special stresses of the children and adolescents from households with adjusted gross incomes above $80-90,000, and their implications for developing better schooling for these students, we must start by analyzing the life-styles and concerns of their parents. Brooks (1989) has done this, and her findings indicate that it is the thoughts and actions of those parents that create many of the stress-related problems that these seemingly golden children and adolescents face. In the preparation of this book, she interviewed a large number of psychologists, educators, and psychiatrists and spoke with many parents, children, and adolescents.

One of her major findings was that these "fast-track" parents were struggling with an obsession with professional success. Although this drive had created luxurious living standards for them, many faced the prospect that their children may not equal their achievements or continue to enjoy the good life unless they hoist their children onto their own fast track as soon as possible.

These parents also see this country as increasingly becoming a meritocracy. Thus their children will not have the chance of making it big unless they attend the best schools, make top grades, and make the right friends. As one consequence of this view of the way things are, these parents place as much pressure on their children to succeed as they place on themselves. Added to this, a high-achieving child also fits the total image they are trying so hard to project, because a successful child is the ultimate proof of their own success.

To guarantee such outcomes, these parents are convinced that they must start their children on the road to success at an early age. This means getting the child into the finest nursery, then the best public or prep school and the finest tutors and extra activities, and culminating with admission to an elite university.

Despite their best efforts, unintended negative consequences sometimes do occur. For those youngsters who are not intellectually and emotionally able to function under such pressure, there is a potential for large amounts of stress and, in some cases, for stress disorders of various kinds. Generally, the children who suffer the most stress are those who are both mediocre in accomplishments and physically less attractive. Moreover, because their parents place such high priority on their own perfection and getting to the top, these youngsters especially worry that their parents won't love them unless they, too, perform according to plan.

It should be noted, however, that others are turned on, rather than off, by the pressure and develop a high level of excellence, although the price for their extraordinary achievement sometimes is high. For example, they may be unable to form close friendships with peers, especially those consistently seen as competitors. In such an environment, very able youngsters also can lose their sense of the value of friendship and cooperation.

In addition, Brooks pointed out that, because the parents of these children often are dashing about on their own fast professional tracks, they have less time for nurturing and use hired help to assist in rearing their children. One consequence is that a growing number of children of fast-track parents are coming to school desperately seeking from teachers the attention, approval, and love that they have not received from their parents. Growing up in a household with other caregivers, and even servants, can also create the impression in some of these children that the world is set up to fulfill their every need. Thus they become very demanding of teachers and others in their school.

Many of these fast-track parents also feel guilty about spending so little time caring for their children, and they alleviate that guilt by showering their children with expensive possessions, often rushing to replace whatever is lost or broken, so that the child does not suffer the consequences of the loss. But this approach can backfire. It can make a child seem greedy and unaware of what it really takes to get by in the world. It also can touch off a cycle of resentment in parents because the child does not seem to be sufficiently grateful.

Having too much can stunt motivation and drive, as well. Why sweat, these children candidly told the author (i.e., Brooks), when you know that your parents will give in to whatever you want anyway? Unfortunately, there is little research on the negative impact of having too much, rather than too little. How much damage these indulgent but well-intentioned fast-track parents do, therefore, is not clearly discernible.

One implication of these findings is that teachers and other school professionals must realize that many of the attitudes and behavior patterns formerly associated with the gilt-tipped edge of society have filtered down and no longer apply to just a very small minority of students. These characteristics are now found among the children of fast-track parents. Increased realization that success and money cannot buy a perfect childhood must also take place. The deck of children of affluence is simply shuffled, substituting one set of stresses and problems for another.

School professionals also need to develop compensating strategies in terms of modifications of the curriculum and in terms of new kinds of parent relations. One possibility is the development of "privileged" studies somewhat analogous to African-American studies and women's studies which have enabled those groups to gain a better understanding of their lives and heritage. In the same way, these "privileged" studies would enable these youngsters to better understand their attitudes and concerns.

Parenting programs and school activities that pay attention to the special stresses and problems of "less able" siblings in fast-track families also might be helpful. Such children are clearly at high risk in a super-achieving, highly competitive environment. Such children, who neither fail as students nor win the accolades, often develop negative feelings about themselves fairly early in life. They call themselves "losers," even though that is not an accurate assessment in the context of the real world. Left unattended, their view of themselves can become a self-fulfilling prophecy. In this connection, a greater awareness among parents and teachers of the stigma attached to failure in fast-track families is crucial. The development of more opportunities among students for cooperation also would help to offset the extreme emphasis on winning that is pervasive in many fast-track families.

In sum, a growing number of children are experiencing high levels of stress and exhibiting behavior patterns that stem from having too much rather than too little. Thus, in analyzing the causes of stress, it is important to look at the special circumstances of the overprivileged as we have traditionally looked at the special circumstances of the underprivileged.

CONCLUDING COMMENTS

The point of departure for this chapter is that, although children and adolescents to a considerable extent create their own experiences from the environments they encounter, the conditions that family, school, peer, and cultural contexts provide for children and adolescents also make differences in their life chances and eventual adult statuses. Thus, analyses of differences in stress, coping, and adaptational outcomes need a focus on what makes *groups* of children and adolescents different from one another in these ways, as well as a focus on analyses of sources of variation in stress, coping, and adaptational outcomes between individuals without regard to their group status. However, *normal* development does occur in a wide range of environments, and unless the environment for a particular group of children and adolescents is outside of this normal range, it is unlikely that stress, coping, and adaptational outcomes will be heavily dependent on the group's defining characteristics. Taking these considerations into account, the sources and causes of variation in stress, coping, and adaptational outcomes for a number of special subpopulations of children and adolescents were examined in this chapter, and one conclusion was that the stress results obtained for one group may have only limited implications for understanding the stress results obtained for other groups.

To sum up, the essence of stress is perceptual-experiential. The stress value of life experiences must be measured in terms of their special meaning to a given group, in addition to their meaning to individuals across a variety of groups. What determines the meaning of life experiences derives from the interplay of the context within which children and adolescents develop, as well as from their unique heritages. Only by understanding some of the complexity of stress, as it relates to the vagaries of circumstance and environment of particular *groups* of children and adolescents, can efforts to understand stress be successful, and attempts at stress intervention in the schools, whether preventive or therapeutic, be effective.

8 STRESS OF FAMILIES WITH HANDICAPPED CHILDREN AND ADOLESCENTS

Beginning in the 1970s, the meaning of "schooling" in this country was redefined and broadened, for handicapped children in particular, to include training toward self-sufficiency. What this redefinition has become, in the context of P.L. 94-142, is indicated by the case of Timothy (see *Timothy W. v. Rochester, New Hampshire School District,* 875 F. 2nd, 1st Cir. 1989). Soon after his birth, Timothy experienced an intracranial hemorrhage, seizures, hydrocephalus, and meningitis. As a result, he was multiply handicapped and profoundly retarded. Timothy's handicaps included cerebral palsy, spastic quadriplegia, and cortical blindness. He also had no language, and his purposeful movements were largely limited to reactions to pain, strong smells and tastes, touch, and familiar voices. He parted his lips when spoon-fed. Nevertheless, the court decided, based on the plain language of P.L. 94-142, that Timothy could not be denied public schooling.

Although this is an extreme case, it points up the possible relationships between stress in the families of children with handicaps and the involvement of parents in the schooling process. This stressful impact has been chronicled through anecdotal reports as well as research. Mullens (1987), for example, reviewed 60 books written by parents of children with handicaps. Among the themes he found were the extraordinary demands placed on families in terms of additional caregiving, time and energy investment, relationship strains, and financial burdens. Such demands included the need to search for the correct diagnosis and treatment and appropriate educational services, a search sometimes exacerbated by the insensitivity of professionals. Significant emotional stress involving intense anguish, recriminations, grief, and worry also was a common theme. On a positive side, many parents also wrote of the special meaning and enrichment added to their lives by their children with handicaps.

STRESS ON MOTHERS AS PRIMARY CAREGIVERS

Research on families with handicapped children has focused on the mother as primary caregiver, although studies of fathers also are available. For example, significantly higher levels of stress have been reported for mothers of handicapped children (Friedrich & Friedrich, 1981; Wilton & Renaut, 1986). In another study by Rodrigue, Morgan, and Geffkin (1990), mothers of children with autism indicated feelings of less parenting competence, family adaptability, and marital satisfaction than mothers of developmentally normal children. Mothers of children with mental retardation also tended to report more depression and lower self-esteem (Harris & McHale, 1989). In a study of parents of chronically ill versus healthy children, parents of ill children also had more depression and a lower sense of competence (Goldberg, Morris, Simmons, Fowler, & Levison, 1990). In this study, mothers also report more stress than fathers, although fathers had greater difficulty adapting to their ill children. Several studies have also noted the tendency of fathers to withdraw from the daily care of children with handicaps (Palfrey, Walker, Butler, & Singer, 1989).

IMPACT OF HANDICAPPED CHILDREN ON PARENT MARITAL RELATIONSHIPS AND SIBLINGS

In contrast, research on the impact of children with handicaps on the marital relationships of parents is more equivocal (see, e.g., Kazak & Marvin, 1984). For example, reviewers of 10 studies (Longo & Bond, 1984) concluded that the quality of marriages tended to remain stable without regard to the disabilities of children. However, in studies cited in Wikler, Haack, and Intagliata (1984) and in Harris and Fong (1985), it was found that unstable marriages were especially vulnerable following the birth of a child with handicaps. In this situation, several factors contribute to marital strain, including: guilt when the condition was genetically based; an unsatisfactory spousal relationship; fear of another pregnancy; and having lost previous children.

The effects that a child with handicaps has on his or her brothers and sisters also present an unclear picture. One review of research findings (Hannah & Midlarsky, 1985) found several common themes, including the presence in siblings of anxiety, withdrawal or depression, aggression and acting out behaviors, and school failure. They further reported that increased responsibilities given to, and increased parental expectations for, nonhandicapped siblings, and parental neglect of the needs of nonhandicapped siblings, were factors in the psychological maladjustment of nonhandicapped siblings. There are some studies, however, which cast doubt on the negative impact of children with handicaps upon their siblings (see, e.g., Lobato, 1983).

The effect of children with handicaps on the family as a system also has been studied. For example, Kazak and Marvin (1984) reported that families with children with handicaps had a parental subsystem relatively exclusive of the father, an arrangement they concluded may be adaptive for such families. It has also been reported by Palfrey et al. (1989) that, although 28 percent of the families reported a direct, stressful impact of a child's handicap on the daily lives of family members, the majority reported no stress associated with rearing a child with handicaps.

MEDIATION OF FAMILY STRESS

Research has indicated that the stressful effects on the family of the child with handicaps may be influenced by several factors. One is socioeconomic status (SES) because there is a higher level of family stress in lower-SES families with children with handicaps (e.g., Palfrey et al., 1989). Among other findings, this study found that mothers with higher education levels were more likely to report stress that was associated with their children's handicaps. However, in a study of families that had adjusted well to the birth of a child with handicaps, there was no significant relationship between family income and overall level of family functioning (Trute & Hauch, 1988). There also are other studies that don't find such a difference (e.g., Flynt & Wood, 1989), perhaps because lower social class also is associated with a higher tolerance for deviance from the norm (see, e.g., Seligman & Darling, 1989).

RACIAL-ETHNIC INFLUENCE

There are few studies of racial-ethnic influence on the stress of families with handicapped children, although in one longitudinal study Anglo families reported less stress than non-Anglo families (Beckman & Pokorni, 1988). In another study, however, there were no significant differences among African-American, Hispanic, and Anglo parents in their initial reaction to the birth of a child with a handicap (Mary, 1990). African-American mothers also were found to be less likely to report negative effects associated with rearing a child with handicaps (Flynt & Wood, 1989; Palfrey et al., 1989). In addition, Seligman and Darling (1989) have noted that cultural differences may contribute to greater acceptance of and/or less difficulty in coping with children with handicaps by Hispanics and African Americans.

IMPACT OF CHILD CHARACTERISTICS

The impact of child characteristics on families of children with handicaps has been the focus of considerable research, although it is difficult to conclude with any certainty how the type of disability of a child will affect the family. One contentious topic in the literature is the influence of the severity of the child's handicap on the family. For mothers of severely handicapped children, high stress levels have been found, although no difference in stress levels was found between mothers of mildly and moderately handicapped children (Kazak, 1986). In a comparison of levels of severity of mental retardation, parents of children with severe mental retardation reported the greatest negative influence on family adjustment (Seligman & Darling, 1989). Families with children with severe disabilities have also been reported to be more restricted in social activities (McCubbin, 1988). However, Lyon and Lyon (1991) contend that summaries of the literature show little support for the negative impact on the family of a child's severe disability. Likewise, Sloman and Konstantareas (1990) question the positive correlation of severity of handicap with family stress. They and others believe that systems outside the family, rather than severity of the child's disability, are responsible for the additional family stress.

The caregiving demands placed on the family by the child's disability (e.g., feeding, handling, medical care) constitute another important source of stress for the family (Quine & Pahl, 1985). Although lone impairments

such as incontinence, lack of mobility, and lack of self-help and communication skills were not associated with higher stress in mothers, multiple
impairments were associated with elevated levels of stress. The child's
communication skills and cognitive abilities were also related to parental
adjustment (Frey, Fewell, & Vadasy, 1988). However, the particular handicapping condition or diagnostic category assigned to a child has little
differential relationship to impact of the handicapped child on stress in the
family (see, e.g., McKinney & Peterson, 1987; Quine & Pahl, 1985).
Results such as this led Kazak (1986) to suggest that more difficult child
behaviors, rather than the diagnostic category per se, tended to be associated with higher levels of maternal stress. As evidence of this, the
stressful impact on the family of behavioral disturbances in children
with handicaps has appeared repeatedly in the literature (see, e.g.,
Seligman & Darling, 1989).

The child's gender and age have also been found to influence the
family. Consistent research findings support the increased difficulty of
parental adjustment to male children with handicaps (Frey, Greenberg, &
Fewell, 1989). Increased stress has also been associated with the child's
increasing age, primarily because differences between the child or adolescent with handicaps and his or her peers become more noticeable and the
larger child or adolescent becomes more difficult to manage (Minnes,
1988). Some researchers believe, however, that life cycle stage of the
family, rather than child or adolescent age, is a more meaningful concept.

IMPACT OF THE LIFE CYCLE

Most research regarding the impact of the life cycle has focused on
families with a child with mental retardation. In such families, additional
responsibilities have been noted at each stage of the life cycle (see, e.g.,
Turnbull & Turnbull, 1986). For example, they noted that stressors associated with school age include: dealing with school personnel, adjusting
to the educational implications of the child's disability, dealing with the
reactions of the child's peer group, arranging for extracurricular activities,
and locating community resources. They also pointed out that as the child
with handicaps ages, the shift away from parenting responsibilities expected in the family life cycle does not take place due to the child's
continued dependence on his or her parents. Transitional periods between
life cycle stages, especially entrance into adolescence and adulthood, also
are associated with increased family stress (Black, Molaison, & Small,

1990). For example, the termination of school services at age 21 is associated with increased family stress. It also should be noted that, for families with mentally retarded children, stress is chronic across the life cycle (Flynt & Wood, 1989). Parent utilization of professional and personal support also has been found to vary over the life cycle, with parents of older children being more resistant to normalization efforts (Suelzle & Keenan, 1981).

EARLY INTERVENTION PROGRAMS

Traditionally, early intervention efforts for handicapped children were child focused and resulted in a failure to understand the broader-based context of the child and family and the relations between the family and other social systems. More recently, an understanding of the family context has been considered important in order for professionals and families to collaborate on goals and intervention activities.

Although research has documented the benefits of parent participation in early intervention programs (e.g., Seligman & Darling, 1989), the involvement of parents has often been variable, with only 20 to 40 percent of parents being actively involved in early intervention programs for their infants or toddlers. For children with severe handicaps, the situation is no better. According to Meyers and Blacher (1987), family–school communication was rare for 31 percent and nonexistent for 3 percent of these children. In addition, about 50 percent of the parents reported that they had some, little, or no involvement in assessment, IEP development, or parent groups.

As the focus in early intervention expands from children to family systems, and even to social systems, it is important to include a philosophical and theoretical framework that supports and justifies the methodology. Research that recognizes the interrelationships of factors involved in the stress and coping process will help to facilitate the development of family-focused early interventions aimed at supporting and enhancing adaptive coping efforts. The importance of a multivariate approach in examining factors internal and external to the family that contribute to stress and coping efforts has also been articulated by several investigators (see, e.g., Kazak, 1986). Such research efforts will promote a greater understanding of the factors affecting family stress, coping, and adaptation and lead to the provision of more appropriate and effective early intervention services.

ROLE OF SOCIAL SUPPORT

Investigations of the role of social support in ameliorating family stress have appeared frequently in the literature (Seligman & Darling, 1989). Both its direct influence on recovery from stress and its protective function against stress have been investigated, although investigators have differed in the definition of social support used. The most widely used definition involves the exchange of information at the interpersonal level which serves to provide emotional support (prompting belief that the individual is the focus of love and caring), esteem support (prompting belief that one is valued), and network support which prompts the belief in membership in a communication network of mutual understanding and obligation. McCubbin and McCubbin (1989) have expanded this definition to include appraisal support or evaluative support or reciprocated goodwill from others. Social support has also been defined from an ecological perspective, which emphasizes the sources of support, i.e., family, friends, and the community (Seligman & Darling, 1989). These sources of support can be divided into sources of informal support (family, friends, neighbors, colleagues) and sources of formal support (schools, community groups, professional service providers).

The role of social support as a resource for the stressful effects of rearing a child with handicaps has been discussed widely in the literature. In a review of research regarding families of children with physical and mental handicaps, Kazak (1986) noted the social isolation of such families from both formal and informal sources of support. Wikler and his colleagues (1984) noted that parents of a child with handicaps are less able to visit friends, take vacations, or run errands due to the demands of child care, stigmatized encounters, special transportation needs, lack of babysitters, and loss of income as a result of the mother's inability to work outside the home. The isolation felt by two-parent families may be even greater for single-parent families, For example, Wikler et al. (1984) found that almost one-third of single mothers of children with handicaps were extremely socially isolated. The importance of emotional support from spouses has also been supported in the literature (Kazak & Marvin, 1984).

Several studies have supported the buffering effect of social support for families with children with handicaps. For example, Peterson (1984) found that support available to mothers of children with handicaps served as a buffer against problems in maternal health and adjustment, i.e., mothers with high stress but high levels of support had fewer problems than mothers with high stress but low levels of support. Intrafamily and extrafamily support independently account for a significant amount of the variance in mother's well-being, and intrafamily support also contributes to the mother's commitment to implementing a child-level intervention.

According to Kazak (1986), one of the most conceptually clear methods of study in the area of social support has been analysis of social support networks in terms of the group of people with whom families with children with handicaps interact. Most research has focused on network size and has indicated that parents of children with handicaps have fewer sources of support. The higher stress levels in mothers of the handicapped are also associated with the greater density of their social networks, where density is the degree of network members' interactions with one another apart from the focal person (Frey et al., 1989). Mothers of children with handicaps have also been found to rely more on family than friends for social support (Kazak, 1986; Trute & Hauch, 1988).

Although social isolation and smaller network size have been found for families with children with some types of handicaps, a study comparing three samples of children with different handicaps with three matched control groups found no differences in the size of the social support networks and no social isolation for families with children with handicaps (Kazak, 1987). However, the networks of the groups with children with handicaps were found to be denser, and differences in both network size and density were found when the three groups of children with handicaps were compared, which reinforces the idea of heterogeneity when considering families of children with handicaps.

Other authors have suggested that parental satisfaction with social support is a more important variable than network size or density (see, e.g., Erickson & Upshur, 1989). In support of this contention, satisfaction with the perceived level of social support has been found to be related to lower stress levels (Factor, Perry, & Freeman, 1990). Perceived adequacy of social support has also been shown to differentiate highest from lowest stress groups in parents of children with autism (Factor et al., 1990). In comparing families with children with autism who were users and nonusers of respite care, they reported that nonusers indicated more perceived social support and less stress than users of respite care. Greater satisfaction with social support has also been reported for mothers of infants with developmental disabilities when compared to mothers of nonhandicapped infants, a result attributed to the involvement of mothers of infants with handicaps in early intervention programs (Erickson & Upshur, 1989).

Although informal sources of support (family, friends, neighbors) have generally been shown to act as buffers against the stress of rearing a child with handicaps, the benefits to the family of interaction with formal sources of support are not so clear. Mothers of infants with handicaps have reported more sources of social support overall than mothers of nonhandicapped infants due to an increased number of contacts with sources of formal support (Gowen, Johnson-Mattin, Goldman, & Appelbaum,1989). However, in another study (Beckman & Pokorni, 1988), formal support utilized by mothers of infants with handicaps was not correlated with mothers' stress at any of three age levels, although informal support was negatively correlated with mothers' stress at two of the three age levels. Although professionals are often listed as resources by parents of children with handicaps, and community services have been called a crucial factor in the family's adaptation, it has been suggested that interactions with formal sources of support may be more stressful than supportive (Turnbull & Turnbull, 1986). In fact, research has shown that external family support from professionals is positively correlated with higher levels of stress in parents of children with handicaps (Minnes, 1988). In a study of mothers of children with mental retardation, 40 percent reported difficulties with community programs or professionals, whereas dissatisfaction with support from friends and family was the least frequently mentioned problem area (Harris & McHale, 1989). On the other hand, services provided by school personnel, medical facilities, and professionals were identified as highly supportive by parents in a study of positive adaptation to a child with disabilities (Weber & Parker, 1981). The hazards of parental over-reliance on community services have also been noted in the literature (Farran, Metzger, & Sparling, 1986). For families with school-age children and adolescents with handicaps, the school system has the potential to be an important source of formal support, although there has been little research in this area (Kazak, 1986).

PARENTS WHO ADOPT HANDICAPPED CHILDREN

There are an increasing number of studies of adoption (e.g., Brodzinsky, Singer, & Braff, 1984; McRoy, Grotevant, & Zurcher, 1988), but few studies of families that adopt handicapped children. An example of such a study is the one by Glidden (1989). It describes the decision to adopt, the process of adoption, and adoption outcomes in 42 British families who adopted 56 mentally retarded children. As to the decision to adopt, in 39 of the 42 families at least one parent had prior experience with handicaps, adoption, or fostering. Glidden also attempted to portray the path between entrance of a handicapped child into the family and the family's adjustment, taking into account both existential crises and reality burdens with which the family had to cope. Existential crises included the feelings of disillusionment, vulnerability, and loss of immortality that might be experienced with the birth of a handicapped child. Included among reality burdens were the day-to-day difficulties of caring for a handicapped child.

One of Glidden's goals was to tease apart the relative contributions of these two crises by comparing parents who adopted handicapped children with parents who gave birth to a handicapped child. According to the reasoning put forward, parents who gave birth to a handicapped child would need to deal with both existential crises and the daily reality of caring for such a child, whereas parents who choose to adopt such a child would have the same reality burdens but would be immune to the existential crises because the child was not born to them. Although this aspect of the study had a problematic quality, the findings of other aspects of the study make a worthwhile contribution. Of special note, Glidden used the Holroyd Questionnaire on Resources and Stress (Holroyd, 1987) to identify factors that differentiated between the families of her sample who had satisfactorily adjusted to the adoption and those who had not. These differentiating factors included prior experience with handicaps, a humanitarian outlook, patience, optimism, energy, and commitment.

PARENTAL INVOLVEMENT IN SPECIAL EDUCATION

Whereas parental involvement in regular education may be actively sought and encouraged by school policy and practices, parent involvement in the special education process for children and adolescents with handicaps is legally mandated and prescribed by federal statutes and regulations (especially P.L. 94-142 and amendments). In spite of, or perhaps due to, the legal requirement, parent participation in special education is problematic and sometimes marked by conflict between parents and school professionals, and its appropriateness for all families with children and adolescents with handicaps has been questioned (Hill, 1986; Winnick, 1987).

Legal Mandates

Parental rights to involvement in the special education of their children and adolescents with handicaps are legally grounded in four major pieces of federal legislation: the 1974 Family Educational Rights and Privacy Act (FERPA), the 1975 Education for All Handicapped Children Act (Public Law 94-142), the 1986 Education of the Handicapped Amendments (Public Law 99-457), and the 1986 Handicapped Children's Protection Act (Woody, Yeager, & Woody, 1990). Whereas FERPA was designed to be instrumental in protecting parents' and students' rights to access and disclosure of educational records, 94-142 (now called the Individuals with Disabilities Education Act) was the most influential legislation regarding parent involvement in the special education process, giving parents of children and adolescents ages 5–21 the power to participate in and influence educational policy and resource allocation in regard to their children and adolescents. Key provisions of 94-142 were that services would be provided for all children and adolescents with handicaps, diagnosis and treatment would be unbiased (particularly with regard to minority students), each child or adolescent would have available a clear set of educational objectives (an individualized education plan or IEP), and parents would be given an opportunity to take part in planning the child's or adolescent's educational program (Gallagher, 1989).

A complex set of due process safeguards also was included to enable parents to challenge decisions regarding the child's or adolescent's identification, evaluation, and placement in a special education program. According to Turnbull and Leonard (1981), the implicit assumption of 94-142 was that the child's or adolescent's interests would be protected if the parent participated in decisions regarding the educational program. An additional safeguard was added by the 1986 Handicapped Children's Protection Act which provided for the payment of parents' attorneys' fees and court costs when parents prevail in litigation against schools.

Public Law 99-457 was a downward extension in age that mandated the provision of 94-142 rights and services to children ages 3–5 (although voluntary services to this age group were included in 94-142). This law also created the Handicapped Infants and Toddlers Program which provides services to at-risk infants and their families and requires significant parent involvement in the development of an Individualized Family Service Plan (Gallagher, 1989).

Parent Participation in and Satisfaction with
Special Education Services

Research regarding parent/family involvement in the special education process has generally focused on parent participation in IEP meetings, parental satisfaction with special education services, and parental preferences regarding involvement. The attitudes of special educators also have been studied.

Results of research regarding parent attendance at IEP meetings have varied according to parent characteristics and the site in question. Low SES and minority group status have been related to low levels of attendance at such meetings (Leyser, 1985; Palfrey et al., 1989; Weber & Stoneman, 1986). A study comparing consistent attendees, inconsistent attendees, and nonattendees revealed that nonattendees tended to have the lowest levels of parental education and were more likely to be single-parent and minority families (Weber & Stoneman, 1986). In another study that encompassed five large urban school districts from different parts of the nation, attendance at IEP meetings varied significantly by site, ranging from 34 to 95 percent (Palfrey et al., 1989). In this study, parents who were single, non-White, and had not graduated from high school were also least likely to attend.

Research has also shown that parents who attend IEP meetings tend to participate passively and have little knowledge of the specific provisions of the child's or adolescent's educational plan (Allen & Hudd, 1987). Although parents have indicated that they benefited from attendance at IEP meetings, their presence was not seen as affecting the educational plan (Weber & Stoneman, 1986), and in many cases the IEP had been developed prior to the meeting (Turnbull & Turnbull, 1986).

Although research does not show that parents are active educational decision makers (Allen & Hudd, 1987), studies of parental satisfaction with the special education process indicate that parents are generally satisfied with the special education services their child is receiving (Lowenbraun, Madge, & Affleck, 1990; Meyers & Blacher, 1987; Stein, 1983). However, parent satisfaction with IEP staffings has been related to the time allotted for staffings, being blamed for their child's problems, and multiprofessional involvement in the process (Witt, Miller, McIntyre, & Smith, 1984). Parents also prefer informal communications with the teacher and the role of giver and receiver of information rather than the role of active decision maker (Turnbull & Turnbull, 1986).

Professional attitudes have also supported the role of the parent as a passive participant in the educational process. A 1978 survey of educators supported the parents' role as giver and receiver of information and rejected more active participation by parents (Witt et al., 1984). Another survey of IEP meeting participants revealed that parents were seen as high in status prior to the meeting but afterward were rated low in terms of their contribution to the meeting (Turnbull, 1983). Another study that surveyed special educators revealed diverse opinions regarding parent participation in the development of the IEP, with about 50 percent seeing merit in parent participation and 71 percent of teachers advocating a parent waiver of their right to participation (Gerber, Banbury, Miller, & Griffin, 1986).

Improving Parent Relationships with School Professionals

One result of the aforementioned special education laws was to make the parent–professional relationship more equal than it had been in previous years. However, there still are significant problems in the relationship between parents of children and adolescents with handicaps and the professional service providers they encounter in the schools and elsewhere (Foster, Berger, & McLean, 1981; Turnbull & Turnbull, 1986; Waggoner & Wilgosh, 1990).

Although parent–professional problems may initially involve the medical profession, school personnel become the focus when the child reaches school age. The nature of the child's or adolescent's educational program often becomes a source of conflict, with numerous areas available for potential disagreement (Margolis et al., 1987). For example, belief in the inadequacy of professional recommendations and fear that the child's chances for self-sufficiency will be compromised have been attributed to parents, as has the belief that recommendations from school personnel are more influenced by bugetary constraints and program availability than by the needs of the individual child. The high potential for conflict at parent conferences and meetings where the child's or adolescent's IEP is developed also has been noted, indicating that, besides negative professional attitudes, parents face problems of poor coordination and communication, professional availability, and pressure to approve inappropriate educational plans. The potential for conflict at such meetings is great due to the different perspectives that parents and professionals bring to the meeting (parents view decisions at the meeting as critical to the child's or adolescent's future whereas professionals may consider it routine) and due to the possible evocation in parents of strong and unexpected emotions as the meeting reminds them of the impact of the child's or adolescent's handicaps on their lives (Margolis et al., 1987).

Several suggestions for improving parent–professional relationships have appeared in the literature (e.g., Kroth, 1987; Turnbull & Turnbull, 1986). The need for professionals to understand the chronic grieving process that parents of children with handicaps go through rather than pathologizing it has been recognized. The stress placed on parents by expectations of involvement in home programs and educational decision making also has promoted suggestions for professionals to recognize that parents have responsibilities outside their role as parent of a child or adolescent with handicaps and to take into account the needs of the entire family. Recognizing that parents are family members with myriad responsibilities and individual needs and preferences can have profound influence on parent–professional relationships in special education settings.

Such efforts will also need to deal with other barriers to parental involvement, because in addition to negative professional attitudes regarding their involvement in the special education process, parents have identified several other barriers to their participation. These include logistical barriers (e.g., work conflicts, lack of transportation, and lack of child care) and communication difficulties. Lack of understanding regarding their legal rights, feeling intimidated by school personnel, and uncertainty about their child's or adolescent's handicaps have also been cited as barriers to parent involvement (Turnbull & Turnbull, 1986). In addition, institutional difficulties that interfere with parent involvement include the time and paperwork involved in complying with complex regulations governing the special education process and the lack of training professionals receive regarding how to involve parents.

Negative Aspects of Parent Involvement in Special Education

Although the authors of federal legislation apparently considered active parent participation in special education an asset, mandated parent involvement has also been criticized for its negative effects on the families of children and adolescents with handicaps. Although its benefits have been recognized, it has also been noted that parent involvement contributes to absenteeism from work, decreased leisure time, frustration, exhaustion, feelings that one is unneccessarily involved, and emotional dependence on the school staff. The idea that schools should be a source of support rather than stress has led many authors and researchers to advocate policy changes that individualize requirements for parent involvement on the basis of the needs of the family (Allen & Hudd, 1987; Wiegerink, Hocutt, Posante-Loro, & Bristol, 1980). These are matters that would be addressed, of course, by schools that want to ameliorate the special stresses that many parents of handicapped children experience, and bring about other improvements in the situation.

CONCLUDING COMMENTS

The underlying thesis of this chapter is that, although all children and adolescents and all families are seriously affected by the schools, specific connections with schools are especially important for families with handicapped children and adolescents. Parents of children and adolescents with handicaps need special help, and schools are the one institution that has maximum accessibility to these children and adolescents and their parents.

This chapter reviews studies of the stress of families with handicapped children and adolescents. In much of this work, the handicapped child or adolescent is thought of as a stressor in the family system. It is a stress situation, however, in which family financial and emotional resources serve as a buffer to the handicapped child or adolescent as a stressor. It is not surprising, therefore, that economically disadvantaged families are less able to handle stress of a handicapped child than families that are more well-off, that one-parent families with a handicapped child cope less effectively than two-parent families, and that mothers in less-successful marriages have more difficulty coping with a handicapped child than mothers in better marriages.

There also is an attempt in this chapter to conceptualize the positive, as well as the negative, aspects of families with children and adolescents with handicaps. It is noted, for example, that the presence of supportive social networks leads to better coping on the part of parents. The belief systems of parents of children and adolescents with handicaps also are an important factor in coping. What this means is that if parents feel that they can cope with raising a handicapped child, they in turn experience less psychological distress.

The chapter makes the further point that a change in emphasis from pathology to coping is occurring in studies of families of children and adolescents with handicaps. That is, there is more emphasis on approaching family stress from a family *function* orientation, instead of from the direction of understanding family dysfunction. General systems theory and a contextual approach to the understanding of family stress also are being given additional emphasis.

As to implementational and practical aspects, studies show that parental involvement in special education has produced generally mixed results. For example, mainstreaming handicapped children and adolescents into regular classrooms, though motivated by the best of intentions, has made teaching and classroom management more difficult and has exacerbated the normal stresses of teaching. The potential costs of this situation for many handicapped children and their families should not be overlooked; and in the implementation of such practices, the need for teachers to have additional resources for coping with the added responsibilities should be taken into account. To improve upon this situation, it is important to realize that where a handicapped student receives services — be it in special versus mainstreamed classes — is probably less important than *what* services the student receives. The provision of better stress-related services to families with handicapped children and adolescents also is one of the major challenges to service delivery in the 1990s.

9 STRESS FACTORS ASSOCIATED WITH FAMILY, SCHOOL, AND COMMUNITY VIOLENCE

This chapter examines in some detail the violence found in families, schools, and communities and the potential of such violence to produce high levels of stress in children and adolescents. The implications of these stress experiences, and the ways that schools can help children and adolescents cope with such stressors, also are explored.

PHYSICAL AND SEXUAL ABUSE AS STRESSORS

The family is a common source of stress (Browne & Finkelhor, 1986; Straus, Gelles, & Steinmetz, 1980). When there are aggressive physical reactions against adult family members, it is called spouse abuse, husband/wife battering, or family violence; when the target is a child, it is called child abuse. However, the definition of child abuse has changed over time, although it varies from state to state, from courtroom to courtroom, from professional to professional, and even more so, from country to country. In addition, abuse may be physical, sexual, or emotional, although emotional abuse is more difficult to define (Brassard, Germain, & Hart, 1987). As to incidence, the true incidence of abuse is unknown. For example, the growing numbers of children who sexually abuse *other children* goes largely unreported (Johnson, 1992). Nevertheless, there were more than one million cases of child abuse reported to authorities in 1986 (National Committee for the Prevention of Child Abuse, 1988).

There also are many correlates or consequences of physical, sexual, and emotional abuse (see, e.g., Browne & Finkelhor, 1986; Walker, Bonner, & Kaufman, 1988). These reported effects include: antisocial behavior, apathy, aggression, anxiety, anger, destructiveness, delinquency, depression, fear, low self-esteem, mistrust, mood swings, passivity, compulsivity, dependency, disruptive behavior, eating disorders, poor interpersonal relationships, regressive behavior, school problems, sleep disorders, withdrawal, hostility, hyperactivity, self-destructive behaviors, somatic complaints, and other maladaptive behaviors. It is obvious, therefore, that there are many scars of abuse, some that never completely heal and may surface later in adulthood.

Unfortunately, little has been written about stress as a specific consequence of child abuse, although parental stress is considered to be the major cause of abuse (Gelles, 1987; Straus, 1980). Certainly abuse is stressful to the dependent child, and chronic abuse leads to chronic stress. In addition, the effects of the stress of abuse are more likely to persist when the parent or other offending agent remains in the child's environment. It also is considered more stressful to children to be abused by someone they know and trust. Post-Traumatic Stress Disorder (PTSD) may also be one of the long-term consequences of sexual abuse (Finkelhor, 1987). Witnessing parental abuse may also be as harmful to the child's development as direct abuse (Widom, 1989). For example, seeing or hearing fathers abusing their mothers is a stressful, even frightening, experience for children. Links between spouse abuse and child abuse have also been suggested by Straus and his colleagues (Straus et al., 1980), who reported that when wife battering occurred in a family, the child abuse rate was 30 percent higher than in nonviolent families.

Parents Who Abuse Their Children

There are a number of factors that predispose parents to abuse their children, including: low IQ, unplanned pregnancy, emotional illness, adolescent parenthood, lack of control, parents abused as children, and economic and health stress (Altemeier, O'Connor, Vietze, Sandler, & Sherrod, 1982; Browne, 1986; Browne & Finkelhor, 1986; Sze & Lamar, 1981). In physical abuse, the perpetrator is likely to be the mother, whereas in sexual abuse the perpetrator is more likely to be the father or another male known to the child. When there is abuse by a stranger, the parents are more likely to be supportive of the child, and the child is likely to receive some form of therapeutic intervention, which may prevent or amelioriate acute and chronic stress. However, if the perpetrator is a parent, the child not only receives a negative message about his or her value and the availability of the parent for positive support, but the parent may be prosecuted by the court and separated from the child, which can be an additional source of stress for the child. However, if the parent does not acknowledge and accept responsibility for the abuse, the child may feel responsible for the abuse, and this can create still more stress for the child. Parents may also use bribes and threats and blame the child for the resulting emotional and economic disruption of the family. Overall, this intrafamilial conflict is not only a very bewildering situation for the child, it is a major source of the abused child's stress.

Young Adolescents and Children as Child Molesters

Young adolescents and children molesting other children is a growing problem (Johnson, 1992). For example, statistics from the FBI's Uniform Crime Reports indicate that the number of 13- to 14-year-olds arrested for rape or attempted rape has more than doubled in the last 20 years (cited in Johnson, 1992). A similar increase also is reported for the 10- to 12-year-old group. In essence, sexual abuse of children by young adolescents and other children is on the rise. At the same time, there has been a downward progression in the ages of these abusers.

In addition to coercive forms of sexual activity (as in rape), other forms of sexualized behavior that increase the likelihood of sexual abuse are a growing problem. For example, Johnson refers to a subgroup of sexually active children in which full-fledged sex occurs, but with children who agree to go along. In another subgroup that she describes, there is sexualized behavior, such as excessive masturbation and behaving sexually with adults, that is more advanced than that of their peers.

Children Who Are at Risk

Characteristics of children also contribute to their risk of being abused. For example, being different (e.g., retarded, premature, or hyperactive) or being seen as different by the parent are significant risk factors (Mullens, 1986). The consequences of abuse, as in the case of a change in appearance (e.g., from a disfiguring facial scar) or in behavior (e.g., from a head injury that causes hyperactivity), can also place the child in further jeopardy. In this case, the original stress which caused the parental abuse may be replaced with the stress of dealing with a child whose needs overwhelm the ability of the parent to cope.

We also are seeing more children who are at risk because they act out sexually (i.e., they go beyond the parameters of normal sex play; Johnson, 1992). The problem, in part, is that more children are in highly sexualized homes and sexually charged atmospheres. For example, the mother may be a prostitute or a single parent who may have a man regularly staying overnight. There also may be tremendous amounts of sexual conversation by the man in the house. In addition, children may be exposed to frequent episodes of sex and sexualized conversation on television. Unable to process it all, children may act out sexually, and, in doing this, they increase their vulnerability to abuse, not just by adults but by other children and young adolescents in their lives.

Parental Stress as a Cause of Child Abuse

The focus of much of the literature on abuse is on the relationship between parental stress and the precipitation of abuse (Browne, 1986). In a study by Straus (1980), the most common stressors among a large sample of adults with at least one child between 3 and 17 years of age were death of someone close, and serious problems with the health or behavior of a family member. Parental stressors specifically related to children, in this study, were stress from pregnancy or birth of a child, the arrest of a child for an illegal act, and suspension of a child from school. Child abuse rates also were found to increase as the number of stressors increased, although the relationship differed for mothers and fathers. Fathers with a higher stress score had higher rates of child abuse, whereas mothers, even under low stress conditions, had a higher abuse rate.

Stress may not be preventable, but parents need to learn to manage stress in nonviolent ways, and to do this, both stress management and parenting skills are needed. The lack of knowledge about normal behavior and development is one source of parenting problems, because unsophisticated parents may see a normal child's behavior as abnormal (Showers & Johnson, 1984). As one result, they push the child to perform beyond his or her capacity and punish the child for what they see as intransigence.

Stress Associated with Being Identified as an Abused Child

Children enter the system of abuse identification through various channels. For example, many schools offer prevention programs that teach children about what constitutes abuse and the need to tell, and that also offer children the opportunity to reveal abuse. However, because of guilt from accepting bribes or from passive participation, or because of fear of retaliation, the child may be reluctant to reveal abuse. Why children choose particular individuals and times to reveal abuse is unknown. They must trust the individual to whom they reveal the abuse and overcome the anticipation of possibly being blamed, hurt by the abuser, or of being stigmatized. To reveal abuse, the child also must surmount the stress of the events, the possibility of further events, and the possibility that revealing the abuse will not stop it. As Faller (1984) has pointed out, some children may choose to internalize the stress rather than report the abuse. This is especially likely for children who feel there is little to gain, anticipate being rejected, or fear being held responsible for the potential breakup of the family.

In addition, the system designed to protect the abused child may cause more stress to the child in the process of dealing with the situation. The abuse investigation itself may be stressful, and if the case goes to court, the child may need to testify in a legal environment that is especially stressful for children (Melton & Limber, 1989). There is additional stress when the need to protect the child leads to placement in another home or family, separation from siblings, or school changes (Browne & Finkelhor, 1986).

Children who need therapy are subjected to other sources of stress (Kagan, 1983). Parents may resist therapy for the child who needs it the most and seek it for the child who needs it the least. In other cases, verbal and nonverbal messages from the family, especially if the child is disliked and undervalued and is seen as responsible for the events, may cause the child to guard behaviors that might indicate need for continued therapy. One cannot assume, of course, that the impact of the stress, frustration, and pain of abuse will be the same for all children. The impact of abusive acts will depend on mitigating factors, defense mechanisms selected, consequences of previous trauma, the child's age, and prior interactions with parents.

Prevention of Stress Related to Abuse

Using a standard classification system for the different types of intervention, efforts to prevent abuse stress would be tertiary when directed to abusers to prevent re-abuse; secondary when directed to at-risk child, preparent, and parent populations; and primary when directed to segments of the general population. In recent years, some progress has been made in decreasing stress and other consequences of child abuse. However, the resources of some communities are strained simply to identify abused children, and in such cases only tertiary prevention may be possible. There also are communities where resources are clearly inadequate, and in such communities even the prevention of re-abuse may not be possible. School, and other, professionals also may be reluctant to report abuse to agencies that are deficient in important ways, e.g., they return children to abusive environments, have young and inexperienced workers, or have workers with excessive caseloads. Nevertheless, professionals have a vital role in ongoing efforts to identify and report child abuse, and it is especially important that teachers, school psychologists, and other professionals continue to be active in this role.

Secondary abuse prevention relies on our ability to identify high-risk populations and risk factors. Programs in both schools and community agencies are being directed to serve teenage mothers and emphasize life skills and parenting education (Boukydis, 1987, esp. Section 2), in addition to stress management (Schinke, Schilling, Barth, Gilchrist, & Maxwell, 1986). These same techniques, which may prevent parental stress and attendant child abuse, also are important for other new parents, to maximize development and minimize adverse effects for unavoidable adverse experiences. Parents with babies whose behavior places them at high risk for poor interaction with their parents, and parents of handicapped children who are at high risk for child abuse, especially need such help (Abbott & Meredith, 1986; Futcher, 1988). Most stressed parents, of course, do not abuse.

However, the most popular efforts have been aimed at preventing child sexual abuse, a prevention effort that usually involves education programs that are aimed at children and implemented by teachers (Davis, 1986). Although there are few systematic evaluations of the effectiveness of these programs, efforts have been made to describe and classify their main characteristics (e.g., Finkelhor, 1986). As an additional valuable resource, Tharinger and associates (Tharinger et al., 1988) have provided a thorough overview of the child sexual abuse literature and a most helpful listing of sexual abuse prevention education materials, which they have systematically reviewed and evaluated. Included are materials for children, adolescents, parents, teachers or group leaders, program implementers, and other professionals.

One special limitation of such intervention efforts, however, is that they don't sufficiently take account of young adolescents and children who sexually abuse chldren, which is becoming a more widespread problem (Johnson, 1992). For example, there are increasing numbers of children who coerce others, physically or emotionally, to have sex. These perpetrators, according to Johnson, suffer from a host of behavior problems, including lack of impulse control, aggressiveness, and lack of problem-solving skills. Without proper intervention, child sex offenders are likely to become adolescent, and later adult, sex offenders. Fortunately, some headway is being made with child sex offenders in different treatment programs. Although few involve the schools (and school personnel), some do include parents and other caregivers.

In implementing primary prevention, there also is much to be learned about the origins and expressions of violence, how to minimize stress to children in the face of violence, and the dynamics of abuse (Newberger, Newberger, & Hampton, 1983). To mitigate the possibility of stress, we also must help parents manage the different aspects of stress (i.e., subjective and objective factors and response capabilities in parents, stress stimuli from children, and environmental options). In addition, primary prevention requires a shift in the priorities of schools toward teaching all students life skills, child development, child and adult health, and child-rearing alternatives. To achieve ultimate success, primary prevention will also require a reordering of the priorities of society.

Special Educational Needs of Children and Adolescents Living in Violence

Although it is difficult to assess the relationship between violence and student school performance, there is evidence that family violence influences children's and adolescents' cognitive and social functions, leading to both intellectual and social dysfunction. Craig (1992), for example, provides evidence that family violence has a significant impact on the cognitive and social profiles of children and adolescents. Children and adolescents living in violence also present many competing needs, so that, as a first step in helping these children and adolescents, it is necessary for teachers and related service providers to set educational priorities. The lack of congruence between the life experiences of these children and adolescents and the reality assumed by the school also must be acknowledged. Although the special education approach is most often applied to children and adolescents with developmental disabilities, this way of thinking may be beneficial to these children and adolescents as well. For example, children and adolescents living with family violence may require additional support to complete the ordinary tasks of childhood and adolescence. Teacher assistance teams and other types of prereferral strategies (see, e.g., Zins, Curtis, Graden, & Ponti, 1988) may also be helpful in developing interventions and programs that allow these children and adolescents to function more effectively in the school environment.

INVOLVEMENT OF CHILDREN AND ADOLESCENTS IN ACCIDENTS: ANOTHER FORM OF VIOLENCE

Children and adolescents sustain injuries from many sources, but perhaps the most destructive are those visited on the child or adolescent by a caretaker. However, one must draw a distinction between intended and unintended injuries, although even that distinction is too simple. One may bring about injuries to children and adolescents passively, by neglect, as well as actively, by assault. Parents who are neglectful or who are unconsciously resentful of the child or adolescent will characteristically expose the youngster to the kinds of situations that make for "accidents."

Garbarino (1988) divides child and adolescent injuries into four types: those that occur randomly, those that are preventable, those due to negligence, and those occasioned by assault. Random accidents are those visited on a child or adolescent by genuine happenstance (e.g., the youngster in a car struck by another car whose driver had a stroke). In contrast, preventable accidents involve events such as a child running into the street after a ball into the path of an oncoming vehicle, an accident that might be regarded as a product of poor child training or poor neighborhood planning. This moves us to the third category, child or adolescent injury due to negligence. For example, an adult who does not insist that the child put on a seat belt might well be regarded as negligent. Or an adolescent might be provided with an all-terrain vehicle by indulgent parents despite a known record of dangerous accidents associated with that vehicle. The fourth category, child abuse, has already been discussed in detail.

As to the seriousness of child and adolescent involvement in accidents, according to Baker, O'Neill, and Karph (1984), motor vehicle collisions are the leading cause of adolescent deaths from injury. In addition, males are at far greater risk than females, particularly for serious injury, as are poor and African-American adolescents. Most accidents, of course, are understandable, predictable, and preventable, and avoidable injuries result in great economic costs, as well as lost school days. They also lead to inestimable stress and other psychological costs to children and adolescents and their parents. For these reasons, injury prevention programs that can be implemented in schools, such as those described by Peterson (1988) and Garbarino (1988), are critical to the important school concern for student safety and amelioration of the stress associated with the consequences of accidents.

STRESS RELATED TO VIOLENCE IN THE SCHOOL

School and neighborhood violence will be discussed in separate sections, although they could be lumped together, because schools are imbedded in neighborhoods. The kinds of violence to which children and adolescents might be exposed are many and varied — verbal attack, verbal harassment, threats of attack, name calling, rumors, bullying, theft and robbery, destruction of property, etc. These violent acts may occur either in the school or in the surrounding neighborhood, although there is the geographic reality that the school is imbedded within the larger community. In addition, the kinds, perpetrators, and victims of violence are often the same in both settings.

In general, reports in the newspapers and on television might lead one to conclude that violence in the schools has reached crisis proportions. In contrast, if one turns to the scientific literature, one obtains a somewhat less alarmist picture, although there are only a few broad-based and carefully executed studies. One such study is the national *Violent Schools-Safe Schools* survey (National Institute of Education, 1978) that was conducted in 4,000 junior and senior high schools. From the results of this survey it was concluded that there is a substantial amount of disruption and disorder in many schools. For example, in an average month, 12 percent of the students surveyed reported having more than one dollar stolen from them, and 1.3 percent reported being attacked (with 42 percent of those attacked receiving some injury). Moreover, 28 percent of all schools experienced vandalism in one month, and 50 percent of the teachers reported being the target of swearing or obscene gestures.

As further evidence of the plight of teachers, Goldstein, Apter, and Harootunian (1984) report that assaults on teachers grew from 18,000 in 1955, to 41,000 in 1971, to 110,000 in 1979. This escalation in the level of attacks on teachers has also led to an expansion in the vocabulary of aggression. For example, Block (1977) added the "battered teacher syndrome" to this vocabulary. These are teachers who manifest a combination of stress reactions including anxiety, disturbed sleep, elevated blood pressure, eating disorders, headaches, and depression. Although this kind of behavior toward teachers might not seem extraordinary, most adults not working in schools are probably not subjected to the same level of affront or victimization.

From such reports, one could conclude that there is a significant amount of serious crime in the schools. However, some educators have challenged these 1970s data and the popular idea that crime is rampant in the schools. For example, Scherer and Stimson (1984) pointed out that the "crime" documented in the 1978 National Institute of Education report included few "serious" crimes. For instance, robbery through force or threat accounted for "only" 120,000 of the three million reported crimes. They also argued that although student language and disrespectful behaviors are problematic in the schools, they should not be confused with crime or violence.

Some More Recent Data

After 1978, when the National Institute of Education issued the landmark *Violent Schools-Safe Schools* report, there was not another comprehensive study of school violence until the National Adolescent Student Health Survey in 1987, which was funded by the U.S. Department of Health and Human Services (cited in U.S. Congress, House of Representatives Committee on the Judiciary, 1991). In this wide-ranging new study, based on responses of 8th- and 10th-graders in more than 200 public and private schools (a total of 11,000 students), more than one third reported they were threatened, robbed, or attacked at school during the

1985–86 school year. Such incidents resulted in physical injury to a student more than a third of the time.

Expert witnesses at this committee hearing also testified that the problem of guns in the schools had reached crisis proportions. For example, in California, the only state that publishes annual data on gun incidents in schools, the number of gun incidents increased 100 percent in the 4 years from 1986–87 to 1989–90. It was further noted that school shootings or hostage takings had occurred in 35 states and the District of Columbia during those 4 years. In this same period, 69 children, educators, and other school employees also had been shot and killed in school, and 190 others had been wounded. Nearly 70 percent of these shootings were by students at school.

Another expert witness at that hearing pointed out that, on the basis of National Adolescent Student Health Survey data for the 1985–86 school year, the National School Safety Center estimated there were 135,000 boys in the secondary schools of this country who carried a gun to school daily, and another 270,000 who carried handguns to school at least once. For that school year, the Center also estimated that each month some 5,200 secondary school teachers had been assaulted and about 282,000 secondary school students had been physically attacked at school.

Among other findings of the National Adolescent Student Health Survey that were cited at the committee hearing, 41 percent of boys and 24 percent of girls said they could obtain a handgun if they wanted to. Twenty-three percent of boys also said they carried a knife at least once to school, and 7 percent did it daily. Forty-four percent of boys and 28 percent of girls also reported having been in at least one fight, that involved hitting each other or attacking with weapons, during the school year.

To sum up, except for the two comprehensive national surveys, educators have had to rely primarily on local data as the basis for determining trends in the nature, incidence, and seriousness of school violence. Nevertheless, it now seems clear that the magnitude and social and economic costs of school violence have reached alarming proportions over the last two decades.

School Violence as a Stressor

There is, unfortunately, a paucity of research on the consequences of school violence on children and adolescents. Nevertheless, those familiar with the situation (see, e.g., Harlan & McDowell, 1981) have noted that one can sense that fear associated with school violence has an effect on the learning-teaching process. This point is also more directly addressed in a few studies of violence in the schools. For example, in the *Violent Schools-Safe Schools* survey previously mentioned, students were asked if they avoided places around school because they felt they would be hurt or bothered in those places. Thirty-eight percent of the students acknowledged at least one such place in their school. Furthermore, 20 percent said they were afraid at least some of the time in school, and another 4 percent admitted that they had stayed home to avoid being hurt or bothered at school. Such fears, of course, can include not only fear of physical harm but also of verbal abuse, racial slurs, and insults.

The pervasiveness of the stress associated with violence in and around schools is generally corroborated by another study of students in Philadelphia schools (Bayh, 1979). In Bayh's study, 21 percent of the boys felt that their classrooms were dangerous, 44 percent felt that way about their schoolyards, and 54 percent felt the streets in and around their schools were dangerous. In another major study at about the same time, Hepburn and Monti (1979) surveyed almost 2,000 junior and senior high school students in St. Louis and found, among other things, that 40 percent felt afraid that they might be hurt or bothered at school. In a parallel study of dropouts, Carriere (1979) found that 18 percent of males and 7 percent of females said that they sometimes did not go to school because they were intimidated by would-be attackers. Extrapolating from these data, perhaps as many as 100,000 of the estimated 750,000 youths who drop out of school each year do so because of fear.

Reviewing studies of this kind, McDermott (1980, 1983) and Goldstein et al. (1984) have made a number of observations and suggestions concerning the stressful impact of school violence on children and adolescents. McDermott suggested that there is a relationship between prior victimization and current fear, and that where there is a higher level of crime, there will be a higher level of apprehension even by nonvictims. Fear of crime in school is also related to fear of crime in general and to living in a high-crime neighborhood. These observations are consistent with other research indicating that schools in lower socioeconomic, high-crime neighborhoods have more school violence (Brodbelt, 1978).

Characteristics of schools, such as size and quality of the facility, also are related to the amount of violence (Brodbelt, 1978; Goldstein et al., 1984). Although inner-city students appear most at risk, suburban schools are also encountering higher rates of violence (Bayh, 1979). In general, however, fear of crime is reported more often by African-American than by White students (McDermott, 1980). As a general rule, there also is more crime and fear of violence in secondary schools, where girls are more fearful than boys, than in elementary schools, where the levels of apprehension of boys and girls are similar (McDermott, 1983).

Implications for School Interventions

The stressors associated with school violence embody specific events that often directly impinge on, and demand adjustments by, children and adolescents. Accordingly, we would expect that helping children and adolescents learn behavioral strategies, such as training in social skills, that effectively deal with the problem would be helpful. For example, it might be worthwhile to encourage children and adolescents to tell a school professional or other resource person about their particular problems. This might help them to combat their feelings of powerlessness and to deal more actively with their concerns. The emotional responses children and adolescents have to school violence may also require affirmation. For example, fear of a bully is a normal response, and when parents share their concerns about their children's welfare, they are helping their children bring their coping strategies to bear on the problem. Also, it is probably more beneficial for the child to have a compassionate parent model rather than one who exhibits a "be tough" attitude and macho approach to the problem. However, this is difficult for some parents, due in part to their not having resolved some of these issues themselves. Parents can also be helped to do a better job in giving their children hope for the future and confidence in their ability to shape their destinies, despite the prevalence of violence in their schools.

In regard to the cognitive dimension of the child, it would be well to develop early education programs that restructure children's thinking about themselves with respect to fears associated with school violence. For example, being afraid of the bully can insidiously cause the child to question self-worth. Although the child "owns the problem," it is possible to teach children at an early age that they have certain rights, and that no one has the right to harm them and to make them feel badly about themselves.

Mediation programs appearing in schools across this country that are aimed at the reduction of school violence are another encouraging development (for examples of programs, see Cheatham, 1988). Designed to teach ways of analyzing conflicts, managing conflicts that arise, and resolving underlying issues that lead to conflict, these programs offer another form of intervention for dealing with school violence, especially in junior and senior high schools. Curricula that are primarily school-based also are beginning to play a major role in helping students to develop a better understanding of conflict and make better use of conflict resolution techniques (Community Board Program, 1987).

School programs that use police officers as teachers, role models, and keepers of the peace are also being implemented, especially in inner-city areas. One good example, the innovative School Resource Officer program, that appears to have operated quite successfully for almost 20 years, is described by Scheffer (1987). It is a joint effort of the police department and the public schools that is aimed at reducing juvenile crime and delinquency. The full-time police officers who are placed in junior and senior high schools participate in extra-curricular activities and parent–teacher organizations. What is significant about programs like this is that they shift the focus from the traditional reactive approach to policing to a person-centered prevention strategy. In the process, the focus shifts to dealing with underlying causes of school and community crime.

Some interesting policy-relevant matters were addressed by Gottfredson and Gottfredson (1985), who made sophisticated statistical analyses of data from the previously mentioned national *Violent Schools-Safe Schools* survey. In the process, they generated certain prescriptions or intervention strategies for dealing with disruptive and disordered schools. For example, they found that clear, firm, and fair discipline policies were strongly associated with lower levels of school violence. Close student–teacher relationships, and pupils spending substantial amounts of time working under the same teacher, also were important.

To get a better idea as to exactly what such prescriptions mean, one needs to examine their results more closely. For example, firmness means strictly enforcing rules, where the principal runs the school with a firm hand and students are paddled for serious rule violations. As another example, fairness means such things as fair rules, where everyone knows the rules and punishment for breaking rules is the same no matter who you are. Evidently, good school discipline, which reduces school disruptions and disorder, involves practices that some school professionals would equate with repression. But the practices also mean, at least in the schools surveyed, that fewer students carried weapons to school, fewer personal belongings were stolen or taken by force from students and teachers, and teachers were not humiliated by vulgar insults from students. Some findings of this study (e.g., that continuous student–teacher relationships and smaller junior and senior high schools would be desirable), however, are compatible with major tenets of contemporary psychology and modern educational principles.

Many other solutions to school violence have been tried, of course, some aimed at students, others at teachers, administrators, or the wider community in which the school functions. The sheer scope and number of these intended solutions is well presented by Goldstein et al. (1984) who also examine more promising strategies in depth. They present analyses of behavior modification techniques, psychodynamic interventions, and the teaching of prosocial behaviors and values. They also examine ways that schools can be modified and reorganized to reduce violence.

STRESS OF CHILDREN AND ADOLESCENTS LIVING IN DANGEROUS NEIGHBORHOODS

Developmental challenges faced by children and adolescents growing up in situations of chronic danger linked to neighborhood violence and conflict also need to be taken into account by the schools. An expanded version of the concept of post-traumatic stress disorder is one vehicle for including situations of chronic and ongoing traumatic stress associated with dangerous inner-city neighborhoods plagued by violence and crime. Of particular importance is the impact of chronic stress and danger on the child's and adolescent's social map, and the child's and adolescent's moral development.

But what does the concept of danger mean to a child or adolescent? In a dictionary sense, it means liability to all kinds of harm — injuries that may be physical, psychological, or moral. At the outset, one must recognize that *objective* and *subjective* danger may be weakly correlated. This is true of children, to be sure, and to a lesser extent, adolescents; yet even adults may be unaware of the objective dangers around them and feel safe when they ought to be afraid, and feel endangered when they are at neglible risk of harm.

Danger is about risk, of course, and most children and adolescents seek the thrill that comes with moderate danger; some even seem to thrive on danger, although in some cases the seeking of extreme danger is an expression of psychopathology, as in suicide (Orbach, 1988). But some children are paralyzed by the slightest hint of danger, as a result of the interaction of temperament and parental training.

Acute and chronic danger have a variety of implications for adjustment. Often, acute incidents of danger simply require situational adjustment, although some children and adolescents exposed to acute danger may need supportive assistance, through the schools or other resources, over a period of time (Pynoos & Nader, 1988; Terr, 1988). Also, traumatic stress, if it is intense enough, and chronic danger, if it lasts long enough, may leave permanent psychological scars.

Some studies of children and adolescents also emphasize the influence that chronic danger can have on moral development. Anna Freud's studies of children exposed to prolonged violence during World War II support the view that living under constant danger can have an important impact on moral development (Freud & Burlingham, 1943). A similar theme also emerges in a study of safety issues for children in a public housing project that was saturated with violence (Dubrow & Garbarino, 1988). Mothers in the project identified "shooting" as their major safety concern, and they developed a variety of coping mechanisms to protect their children from immediate harm. This is not to say that such children escape unscathed. There probably is a sleeper effect similar to that found in longitudinal analyses of the impact of divorce on children, where life-adjustment problems have emerged 10 or more years after family dissolution (e.g., Wallerstein & Blakeslee, 1989).

Studies of acute and chronic danger also point to a series of ameliorating factors that may provide a starting point for efforts to understand the special character of coping in the stressful circumstances of sudden or prolonged violence. These convergent findings, which are helpful to school personnel that plan and implement programs designed to help children and adolescents deal with the stress of living with unexpected or prolonged danger, are reported in Hurrelmann and Losel (1990) as:

a. actively trying to cope with stress (rather than just reacting);

b. cognitive competence (at least an average level of intelligence);

c. experience of self-efficacy and a corresponding self-confidence and positive self-esteem;

d. temperamental characteristics that favor active coping attempts and positive relationships with others (e.g., activity, goal orientation, sociability), rather than passive withdrawal;

e. stable emotional relationships with at least one parent or other reference person;

f. an open, supportive educational climate and parental model of behavior that encourages constructive coping with problems; and

g. social support from persons outside the family.

Unfortunately, there also are many maladaptive methods of coping with both acute and chronic danger. The psychopathological dimensions of such maladaptation are now widely recognized as post-traumatic stress disorders. The social dimensions are equally worthy of attention, as when children and adolescents cope with danger by adopting a worldview, or persona, that may be dysfunctional in any normal situation, e.g., if to defend themselves, they adapt to chronic crisis situations by becoming hyperaggressive (which is maladaptive to school success and where such behaviors lead to rejection). Parents, in their adaptations to dangerous environments, may develop child-rearing strategies that impede normal development, as in the case of parents who prohibit their young children from playing outside for fear of shooting incidents. Similarly, the fear felt by parents of children in high-crime environments may be manifest as a very restrictive and punitive style of discipline in an effort to protect their children from falling under the influence of neighborhood gangs. Although such adaptations are well-intentioned and appear to be sensible, their side effects may be detrimental in the long run. For this reason, such strategies may be generally less successful than a strategy of promoting alternatives to the negative subculture feared by parents, alternatives that can be developed and implemented by schools and community agencies in such neighborhoods (Scheinfeld, 1983).

One long-term effect that appears to be very consequential is in moral development because experience of chronic danger seems to be associated with truncated moral development. For example, Field's research (cited in Garbarino, Kostelny, & Dubrow, 1991) in Northern Ireland and in Lebanon identified many children stuck at more primitive stages of moral development. For example, whereas 27 percent of 11- to 14-year-olds in normal environments typically respond at the rational/beneficial/utilitarian fifth stage in the Tapp-Kohlberg scheme, almost none of the 11- to 14-year-olds studied in Northern Ireland or Lebanon did. Why? From what we know of the development of moral reasoning and ego development, the most likely answer mixes temperamental, social, and cultural forces. Advanced moral reasoning of the type measured by the Tapp-Kohlberg assessment seems also to reflect the degree to which children are supported in engaging in issue-focused discussions and social interactions. These interactions invoke the child's emergent capacities and stimulate perspective taking and intellectual encounters with values and principles. In the final analysis, therefore, the issue of stimulating moral development beyond the lower levels becomes in large measure a family, school, and community issue. Do parents and teachers, for example, demonstrate the higher order moral reasoning necessary to move children from the lower to the higher stages of moral development? Do families and schools provide the emotional context for the necessary processing to make positive moral sense of danger? Do inner-city schools have programs designed to help both students and their families deal with chronic stress and danger in constructive ways?

CONCLUDING COMMENTS

The thrust of this chapter is that children and adolescents growing up in America are frequently exposed to various forms of violence, and that this violence represents a stressful intrusion into the child's and adolescent's life and threatens his or her safety and security. As used in this chapter, the term "violence" refers to acts or threats that result in harm or injury to the child or adolescent. Violent acts also are treated as stressors or independent variables that result in stress reactions.

Studies of child abuse and school and neighborhood violence are reviewed, although it is recognized that social and behavioral scientists have given little attention to the impact of school and neighborhood violence on children and adolescents. Nevertheless, a convincing case can be made that serious violence is prevalent in many schools and neighborhoods, and that these violent acts have important negative consequences for children and adolescents. At the same time, the prevalence of child abuse is less at issue, and the ordinarily debilitative effects of such victimization seem beyond question, although the growing phenomenon of young adolescents and children sexually molesting children has not yet received the attention it deserves.

As to implications for school intervention, a variety of strategies are reviewed that seem to help children and adolescents deal with school violence and its stressful consequences. Nevertheless, schools could play a more active role in teaching students to cope more effectively with school violence and related stress. Part of the problem in attempting to deal with the issue of school violence is the ideological polarization that sometimes occurs (i.e., the tendency to construe solutions to the problems of violence in terms of carrots and sticks). For example, there are some who advocate stricter disciplinary measures and a return to the image of the teacher as an authority figure, whereas there are others who advocate the promotion of cooperation and other forms of prosocial behaviors as the way to deal with school violence. The point, of course, is that the two viewpoints are not antithetical — one can shore up disciplinary practices and at the same time develop school curricula and make other efforts to promote prosocial behavior patterns among children and adolescents.

It should also be noted that, although violence in the schools should be the focus of much of the school's intervention and prevention efforts, children and adolescents who experience acute danger or who live in chronically dangerous situations also need special attention. Although it is difficult to assess the relationship between this kind of violence and student school performance, there is evidence that such violence influences children's and adolescents' cognitive and social functions, leading to intellectual impairment and social dysfunction. Children and adolescents living with violence in their families and neighborhoods also present many competing needs, so that, as a first step in helping them, it is necessary for teachers and related service providers to set educational priorities. The lack of congruence between the life experiences of these children and adolescents and the reality assumed by the school must also be acknowledged. Although the special education approach is most often applied to children and adolescents with developmental disabilities, this way of thinking may be beneficial to these children and adolescents as well. For example, children and adolescents living with violence may require additional support to complete the ordinary tasks of childhood and adolescence. Teacher assistance teams and other types of prereferral strategies may also be helpful in developing interventions and programs that allow these children and adolescents to function more effectively in the school environment.

10 WHAT WE CAN LEARN ABOUT STRESS FROM "VULNERABLE BUT INVINCIBLE" CHILDREN AND ADOLESCENTS

How, one might ask, is it possible for an achievement-oriented society like the United States to present such a vast "problem" literature in the scientific study of children and adolescents — a literature often expressing adjustment difficulties, social failures, blocked potentialities, and defeat? It is possible only if researchers and practitioners are predisposed by interest, investment, and training to see deviance, psychopathology, and weakness wherever they look. Fortunately, in research on the stress of children and adolescents, studies of resilience and stress-resistance are becoming an important part of the available literature. Bleuler, the great Swiss psychiatrist, provided one of the earliest portraits of high-risk children and adolescents and their *positive* attributes (Bleuler, 1978). He pointed out that the majority of children of schizophrenic parents are healthy and socially competent, even though many of them had lived through miserable childhoods. In his view, paying attention to the positive development of the majority was just as important as studying the dysfunctional minority. He further emphasized that his studies of such children left him " . . . with the impression that pain and suffering has a steeling — a hardening — effect on the personalities of some children, making them capable of mastering their lives with all its obstacles, in defiance of all their disadvantages" (p. 409).

This is the "paradox" to which other pioneers in the study of vulnerability and coping in children and adolescents have made reference. Murphy and Moriarity (1976), for example, widened the world of childhood and adolescence to embrace more than vulnerability; they added coping and growth. Among other researchers who have traversed a similar path, the work by Werner and Smith (e.g., 1982) is especially noteworthy. Their long-term follow-up of children living in Kauai, an island at the northwest end of the main islands in the Hawaiian chain, has added to our knowledge by demonstrating, as Bleuler has, that even among high-risk children and adolescents there are some who are resilient and invincible. The continuing emphasis of researchers and practitioners on righting this imbalance is further chronicled by more recent reviews of the research evidence (see, e.g., Rolf, Masten, Cicchetti, Neuchterlein, & Weintraub, 1990).

To sum up the situation, "vulnerable" children and adolescents have for too long been the province of mental health professionals. One result of this prolonged neglect of the "invulnerable" child and adolescent — the healthy child and adolescent in an unhealthy environment — has been that it provided us with a false sense of security which led us to erect prevention models, and to develop intervention programs, based more on values than facts. Fortunately, "invulnerable" children and adolescents have continued to be the "keepers of the dream," and in studying the forces that move such children and adolescents to survival and adaptation, there can be long-range benefits to our schools and society. Such benefits can also be far more significant than efforts aimed solely at curtailing the high incidence of vulnerability among children and adolescents. In essence, there is much that can be learned from children and adolescents who overcome severe adversity.

NATURE OF RISK, VULNERABILITY, COMPETENCE, INVULNERABILITY, RESILIENCY, AND PROTECTIVE FACTORS

As mentioned above, early studies of the children of parents with various psychopathologies led to studies of risk factors and vulnerability, and when this research revealed that children facing severe adversity do not necessarily develop psychological or behavioral problems, factors such as competence began to be studied. Then came the study of invulnerability and resiliency, and protective factors. Each of these concepts has a slightly different meaning, but they overlap considerably.

Risk factors are those factors that, if present, increase the likelihood of a child or adolescent developing a psychological or behavioral disorder (Garmezy, 1983). For example, parental psychiatric illness has been documented as a risk factor (Anthony, 1978). In contrast, *protective factors* are attributes of individuals, situations, events, and environments that serve as mitigating factors in regard to the development of psychological or behavioral problems in at-risk individuals (Rutter, 1983b). They provide resistance to risk and stress, and foster outcomes marked by patterns of adaptation and competence. Protective factors, which include both individual characteristics (e.g., IQ, gender) and environmental characteristics (e.g., socioeconomic status, religious affiliation), ameliorate or buffer an individual's response to constitutional risk factors or stressful life events.

However, risk and protective factors cannot always be neatly categorized. Some protective factors can be conceptualized as the reverse of respective risk factors. For example, if poverty is a risk factor, then financial security is a protective factor. But other risk factors, such as those associated with psychopathology, often are culturally bound, whereas many protective factors have a more cross-cultural universality (Werner & Smith, 1982). Existing definitions of risk also present problems, one being the lack of concisely defined and clearly articulated criteria for determining what variables should be considered as risk factors (Seifer & Sameroff, 1987). In some situations, therefore, the identification of protective factors, or determining what differentiates the vulnerable from the resilient child or adolescent, can be a difficult task.

Resiliency (or resilience) is an individual characteristic, whereas protective factors include both individual and environmental characteristics (Garmezy, 1983). Resiliency implies a track record of successful adaptation following exposure to biological and psychological risk factors and/or stressful life events, and further implies that there is the expectation of continued lower susceptibility to future stressors. However, children who have low resiliency or who are vulnerable in infancy or early childhood are not necessarily doomed for life; some become resilient and bounce back (Werner, 1989). Because resiliency depends on both constitutional and environmental factors, the degree of resistance to stress varies over time and is partly dependent on the child's life circumstances.

Invulnerability is usually defined as the display of competent behavior in spite of deleterious circumstances, whereas *competence* has been defined as the ability to cope with events, relationships, and task demands in ways appropriate to the individual's developmental level (Garmezy & Masten, 1986). Thus, any child or adolescent who is at risk but who displays behavior that is consistent with his or her developmental stage could be viewed as competent. *Stress resistence* also is typically used to refer to a greater likelihood of successful adaptation despite exposure to stressful life events (Garmezy, 1983). Generally, resilient children and adolescents can be described as good copers who manifest a high degree of competency, although their ways of coping and their type of competence may vary considerably. Rutter (1987) further pointed out that protection or risk is not a quality of the factor itself, but rather of the way in which the factor interacts with other factors. In fact, in the absence of high stress, "protective" or "risk" factors as such have no impact. Furthermore, one cannot tell whether a factor functions as a direct stressor or as a vulnerability factor from the factor itself. This can only be determined in the circumstances in which the supposed protective or risk factor is studied. For example, loss of a parent is obviously a direct stressor that can be documented as a vulnerability factor, leading to susceptibility to other stresses. Also, stressful factors may be, like immunization, protective in the long run. Thus, these terms for risk and protective factors actually refer to an interactive process, and to emphasize their interactive and contextual nature, Rutter (1987) proposed that the terms *protective mechanisms* or *protective process* and *risk process* would be appropriate substitutes for the usual references in the literature to "factors."

In line with this suggestion, Werner and Smith (Werner, 1989; Werner & Smith, 1982) have made the point that the interaction of risk and protective factors is a balance between the power of the person and the power of the social and physical environment, and as long as the balance between stressful events and protective factors is manageable for an individual, he or she can cope effectively. Although this balance is necessary throughout life, different factors assume different degrees of importance at different developmental stages. Constitutional factors seem to be the most important during infancy and childhood, and interpersonal factors appear to be the most important in adolescence.

To enhance understanding of risk and protective factors further, three models are proposed by Garmezy, Masten, and Tellegen (1984) for analyzing relationships between major situational stressors and individual protective factors. In their *compensatory model*, stress factors and individual protective attributes are viewed as combining additively in the prediction of outcome. In this model, the impact of severe stress can be counteracted by personal strengths. For example, a very intelligent child may be able to overcome the stress and disadvantage of poverty and a dysfunctional family. In their *challenge model*, the relation between stress and competence is presumed to be curvilinear, and moderate stress is treated as a potential enhancer of competence. For example, a resilient child may be spurred to greater growth by having one parent with serious emotional problems, whereas having two parents with serious emotional problems may be overwhelming to the same child. In their *immunity-versus-vulnerability model*, protective factors modulate, dampen, or amplify the impact of stress. This suggests that protective factors impart a kind of "immunity" against stress, because adaptation to a stressful situation will be easier when protective factors are present. For example, a strong social support system may enable a child to weather a crippling injury that could lead to serious emotional problems for the average child. As a final note about these models, it should be understood that they are not mutually exclusive.

PERSONALITY, SOCIAL, AND FAMILY FACTORS IN RESILIENCE

Two assumptions underlie efforts to study resilience in children and adolescents: first, that resilience is a significant feature of behavior and development; and second, that systematic elucidation of such phenomena provides useful information for helping children and adolescents at risk for maladaptation.

Resilience refers to successful adaptation despite challenging or threatening circumstances. Three main types of psychological resilience in children and adolescents have been studied: (a) good outcomes in high-risk children and adolescents, (b) good functioning under adverse conditions (stress resistance), and (c) recovery from trauma or disasters. Some studies have focused on internal adaptation, psychological well-being, and ego resiliency, whereas others have focused on effective functioning in the environment. The book edited by Dugan and Coles (1989) offers a diverse sampling of resiliency research and concepts, and among its highlights are the voices of resilient children and adolescents that echo throughout the chapters. Other reviews of the concepts and research on resilience in children and adolescents also are available (e.g., Arnold, 1990; Rolf et al., 1990). These materials provide orientation to resilience concepts and a wealth of empirical findings.

A contextual perspective on resilience, one that emphasizes the trans-actional nature of adaptation, is evident in much of this research. Other often-made general points are that challenge can evoke resilience, and that children and adolescents may take diverse paths to good outcomes. The study of adaptation across time (in longitudinal studies) also has been critically important to understanding how resilience occurs. The conclud-ing chapter by Long and Vaillant in Dugan and Cole's edited book (1989), which is a revision of their article published in 1984, is one good example. In it, they document the upward mobility over a 30-year period of disad-vantaged youths in Boston. Their data illustrate the dramatically different picture that emerges in prospective studies that follow risk samples over time. It is a picture, in essence, which gives one an appreciation for diversity and resilience that replaces at least part of the gloomy picture so common in retrospective studies of risk. Results from this study, along with other research, suggest that IQ may be a particularly important moderator of risk in disadvantaged boys.

Several bodies of research (e.g., Garmezy, 1983; Garmezy, Masten, & Tellegen, 1984) also point to variables that are related to resiliency. These variables relate to several domains: (1) the child's dispositions or person-ality attributes; (2) family characteristics, including parent strengths and vulnerabilities; and (3) characteristics of the schools and surrounding community. The school and the family are of critical importance. Besides having a *direct* influence on resiliency (e.g., in the development of com-petency skills), the school and the family also affect related personality and social milieu dimensions and thus have an *indirect* influence on stress resistance as well.

Personality Factors

Various personality factors have been linked to resiliency. Werner and Smith (1982) found that, compared to groups of adolescents who had developed serious learning or behavior problems, resilient adolescents scored higher on the Responsibility, Socialization, Communality, and Achievement via Conformance scales of the California Personality Inventory. They also reported that both positive self-esteem and internal locus of control were among the variables that discriminated between good and poor outcomes, although these results occurred *only* for youths who had experienced much stress. Among adolescents who had not experienced a great deal of stress in their lives, these factors did not discriminate the resilient from those with poor outcomes. In this way, Werner and Smith identified positive self-concept and internal locus of control as two ameliorative or protective factors important in counterbalancing the risk associated with stress. In addition, in their study of children in inner London, Rutter and associates (Rutter, Maughan, Mortimore, Ouston, & Smith, 1979) found that good scholastic attainment (which they previously found to be related to higher self-esteem) seemed to have a protective effect in relation to the stress of disadvantaged children. Garmezy (1981) also found that a positive sense of self, as well as a sense of personal power rather than powerlessness, an internal locus of control, and a belief in the capacity to exercise a degree of control over their environment, were factors in the resiliency of African-American children. These qualities were also found by Garmezy (1981) in resilient offspring of psychotic parents.

Competence factors also have been consistently associated with stress-resistent outcomes. In his review of studies of competent African-American children in urban ghettoes, Garmezy (1981) noted that reflectiveness and impulse control were dominant cognitive styles in resilient children. In later work, Garmezy's group (Garmezy et al., 1984) describe significant correlations between measures of intelligence and manifestations of competence. As a requisite for resiliency, competence includes the ability to construct an internal representation of an event, or the ability to construct and order the incoming data so that they can become sufficiently meaningful to be acted upon. Not surprisingly, such competence is viewed as a function of intelligence.

Superior social skills also are contributors to superior psychological outcomes in those exposed to highly stressful circumstances. Garmezy (1981) noted that children previously identified as competent were rated by teachers and clinicians as being friendly and well liked by peers and adults, and as more interpersonally sensitive, cooperative, emotionally stable, and socially responsive. Moreover, the adaptive copings used by children who overcome the risk of severe stress appeared to be linked to these social skills. These stress-resistent children also had the ability to regulate impulsive drives and to delay gratification, as well as to maintain future orientation. Murphy and Moriarity (1976), in their longitudinal study of children in Topeka, Kansas, describe resilient children as having such coping skills as an ability to count on "inner resources," being highly sensitive, and showing strong curiosity about people, things, and ideas. Rutter and associates (Rutter et al., 1979) cited adaptability and malleability among the chief characteristics that protect against psychiatric disorder in childhood and adolescence.

Social Milieu Factors

Rutter and associates (Rutter et al., 1979) underscore the importance of the school environment and the quality of the school as a social institution in the development of resiliency. In this study of behavior and attainments, begun 1 year before the children were transferred to secondary school and continuing for a 7-year period, substantial variations in children's outcomes among schools were found, even after controlling for differences at admission to secondary school. Some secondary schools with a high proportion of children from primary schools who had demonstrable behavioral deviance had low rates of delinquency, whereas other secondary schools with a low proportion of children from primary schools who had demonstrable behavior deviance had high rates of delinquency. From such findings, Rutter concluded that good schools can and do exert an important protective effect.

Rutter's group (Rutter et al., 1979) also noted the possible importance of the scope of opportunities for the child, although the evidence is mostly anecdotal. Based on their observations, ultimate better adjustment is made by those deprived individuals who manage to avoid pregnancy or fathering a child in their teens, who had more education, and who married someone from a more favored background. These decisions help to break the cycle of disadvantage and to broaden the range of possibilities open to the youth. Greater opportunities, however, may simply be the by-product of resiliency, and work is needed to elucidate what mechanisms permit this greater range, both in terms of situational factors and individual differences.

The ameliorative role of social support systems in the community is also emphasized by Garmezy (1983), Werner and Smith (1982), and Rutter (Rutter et al., 1979). Werner and Smith found that resilient adolescents made extensive use of the informal assistance of peers, older friends, teachers, and ministers. Murphy and Moriarty (1976) also found this to be true in their observations and conceptualize the observations in terms of the importance of "identification with resilient models."

The number of life stresses to which youth are exposed also relates to resiliency. Werner and Smith (1982) reported that the resilient adolescents in their study were exposed to significantly fewer stressful life events than those children who developed serious problems. Rutter and colleagues (Rutter et al., 1979) also demonstrated that stressors have interactive effects. Identifying six chronic family stress variables that were strongly associated with child psychiatric disorder, they found that a combination of chronic stressors was associated with poorer outcome than a summation of the effects of the individual stressors considered singly.

Family Factors

With the growing influence of family systems theory and research, the family has received increasing attention as a major influence in the protection of children and adolescents from stress risks and poor developmental outcomes. In terms of home environment, Garmezy (1983) and Werner and Smith (1982) found less physical crowding to be associated with better outcome. In Garmezy's report, higher achieving lower-class African-Americans were described as having households that were less cluttered, less crowded, and cleaner. On the other hand, both Garmezy and Werner and Smith found no consistent correlation between two-parent homes and outcome. Another finding reported by Garmezy is that, in father-absent homes, the mother's style of coping and compensating was a powerful redemptive factor. However, Werner and Smith determined that additional caretakers (e.g., extended family, siblings) were essential in mediating the effects of the stress of single parenting on the offspring.

Parental attitudes have a major influence on the well-being of the child. Werner and Smith (1982) reported that resilient adolescents live in homes where there were consistently enforced rules. In a similar vein, Rutter (Rutter et al.,1979) concluded that good supervision and well-balanced discipline may protect children from high-risk backgrounds. Support for this conclusion also comes from other studies. For example, Wilson (1974) reported that in conditions of poverty, strict parental supervision was more effective than a happy family atmosphere in preventing delinquency.

The quality of the relationships between parents, and of parents with their children, also is important. In Werner and Smith's longitudinal study

(1982), resilient adolescents had parents who were described as more understanding and supportive than were parents of troubled youngsters. They found, as did Murphy and Moriarty (1976), that these families expressed closeness and respect for individual autonomy. In cases of an extremely troubled home environment, Rutter (Rutter et al., 1979) observed that a good relationship (high warmth and absence of severe criticism) with one parent provided a substantial protective effect. Garmezy (1981) also noted the importance of an adequate identification figure in higher achieving lower-class families. In later work, Garmezy and his associates (Garmezy et al., 1984) found that positive family attributes (e.g., good family communication, high degree of parental perceptiveness about their children) were related to more adaptive behavior under stress. The importance of healthy communication in families in providing the high-risk child with the resources and coping strategies underlying resiliency and healthy functioning also was emphasized by Wynne, Jones, and Al-Khayyal (1982).

THE SPECIAL ROLE OF THE SCHOOL IN RESILIENCE

According to Kellam, Ensminger, and Turner (1977), resilient children of all ages seem to enjoy school. They further noted that a positive school environment that has a responsive and nurturant atmosphere mitigates the effects of stress. For example, Rutter and his colleagues (Rutter et al., 1979), who studied students attending secondary schools in poor sections of London, found that a positive school environment can mitigate the effects of home stress. Characteristics of the schools that had the most beneficial effects included high academic standards, praise, incentives, rewards, feedback, and opportunities for students to obtain positions of responsibility. Wallerstein (1987) found similar school characteristics, including an organized and predictable environment, to be helpful to children successfully adapting to parental divorce. Structure within the school setting was also found to be important to high academic achievers in divorce-prone homes (Wallerstein & Kelly, 1980), and for talented, high-achieving Hispanic females (Gandra, 1982). However, in the study by Hetherington, Cox, and Cox (1982), different characteristics of the schools were found to be more important to boys than to girls. More important to boys was an environment with structure and control, whereas resilience in girls was fostered by a nurturing environment that allowed for the assumption of responsibility. These are the same characteristics that are associated with the differing home environments that foster resiliency in each sex.

Support from societal sources, including schools, has been found to serve as a buffer from the physiological and psychological consequences of exposure to stressful situations. Social support, in particular, is an important "resistance resource" that strengthens an individual in the presence of stress. From whatever source the child receives support, an essential protective factor for resilient children appears to be a significant adult who can provide a support system important to the child's well-being (Werner, 1989). Resilient children who were able to overcome economic and social disadvantages had at least one adult who had a significant influence on their lives. For many of these children, the significant adult was a teacher. In the Kauai Longitudinal Study (Werner & Smith, 1982), the most frequently identified positive role model and confidante identified by the children was a teacher, which is but one example of the tendency of resilient children to rely on friendly teachers and other school affiliations in times of stress and crisis (Werner, 1989).

The ability of resilient children to garner support may also be a key to their resiliency. In the Kauai Longitudinal Study (Werner, 1989; Werner & Smith, 1982), school-age "vulnerable but invincible" children were reported by their teachers as being highly sociable. Sociability also is a characteristic of resilient school-age children in other studies (see, e.g., Anthony & Cohler, 1987).

Intelligence is another important factor in stress resistance (Garmezy et al., 1984). There is evidence, for example, that children with higher IQs and scholastic achievement are protected from the otherwise adverse effects of moderate to high family stress levels, although it is important to point out that less intelligent and less scholastically competent children deteriorate with the same level of family stress. As to factors that might be involved, children with higher IQ scores tended to describe themselves as more poised and self-confident, as having a greater sense of self-worth, as being better socialized, and as being more flexible (Rutter, 1987). Thus, it is not surprising that school achievement and social competence are reliable predictors of stress resistence in children and adolescents. In summary, the resilient child and adolescent is a good student, has a fairly high IQ, and is high achieving and future oriented. This child or adolescent also is well liked by teachers and peers, develops friendships, and has a strong self-concept.

INFLUENCE OF STRESSFUL LIFE EVENTS AND GENETIC FACTORS ON CHILD AND ADOLESCENT PSYCHOPATHOLOGY

Over the years, there has been much research documenting the association between stressful life events and psychopathology that has supported the development of a stress model of psychopathology. However, relationships that have been found between stressful life events and psychopathology typically have been weak, leading some researchers to look for better ways to assess life events. Interview approaches have proved to be a promising alternative to typical self-report methods. In interview approaches, attempts are made to ascertain whether or not the events in question occurred independently of the respondent's prior symptoms and behavior. As a result, strong relationships between the occurrence of independent events and risk for psychopathology have been demonstrated (Coyne & Downey, 1991).

There also are other reasons for giving more consideration to stress that cannot be presumed to be independent of the psychological state and behavior of the child or adolescent confronting it. For example, for children and adolescents there is the likelihood that the tendency to experience adversity is familial. If we take seriously the need for an interactive developmental conception of psychopathology, we must study potentially nonindependent events that may both express and influence the vulnerability of children and adolescents to psychopathology.

A sole focus on life events also may detract from the problematic and relatively intractable continuities in the lives of children and adolescents. That is, both "independent" stressful events and chronic stressors are more likely to befall children and adolescents raised in adverse environments. We should be careful not to minimize such continuities in children's and adolescents' life situations. We must also be careful not to infer personal shortcomings, poor coping, or incompetency from what are actually effects of enduring features of life situations.

Some researchers also have looked for other factors that can influence the development of psychopathology. In recent years, one result has been that psychopathology has become an active area of behavioral-genetic research. For example, there are studies reporting results suggesting a common familial factor predisposes children both to depression and to behavior associated with stressful life events (McGuffin, Katz, & Bebbington, 1988a, b). Evidence also exists for a common genetic component that influences both symptoms of depression and anxiety (Kendler, Heath, Martin, & Eaves, 1987).

Other accomplishments of ehavioral-genetic research, in relation to the development of psychopathology in children and adolescents, include:

1. In a review of the world literature on juvenile delinquency and adult criminality in twins, Cloninger and Gottesman (1987) have shown that there is a considerable influence of shared family environment for juvenile delinquency. In contrast, studies of adult criminality point to substantial heritability, with much less indication of shared family environmental influences. One implication of these findings is that the bulk of juvenile delinquency arises from environmental factors, although there is a sub-group of juvenile delinquents who go on to become adult criminals who may have a genetic liability. As one indication of this situation, longitudi-nal studies indicate that primary-grade children with a diagnosis of atten-tion deficit disorder are at a high risk of later juvenile delinquency, as well as drug abuse and teenage diagnosis of conduct disorder (Satterfield, Hoppe, & Schell, 1982).

2. Anorexia nervosa, an eating disorder predominantly affecting fe-males, is characterized by a fear of fatness, the preoccupation with and pursuit of thinness, and amenorrhea. Scattered data suggesting a genetic component to anorexia are available (e.g., Holland, Hall, Murray, Russell, & Crisp, 1984).

3. There is no doubt that infantile autism (which includes autistic alone-ness, speech and language disturbances, and an obsessive desire for sameness that occurs before 30 months) runs in families, being 50 to 100 times more frequent than in the general population (Rutter & Garmezy, 1983). Other studies suggest a strong genetic component (e.g., Smalley, Asarnow, & Spence, 1988). Nevertheless, the origins of the disorder remain mysterious.

4. Studies of schizophrenia have also yielded important information in the past few years. A study by Gottesman and Bertelsen (1989) suggests a genetic diathesis that requires an environmental mental stressor to trigger schizophrenia. The longitudinal Finnish Adoptive Family Study of Schizo-phrenia has provided continuing evidence of a genetic contribution to schizophrenia as well as a possible genotype-environment interaction in which a genetic predisposition (a schizophrenic biological mother) in combination with a dysfunctional adoptive family environment increases the likelihood of severe disturbance (Tienari et al., 1989). It should be noted, however, that the predisposition to schizophrenia in a child could also result in a disturbed family environment.

Despite important accomplishments like this, the fundamental strength of behavioral genetics has been its use of methods that assess both genetic and environmental influences rather than assuming that either nature or nurture is omnipotent. It is important therefore that this second message of behavioral genetics be heard, that is, that the same data that point to significant genetic influence provide the best available evidence for the importance of nongenetic factors. Rarely do behavioral-genetic data yield heritability estimates that exceed 50 percent, which means that behavioral variability is due as much to environment as heredity. In behavioral genetics, the word *environment* includes any nonhereditary influence, such as biological factors (e.g., physical trauma, nutritional factors) in addition to psychosocial environmental factors. Behavioral genetics can also do much more than merely point to the other component of variance and note its importance. In actuality, behavioral-genetic research has revealed as much about environmental processes as it has about heredity.

One of the most important discoveries in recent behavioral-genetic research is that environmental factors important to development are experienced differently by children in the *same* family. In the past, the reasonable assumption was made that resemblance within families was caused by environmental factors shared by children growing up together in a family. However, behavioral-genetic research indicates that siblings resemble each other for genetic reasons. What runs in families is DNA, not experiences shared in the home. In effect, the significant environmental variation lies in experiences *not* shared by siblings (see, e.g., Plomin & Daniels, 1987).

The conclusion that environmental factors operate in a nonshared manner creates new research opportunities for studying environmental influences (including influences on stress and coping). It suggests that instead of thinking about the environment on a family-by-family basis, we need to think on an individual-by-individual basis. The critical question is, Why are children and adolescents in the same family so different? The key to solving the puzzle is to study more than one child per family. The message is not that family experiences are unimportant. The argument is that environmental influences in individual development are specific to each child or adolescent, rather than general to an entire family.

According to recent developments in research on nonshared environment, aggressive behavior and delinquency show some shared environment, but other areas of personality and psychopathology do not (Plomin,

Nitz, & Rowe, 1990). A surprise, however, is that nonshared environment is of prime importance for IQ (as well as personality and psychopathology). IQ has been thought to be an exception to the rule that environmental influence is nonshared. The findings of recent research (e.g., Plomin, 1988) also suggest that the influence of shared environmental influences, although important in childhood, wanes to negligible levels during adolescence, and, in the long run, environmental effects on IQ are nonshared. In addition, efforts are now underway to identify specific experiences of siblings that differ. According to Dunn and Plomin (1990), siblings growing up in the same family will experience different environments owing to their parents' treatment of them, their interactions with their siblings, experiences beyond the family (e.g., in schools), and chance.

GENETIC COMPONENT OF STRESS
AND MECHANISMS OF COPING

Adaptation is viewed as a complex interplay of a child's or adolescent's vulnerabilities, genetic and acquired, and the challenges and opportunities that unfold in their lives. There also are maturational changes and developmental changes in adaptational style that occur in conjunction with newly emerging resources and changing demands from the environment. It is a process, therefore, in which genetic vulnerabilities and assets combine with environmental factors in the development of the individual to produce different pathways to adaptational outcomes.

There is also, of course, a significant role for stress and coping in these transactional processes and adaptational outcomes, although the impact of stress depends both on the current vulnerability and resources of the child or adolescent and the intensity and duration of the stress. For this reason, it is unfortunate that there is next to no research on the genetic sources of stress and mechanisms of coping. The key feature of this problem is that there is a dearth of research on *individual differences* in stress and mechanisms of coping. A major new approach to the study of stress in children and adolescents, therefore, would be behavioral-genetic analyses of individual differences in stress, stress appraisals, and coping processes. Through such research we might better understand the genetic and environmental origins of relationships between stress and coping and school achievement and other adaptational outcomes for children and adolescents.

CONCLUDING COMMENTS

What, then, are some of the implications of these findings on vulnerable but invincible children and adolescents?

We know that, in the course of development, many children and adolescents are exposed to situations and conditions that place them at serious risk for unsuccessful adaptation. In spite of these vulnerabilities, however, a great majority manifest no developmental arrests and appear to make an adequate and even superior adjustment. This positive side of development has, in the last decade, become an increasingly prominent topic for investigation. Various genetic, personality, social milieu, family, and school factors have been found to be associated with resiliency. Although it is probable that these sets of variables, in varying combinations, contribute to the development of stress resistance, there is reason to believe that schools can play an increasingly important direct as well as indirect role (e.g., by influencing family processes) in developing stress resistance in children and adolescents.

We also know that, even in experiences of the most severe stress, some children and adolescents exhibit an ability to cope adaptively. Because such stress resistant youngsters manifest the ability to deal effectively, even gracefully, with events that traumatize their peers, findings concerning the coping reactions of these children and adolescents may help schools to teach stress competence to all children and adolescents. Although the idea of "immunizing" children and adolescents against the worst effects of stress should be examined by the schools, it is important to recognize that there is no general "immunity" to stress. Instead, there are different patterns of stress responding that are more or less adaptive, depending on the context, the circumstances, and the developmental stage of the child or adolescent.

We also know that, although the focus has been on stress-resistant children and adolescents in the studies done, one can be impressed by the fact that some high-risk families protect their children from the dangers that surround them. In these cases, it seems as if it is the *families*, rather than the children and adolescents, *that are stress-resistant.* This is not to deny, of course, that there are factors in the children and adolescents that help them resist the influence of a high-risk environment.

We also know that genetic factors may operate to create environmental risks, and that environmental factors operate in a nonshared manner. For example, parental psychopathology may lead to family discord and disruption, with adverse consequences for the children being dependent as much on the discord experienced as on any direct genetic vulnerability. Also, instead of thinking about stress influences and stress interventions only on a family-by-family basis, one also needs to think about stress influences and stress interventions on an individual-by-individual basis. In thinking about stress influences and stress interventions, differential experiences beyond the family (e.g., experiences with teachers, peers, and friends) also need to be examined.

There is more, so much more, one can extract from this literature. We know, for example, that resilient individuals, as children, have pronounced autonomy and positive social orientation. They also possess good problem-solving and communication skills. As adolescents, they have a more internal locus of control, a more positive self-concept, and a more nurturant, responsible, and achievement-oriented attitude toward life. Schools, of course, can and should provide additional support and direct help to vulnerable children and adolescents where these resources are lacking.

These personal qualities, and other cited research, also bear on another important point: that the child or adolescent who lives in an adverse environment is especially likely to learn to solve stress problems through participation in problem-solving tasks under the tutelage of more skilled members of society. Applying this metaphor of the child and adolescent as apprentice to planning stress interventions, this means that a key mechanism for the development of adaptive coping processes and skills is the concept of *guided participation.* This is a process whereby teachers, parents, other adults (and for children, older peers) provide bridges for children and adolescents between already developed coping skills and those needed to solve present or emerging stress problems. This model of stress intervention further assumes that coping is a multidirectional process. That is, from this perspective, the diverse tasks of coping, the value assigned in different communities and groups to different types of coping skills, and the kinds of arrangements required to guide children's and adolescents' acquisition of new coping skills, need to have a central role in the planning of stress interventions in the schools.

It also is evident from the studies reviewed in this chapter that it is important to distinguish between interventions aimed at optimizing *positive* experiences of well-being and self-efficacy and those aimed at preventing, ameliorating, or overcoming *negative* experiences of stress and disorganization. The consideration of individual differences also is important in planning stress interventions in the schools. For example, those planning prevention programs aimed at improving the general capacity to adapt to stressors must be mindful of the role that needs of individual children and adolescents play in the stress intervention process.

Nevertheless, understanding resiliency can provide guidance for a wide range of efforts to promote effective adaptation. Diverse investigations over the past two decades have identified many of the underlying skills and behavioral correlates of resilience, and these findings can be translated into a variety of social skills training and other programs in the schools. Such programs not only hold considerable promise for children and adolescents who grow up in very high risk environments, but they also hold promise for preventing the development of maladaptive behavior in other children and adolescents that might arise as a consequence of specific and unavoidable life stressors. The content of such training should, of course, be targeted to the pertinent life stressor (e.g., parental divorce). Similarly, the concept of "stress inoculation training" can be applied to vulnerable as well as other children and adolescents, so that they gain the confidence in coping with stress that will facilitate future adaptation. In essence, stress interventions in the schools can be aimed at expanding the repertoire of children's and adolescents' resources for coping with stress or by helping them to use more effectively the resources they already have.

11 STRESS OF TEACHERS IN THE PUBLIC SCHOOLS

Those who have studied the schools of this country realize that it is not only students who have serious stress problems. There is evidence that a substantial proportion of teachers also are experiencing high levels of stress. This is indicated by various kinds of evidence collected during the 1980s. For example, the rate of attrition for teachers in their first 5 years on the job is around 50 percent (e.g., Olson & Rodman, 1988). Also, in a typical year one out of every four teachers is seriously thinking about leaving teaching as a career (Harris & Associates, 1988). Since the acceleration of the school reform movement in the early 1980s, there has also been a substantial decline in teacher morale (Boyer, 1988), a decline that probably has continued into the 1990s. Although comparing present rates of teacher dissatisfaction with rates in earlier decades (e.g., the 1950s) is problematic, it is safe to conclude that too many teachers today are dissatisfied with their lot, and that this situation is seriously undermining the health of the public schools.

In addressing the extent and seriousness of teacher dissatisfaction and stress, the question of how teachers compare with other school professionals, and with people in other professions and occupations, also needs to be raised. Although there are methodological problems in making such comparisons, they can help to put the problem of teacher stress in perspective. As to the prevalence of debilitative stress among teachers, Farber (1991) cites several unpublished studies specifically focused on stress in which the percentage of teachers reporting high levels of stress ranged from 16 to 53 percent. In other studies focusing on such variables as satisfaction with teaching, whether they plan to leave teaching, or would choose teaching again, similar results were obtained (e.g., Carnegie Foundation, 1988). With regard to the stress situation in other professions, studies of other professionals, including psychologists (Kilberg, Nathan, & Thoreson, 1986), school psychologists (Huebner, 1992; Wise, 1985), school administrators (Tung & Koch, 1980), doctors (Altman & Rosenthal, 1990), lawyers (Margolick, 1990), and social workers (Eaton, 1980), found results on dissatisfaction and stress that were similar to those obtained for teachers. Therefore, when compared to other professionals, it would appear that teachers, as a group, are not especially vulnerable to stress. Nevertheless, there are clear indications that a substantial proportion of teachers are experiencing high levels of stress, especially in inner-city schools, and they deserve and need special attention.

THE MEANING OF TEACHER STRESS

Teacher stress was defined by Kyriacou and Sutcliffe (1978a) as "a response syndrome of negative affects (such as anger or depression) resulting from the teacher's job" (p. 159). Similar to Lazarus' theory of stress (Lazarus & Folkman, 1984), they also recognized that teacher stress is mediated by the teacher's perception of threat to his or her well-being, and that coping mechanisms are activated to reduce the perceived threat. If these coping actions are unsuccessful in reducing perceived stress, a number of psychological and emotional reactions are experienced. Further, continued exposure to stressful situations without a corresponding increase in coping resources will bring fatigue, exhaustion, and burnout (Dunham, 1984).

Some other teacher stress models also have been developed (e.g., Farber & Miller, 1981; Moracco & McFadden, 1982; Phillips & Lee, 1980; Tellenback, Brenner, & Lofgren, 1983). But most models of teacher stress are quite similar, and one might go so far as to say that in many cases one can be substituted for another by simply changing the nomenclature.

Moracco and McFadden's model consists of seven components, adapted from Kyriacou and Sutcliffe's model (1978a). These components include: (1) potential stressors (societal, occupational, and family), (2) appraisal mechanisms, (3) actual stressors (teacher perceived stressful situations), (4) coping mechanisms, (5) manifestations of stress (physical and/or psychological), (6) burnout and chronic symptoms (the ultimate effect of prolonged stress), and (7) teacher characteristics (age, past experiences, personality traits, and belief systems).

Another model, developed by Tellenback et al. (1983), is somewhat different from Moracco and McFadden's. Their model incorporated a new component, neighborhood characteristics. The model suggests that the frequency of stressors will be affected by the social context of the school, and that schools with different neighborhood characteristics will attract teachers with varying demographic and personal characteristics.

In both Moracco and McFadden's model and the model by Tellenback et al., the components of teacher characteristics, potential stressors, actual stressors, and outcomes of teacher stress (e.g., manifestations of stress or health and well-being, and chronic symptoms and burnout or withdrawal) are included. However, the former includes the components of teachers' appraisal and coping mechanisms, whereas the latter does not.

Like Kyriacou and Sutcliffe (1978a), in Moracco and McFadden's model, the mechanisms of appraisal and coping are generalized notions. They do not elaborate the constructs of teachers' appraisal and coping. For this reason, the theory of stress and coping developed by Lazarus would provide a more comprehensive theoretical base to investigate the nature of teacher stress and to provide a framework for the development of stress interventions.

SOURCES OF TEACHER STRESS

Many sources of teacher stress have been identified, although the main sources of stress for an individual teacher in a particular school may vary greatly (Kyriacou, 1987). There also is a general consensus that teacher stress can originate from three main sources: the characteristics of the teacher, the school environment, and out-of-school sources that include family problems, life crises, social pressures, or financial difficulties (Forman & Cecil, 1986).

As to the identified sources of school-related stress, they appear to fall into six major categories (Farber, 1991; Kyriacou, 1978b,1989; Phillips & Lee, 1980). These are: (1) poor motivation of students, (2) poor student discipline, (3) poor working conditions, (4) time pressures, (5) low status, and (6) conflict with colleagues. Of these school sources, student-related stressors (e.g., students' poor attitudes toward school and their lack of motivation, and students' misbehavior) have consistently been identified as a major source of stress. After reviewing the literature, Makinen and Kinnunen (1986) concluded that "the major correlates of serious teacher stress refer to disturbances in the interpersonal contacts inherent in the profession" (p. 56). This includes teacher–student interaction, among other things.

The literature on sources of teacher stress also was reviewed by Turk, Meeks, and Turk (1982). They found that students' misbehavior was one of the problems consistently identified as a source of teacher stress in the 49 studies they examined. They concluded that the mere presence of a particular problem did not cause teacher stress, but rather that it was the intensity and chronicity of the problem, and their coping strategies and concurrent concerns, that caused teacher stress.

There also are other factors that can contribute — alone or in combination — to high teacher stress. Researchers have listed school climate, coping resources, work overload, lack of control, and isolation as significant factors (Blase, 1986; Farber, 1991; Kremer-Hagon & Kurtz, 1985; Litt & Turk, 1985; Mazur & Lynch, 1989; Parkay, Greenwood, Olejnik, & Proller, 1988; Phillips & Lee, 1980). Teachers working with early adolescents in junior high and middle schools also have more feelings of stress than teachers who teach in elementary schools (Gold, 1985). Also, contrary to expectations, teachers of nonhandicapped students report significantly fewer feelings of success and competence and have more impersonal attitudes toward their students (Beck & Gorgiulo, 1983).

SPECIAL FACTORS CONTRIBUTING TO TEACHER STRESS

A number of other, more special factors have been linked with the occurrence of stress in teachers. These include public criticism that shows a noticeable lack of respect for teachers and lack of appreciation of their efforts. Charged with the task of educating and socializing millions of children and adolescents, teachers are constantly reminded of and excoriated for their failures, but rarely praised for their successes. Teachers also feel a loss of autonomy and sense of professionalism, inadequate salaries and a lack of promotional opportunities, and they struggle with issues and problems associated with role ambiguity and conflict. Other special stressors that impinge on teachers, and which are illustrative of the generally stressful condition of teachers, are discussed below.

Increased Standardized Testing as a Source of Teacher Stress

The growth of testing in recent years has been spectacular, with a parallel increase in pressure on teachers to improve test performance. In many states, competency testing has been legislatively mandated, and schools failing to achieve certain standards are subject to review and some form of remedial action. One consequence of these policies is that schools have increased efforts to prepare students to take tests. Another is that they have taken steps to gear their curricula and teaching to test content. Thus standardized achievement testing has become an increasing influence on teaching and learning.

The improvement of achievement is of course a desirable goal, and one cannot condemn the use of standardized tests to help achieve it. But there is a concern that increasing reliance on standardized achievement tests may be contributing significantly to the stress experienced by teachers. For example, Smith (1991) has reported on a qualitative study of how teachers are affected by standardized achievement testing. Among other things, she found that the public dissemination of information about classes with below grade-level test scores was a source of feelings of embarrassment, shame, guilt, and anger in many teachers. Even teachers whose students scored above grade level were not immune from such stress. Some administrators in high-scoring districts apply pressure to teachers to keep scores high or raise them because they use such data as symbols of status and to ward off outside interference from parents and others.

There also are some teachers who believe that standardized tests are invalid, and the necessity to raise scores sets up feelings of dissonance and alienation that can be sources of stress. Other teachers are concerned about the emotional impact of standardized achievement testing on students. Teachers also are stressed by the scheduling of standardized tests, although they try to remain calm and nonchalant about the testing.

Other effects of standardized achievement testing, such as reducing the time available for instruction, can also be a source of stress. Teachers work with what might be called a packaged curriculum that often exceeds their ability to cover all that is expected. There also can be a focus on material that the standardized test covers, which in turn can result in a reduction in the teacher's ability to adapt, create, or diverge — which can be a special source of stress for some teachers.

The implication, of course, is that these effects of testing can increase the stress of teachers and also lead to negative teacher effects on students.

A Growing Gap Between a Teacher's Self-Efficacy and Outcome Expectancy: A Potentially Important Source of Stress

Bandura (1986) distinguishes between self-efficacy (the person's view that he or she is capable of performing a task) and outcome expectancy (the idea that a certain action will lead to a desired outcome). Bandura gives the example that a person may feel that a certain action will produce the desired outcome yet not feel capable of performing that action. In that case, the person would have high outcome expectations for action but low self-efficacy about his or her ability to perform the action. In this connection, Dembo and Gibson (1985) noted that teachers who believe in the efficacy of their teaching are more successful than those teachers who do not. However, they also pointed out that teachers' sense of efficacy varies with experience. In general, efficacy scores decreased with experience. This was true across groups of preservice and experienced teachers, as well as across years of teaching. Interestingly, this was in opposition to the trend for teachers' perceptions of their teaching skills.

What Dembo and Gibson found out, therefore, is the reverse situation of the example described by Bandura (noted above). That is, as teachers gain confidence in their skills and knowledge of good teaching techniques (self-efficacy), they lose confidence in their ability to enable students to learn (outcome expectancy). This may be due, in part, to the fact that more experienced teachers are increasingly aware of external factors not related to teaching (such as home environment, peer systems, socioeconomic status and specific problems such as drug abuse, pregnancy, delinquency, and mental or emotional status) that may affect their students' ability to learn. This difficult and persistent problem can, of course, become a major source of stress for some teachers.

Effects of School Decline on Teacher Stress

The declining performance of a school focuses the attention of the principal and teachers on the task of managing decline. Decline, too, is organization development, possibly as natural as growth and revitalization. Research and theory on decline are available in the organization and change literature, although more attention needs to be given to decline in schools (Nicoll, 1982).

Undoubtedly, the decline of a school creates stress. Hostility, denial, and anger may be part of the community climate, whereas sadness, fear, and embarrassment may be important school factors. The principal and the teachers also face many dilemmas, one of the most important being how to handle blaming — placing it on the external environment (e.g., the changing neighborhood), accepting it in the school and classroom, or scapegoating others (especially the students). The bottom line, of course, is that declining schools create additional sources of stress for teachers.

Gender as a Source of Differences in Teacher Stress

A large majority (about 75 percent) of the teachers in the public schools are women. For this reason, sex differences in level and forms of stress, in adaptive resources and processes, and in other factors, can be important determinants of the overall effectiveness of the teacher workforce. The issues are complex, however, because sex or gender differences in stress and adaptation to stress are not simple and uniform and because they represent bio-psychosocial phenomena (Barnett, Biener, & Baruch, 1987). Therefore, to deal with these differences and their stress implications, a good balance of psychological, sociological, and biological perspectives is necessary. However, it is only in the past decade that problems of gender differences have come to the fore in stress research. For example, patterns of gender differences in health that have been examined hold the potential for stress differences between male and female teachers. Men have higher rates of life-threatening illnesses and some psychological disorders (e.g., alcoholism), whereas women have more overall physical complaints and ailments and higher rates of prevalent affective disorders such as depression.

Another source of potential stress differences between male and female teachers involves the movement of women into the labor force in increasing numbers. Research on the impact of work roles and the effect of holding multiple roles on the stress of men and women has increased (see Barnett et al., 1987). The research suggests that holding multiple roles is not inherently detrimental to the well-being of men and women, although men may be more exposed or responsive to stress at work, and women to stress in family roles. However, excessive stress in any one, or a combination of roles, is detrimental, and men and women differ as individuals and as groups in their responses to these stresses.

Many women teachers also have young children. For example, since 1970, in the workforce as a whole, the proportion of mothers with young infants has doubled (Clarke-Stewart, 1989). As a result, problems in providing child care have become a major factor that causes families stress. To obtain child care, families frequently are forced to make multiple kinds of arrangements (Kamerman, 1980). These involve schools, spouses, relatives' homes, and teenage baby-sitters. With two or more children such "packages" are even more likely. In the 200 families Kamerman studied, more than one in four of the families used four to six types of child care per week. The stress involved in keeping a system of multiple-care arangements going falls primarily on women.

Another well-documented stress factor in the lives of working mothers is multiple-role stress (McBride, 1990). When mothers enter the workforce, husbands usually do not significantly increase their household and child-care responsibilities (Scarr, Phillips, & McCartney, 1989), and this unequal sharing of responsibility for family management is an important cause of marital conflict and stress. This is important because it has been shown that the presence of accessible child care and a husband's willingness to share responsibility are related to decreasing role stress for mothers (e.g., Ross & Mirowsky, 1988).

A new focus on gender in stress research has also pointed up the need to attend to potential sources of stress that may be relatively unique to men or women. However, much of the available research has focused on phenomena especially stressful to women, including sexual discrimination and harrassment, victimization, and physical appearance and weight.

Discontinuity of Experience in Child Care: Another Potential Source of Teacher Stress

The assumption that continuity of experience promotes optimal child development is an integral component of concerns regarding day care for children, although Peters and Kontos (1987) offer the conclusion that the validity of this argument has yet to be established. They, and chapter authors, examined the existence amd importance of continuity, congruence, consistency, and stability of children's care experience (in particular, home and day care), and the two themes that emerged concerned (1) parent–care provider relationships, and (2) the integration of parental goals with policy and program development. In discussions of relationships between parents and care providers, the asymmetry of these relationships was underscored. For example, data reported in several chapters led to the conclusion that parents hold generally positive evaluations of child-care providers and experiences, whereas providers generally hold more negative evaluations of parents, and view the day care environment as compensatory. It would appear, therefore, that teachers, as parents, must assume primary responsibility for promoting environmental continuity by means of their choice of child-care settings and by adopting attitudes and behaviors similar to those of child-care providers. However, the situation is not that "simple" because there is other research indicating that the most salient factors in child-care selection are proximity to home or workplace and cost.

Although the authors collectively argued that discontinuity is not necessarily harmful to children, one is not left with the conclusion that continuity is unimportant. For example, policy recommendations emphasizing care provider–parent interaction and communication illustrate this point. It also is suggested that child characteristics are the primary source of discontinuity, rather than caregiver factors, and it is then argued that such discontinuity can be adaptive. At the same time, these several chapters strongly recommended policies that would facilitate continuity between family and child care. This tension is illustrated, for example, by underscoring the importance of a range of child-care alternatives that would promote continuity according to the needs of a variety of families.

A contextual analysis regarding the various levels at which continuity may or may not be beneficial also would aid integration of these viewpoints. For example, although lack of continuity of programming may not be directly harmful to children (e.g., in terms of higher stress levels), the lack of understanding of the values and goals of the caregivers involved may indirectly influence children through higher levels of stress and tension that occur in both parents and caregivers. The broad range of populations involved is a related consideration. The potential for discontinuities (and higher levels of stress) at the interface between family structural variables (e.g., socioeconomic status, marital status) and type of day care chosen is one such important instance.

Because many teachers use day-care facilities on a regular basis, and most schools don't provide such facilities, these can be issues that are the source of much frustration and dissatisfaction, and increased levels of stress, for many teachers. One solution, of course, would be for more schools to provide child-care facilities on school campuses, in part justifying this action as a stress intervention.

CONSEQUENCES OF TEACHER STRESS

Stress in teaching has been assumed to have deleterious consequences on teacher performance, and it is reasonable to believe that this would affect student performance and learning. However, most concerns about consequences of teacher stress, especially in terms of impact on students, are still largely speculative. For example, Phillips and Lee (1980), stated that "one might hold that teacher stress does frequently lead to teacher anxiety and other problems and that these teacher problems in turn do lead to lower teacher effectiveness" (p. 104). In contrast, the effects of job stress on a worker's well-being and health have been well documented in business and industry (Karasek & Theorell, 1987). Because these effects may be considered very similar to those in the school workplace, this in turn may partly account for why so little literature is found on the consequences of teacher stress.

One consequence that is frequently discussed in the teacher stress literature is teachers leaving the profession (e.g., Cunningham, 1983; Dunham, 1984; Farber, 1991; Kalker, 1984). However, what is perhaps more damaging than a desire to leave the profession is the development of negative attitudes and diminished capacities among highly stressed teachers who stay on the job (Farber, 1991; Kalker, 1984). The importance of this point is that these negative attitudes may also be reflected behaviorally in actions that are generally aggressive, involve a decreased ability to deal with classroom problems, and include general irritability and hypersensitivity to criticism.

At a more physical level, teacher stress has been linked to fatigue and exhaustion (Farber & Miller, 1981; Needle, Griffin, & Svendsen,1981); psychosomatic disorders, depression, and anxiety (Dunham, 1980; Phillips & Lee, 1980; Truch, 1980); as well as mental illness and substance abuse (Dunham, 1980). As Kalker (1984) has pointed out, the ultimate sufferers of the consequences of teacher stress are students. When teachers are highly stressed they are unable to dedicate themselves to giving a good, honest effort.

Among authors describing consequences of teacher stress, Dunham (1980) also suggested that stress in teaching may have positive outcomes. Dunham pointed out that a positive consequence of teacher stress may be the development of new coping skills. He also suggested potentially positive outcomes including an increased sense of self-concept derived from having successfully solved problems and developed new skills useful in similar situations that may arise in the future. Other potentially positive results of teacher stress are the development of a more effective teaching style and behavior, the development of more positive relations with students, and improved interpersonal relationships with other teachers.

STRESS AND TEACHER COPING STRATEGIES

As to the coping strategies of teachers, the research evidence indicates that, in general, people use both problem-focused and emotion-focused coping in managing stressful situations (Gass & Chang, 1989; Lazarus & Folkman, 1984). However, the literature also indicates that an individual's choice of coping strategies is associated with his or her appraisal of stressful situations (Folkman & Lazarus, 1985). That is, people use more problem-focused forms of coping in encounters they appraise as changeable, and more emotion-focused forms of coping in situations they consider to be unchangeable.

However, there is no clearcut consensus about which coping strategies are most effective (Aldwin & Revenson, 1987). Few studies have examined the relationship of coping to some outcome measure, and even those that have been conducted have produced inconsistent results. For example, some studies have found that problem-focused coping decreases emotional distress, whereas emotion-focused coping increases it (Baum, Fleming, & Singer, 1983; Felton & Revenson, 1984; Mitchell, Cronkite, & Moos, 1983; Nezu & Ronan, 1985). However, Gass and Chang (1989) found that more problem-focused and less emotion-focused coping had direct effects on reducing psychosocial health dysfunction. In another study, problem-focused coping had little effect on emotional distress but decreased subsequent problems (Menaghan, 1982). And Etzioni and Pines (1986) found that inactive and indirect types of behaviors were less effective than were more active/direct strategies.

With regard to coping effectiveness in reducing teacher stress, Long and Gessaroli (1989) found that male teachers felt that avoidance coping was more effective, whereas female teachers felt that problem solving was more effective. On the other hand, the use of certain coping strategies tends to contribute to rather than reduce the pressure of stress in classroom teachers. For example, the use of escape/avoidance coping tends to increase teachers' emotional exhaustion and depersonalization. In contrast, the use of problem solving decreases depersonalization and increases personal accomplishment.

There also have been some studies that found that teachers' coping strategies are not related to any substantial decrease in stress level (Kyriacou, 1980; Litt & Turk, 1985; Needle et al., 1981). For example, Litt and Turk found that teachers' coping resources were not related to job satisfaction or physical stress but were related to intention to leave teaching.

However, from a broader mental health perspective, it is clear that many factors can influence the relationship between coping and outcomes (Aldwin & Revenson, 1987). For mental health outcomes, the type of problem faced and the degree of stress experienced are recognized as the most notable factors. According to Folkman and Lazarus (1988a, b), the adaptive value of the coping process also often depends on the context of the stressor. A similar result was also observed by McCrae (1984).

SOME GENERAL APPROACHES TO REDUCING TEACHER STRESS

Many solutions have been offered to reduce teacher stress, although usual solutions are ineffective because of their short-term nature (Farber, 1984). Some of the solutions offered that may be more beneficial include improving teacher morale, boosting a sense of cooperation, and increasing peer support (Litt & Turk, 1985). Focusing on participatory decision making may increase organizational competence and give teachers a greater sense of control (Cherniss, 1985). In contrast, Stevens and Pfost (1983) suggested reducing the number and intensity of stressors and facilitating more effective coping skills. Interventions based on a holistic and comprehensive approach should also be utilized, so that more effective coping skills can be learned (Parkay et al., 1988).

The social problem–solving approach advocated by Stevens and Pfost (1983) consolidates goals of these kinds of interventions, although the treatment activities incorporated in this approach have limited scope. They elaborated four features of problem solving. First, it is a generic approach that transcends organizational or person-oriented strategies. Second, the model can be applied separately to each identified aspect of stress. Third, process itself can increase self-efficacy which can indirectly counter stress. And last, the model includes a feedback loop that allows for monitoring, evaluation, and modification of the intervention, if necessary.

However, social problem-solving and other cognitive-behavioral approaches to reduce stress-related disorders haven't been implemented in many schools. As to why, part of it has to do with the organizational system. There are few nationwide or statewide programs aimed at improving teacher working conditions, and school districts that make such efforts do so without regard to system effects. Nevertheless, the stress of teachers is a problem of far-reaching consequences, and powerful, comprehensive approaches to stress interventions are needed.

TAKING IMPLICIT THEORIES OF TEACHERS SERIOUSLY IN EFFORTS AIMED AT REDUCING TEACHER STRESS

School psychologists and counselors, as well as other professionals who want to implement programs designed to relieve the classroom-based stress of teachers, need to be aware of Hunt's (1987) challenge to Lewin's (1951) much-quoted maxim that there is nothing as practical as a good theory. Hunt offers and demonstrates the reverse form of the maxim, i.e., that there is nothing so theoretical as good practice. It's not easy to summarize briefly Hunt's argument, but some of the most important points he makes, that are applicable to interventions aimed at ameliorating stress associated with classroom teaching, are:

1. The teacher "reads" others and "flexes" in responding to what they say, need, want, or do in accordance with his or her own implicit theories. Each teacher may be partisan to particular formal or abstract theories of behavior, but in the world of minute-to-minute classroom teaching and social interaction (including interaction with stress interventionists), his or her implicit theories are crucial in determining how he or she reads and flexes.

2. Teachers are "psychologists" who are constantly diagnosing and acting (i.e., reading and flexing) in terms of implicit theories they are usually unaware of, or are not encouraged to explicate. Nevertheless, these implicit theories represent a fund of teacher experience and knowledge that stress interventionists should not undervalue.

3. To the extent that teachers are not helped, as part of the implementation of a stress intervention, to become aware of their implicit theories and learning styles, i.e., the conditions and experiences that made them the kind of learners they are, they are rendered insensitive to dimensions of the stress intervention to which they must constructively respond.

In essence, the practical value of a stress intervention with teachers is diluted, if not subverted, if the intervention is applied without also helping teachers come to grips with their own learning styles and implicit theories. In the process of taking that injunction seriously, the stress interventionist may even find that the formal, abstract theory underlying his or her intervention may need to be changed.

SOCIAL SUPPORT AND TEACHER COPING

With regard to social support and coping, several researchers have suggested that increasing the social support available to teachers may be a useful strategy for preventing teacher stress (Kirk & Walter, 1981; Moracco & McFadden, 1982; Paine, 1981; Russell, Altmaier, & Velzen, 1987). However, empirical evidence concerning the impact of social support on teachers' stress and coping is limited.

A more general finding of effects of social support has been that a relationship exists between social support and the experience of job stress (Ford, 1985). For example, in a group with lower occupational status, Marcelissen, Winnubst, Buunk, and Wolff (1988) found that social support had a causal effect on most stressors, indicating that social support does reduce role ambiguity, role overload, role conflict, and future job uncertainty. In a related study, Wills (1985) suggested that the perception that support is available for providing needed aid and resources can enhance feelings of personal control which lead to problem-focused coping.

Evidence also reveals that social support affects the appraisal of threat and buffers people against stress by helping them to redefine a situation as less threatening (Gore, 1978). In the same vein, McNett (1987) reported that individuals who perceived higher availability of social support tended to use problem-focused coping strategies, and those who perceived lower availability of social support tended to use emotion-focused coping strategies. Billings and Moos (1981) also found that persons engaging in avoidance coping behavior tended to have less social support. In addition, House (1981) noted that emotional support seems to be the most important of the various types of support. Ford (1985) also found that emotional support was more important than other facets in the prediction of work outcomes.

The importance of supervisor support in alleviating or reducing job stress also has been suggested by many researchers (e.g., Marcelissen et al., 1988; Russell et al., 1987). In a longitudinal study, Marcelissen and his colleagues examined the effect of support provided by supervisors and co-workers on the reduction of job stress. For persons at lower occupational levels, they found that social support provided by supervisors played an important role in reducing or eliminating stressful circumstances at work.

For teachers in particular, the results of the study by Russell and associates indicated that support received from supervisors was the only significant predictor of teacher burnout. Teachers with supportive supervisors reported less emotional exhaustion, more positive attitudes toward students, and greater personal accomplishment. Supervisor support was also found to interact with job-related stress in predicting depersonalization. This result was consistent with the buffering hypothesis. That is, as the level of supervisor support increased, the strength of the relation between job-related stress and feelings of depersonalization decreased.

Studies of other occupational groups, such as nurses (Constable & Russell, 1986) and factory workers (House, 1981), have also found that supervisor support has positive effects on the physical and mental health of workers. These findings suggest that supervisory personnel should be the focus of intervention programs designed to increase the social supports available to teachers.

Russell and his colleagues (1987) also suggested that reliable alliance support was found to be predictive of teacher burnout. According to Weiss (1974), kin relationships are typically the source of reliable alliance support. In addition, friends and family relationships also serve as a source of reliable alliance support (Russell et al., 1987). This has broad implications, of course, for the development of social support systems that protect teachers from stress.

CONCLUDING COMMENTS

Solutions to the stress of teachers have been suggested at the individual and system levels. Unfortunately, those aimed at helping individual teachers better cope with stress have had limited success in reducing work-related stress, in part because school work environments, like other work environments, are impersonally organized and hence impervious to individual coping efforts. On the other hand, second-order change strategies that involve restructuring of the schools are only now getting underway on a very limited basis under the aegis of the school reform movement. The problem here, of course, is implementation of the far-reaching changes in schools that can help teachers to better withstand the impact and negative consequences of stress.

One necessary change is a reappraisal of the condition of the public schools. According to much of the media, the public schools are moribund, even beyond reformation, and only a crusade will save them. Although there is much evidence that students in this nation's schools are performing poorly, to blame the schools and their teachers alone is to promote the absurdity that the schools are solely responsible for the education of children and adolescents. The public schools serve a multiplicity of purposes and are woven into the institutional fabrics of the nation. To succeed in the schools, children and adolescents must have the personal resources to attend to the demands of school, and they also must have the economic support and family structure and stability that is essential to school success. In essence, the problems of America's schools stem in part from causes deep in the national experience. More work on these problems of the public schools, and less school- and teacher-bashing, would do much to relieve the stress of teachers.

Another necessary change is the reconceptualization of what it means to be a teacher. That is, the overall reduction of teacher stress will require a redefinition of the nature of a teacher's role. What is needed is schools of the future that make it possible for teachers to assume a variety of roles. Roles are needed that include mentoring responsibilities for new teachers by veteran teachers. There need to be opportunities for teachers to engage in curriculum development and to develop better assessment methods. There also should be opportunities for teachers to carry out research with their colleagues, other school professionals, and with researchers from universities. In short, the school of the future itself must be a center for professional growth for teachers as well as students.

12 KEY TASKS UNDERLYING SUCCESSFUL AND ENDURING STRESS INTERVENTIONS IN THE SCHOOLS

Diverse approaches to stress intervention have been described in prior chapters, although it has been difficult to determine their effectiveness, especially in terms of long-term adaptational outcomes. There also is clear evidence in prior chapters to support the assumption that environmental and individual stressors and resources influence the school problems of children and adolescents. The larger question, however, is how environmental and individual resources are best strengthened and deleterious environmental conditions and individual characteristics modified. A framework for looking at some of the problems in achieving this goal is presented in this chapter.

WORKING WITHIN CONSTRAINTS OF "REGULARITIES"

Although there are a wide variety of organizational environments that impinge on children and adolescents, school settings account for the largest number of daily interpersonal interactions. Children and adolescents also spend as much time at school as at home, and as children grow older, school friends take on increasing importance as sources of social support (Cauce & Srebnik, 1989). In recognition of this, programs utilizing individual and family resources have been developed that have an impact upon the lives of individual children and adolescents. However, programs that rely primarily on in-school resources are less in evidence because schools and the nature of the learning enterprise are much more difficult to change. The dilemma is that, while schools are being pushed by external forces to change (e.g., responses to court-ordered desegregation, the advent of P.L. 94-142 concerning instructional planning for handicapped students, the rise of teachers' unions, and the widespread adoption of preschool education), there also are intractable internal aspects of schools that tend to mute attempts at innovation that changes basic structures (Sarason & Klaber, 1985). For example, Sarason and Klaber noted that the assumption that education takes place best inside encapsulated classrooms in encapsulated schools is rarely questioned.

Designers of stress intervention programs in the schools therefore must, of necessity, learn to work within the constraints of school setting "regularities" (Sarason, 1982). The working axiom is that effective school stress projects are those whose critical elements are integrated into the structures of the school setting (Elias, 1989). A key factor in adoption is organizational readiness, which, in the case of stress intervention projects, can be assessed by the awareness and acceptance of the problem of student stress by the school; the attitudes, motivation, and practices of school staff; and the resources and organizational structures available to support stress-type interventions. In addition, to implement stress projects successfully in the schools, attention must be paid to school–family contexts — by involving parents, and by being culturally sensitive.

GENERAL LOW QUALITY OF INTERVENTION PROGRAMS

Advances in stress interventions in the school, especially those aimed at prevention, will likely have to follow a difficult path because of the general low quality of intervention programs. Although there are many studies that document the positive outcomes of intervention programs, the relationships typically found are weak and the studies themselves often are a source of frustration. This is the message of a book edited by Price, Cowen, Lorion, and Ramos-McKay (1988). The book was a product of an

American Psychological Association task force that contacted 900 experts knowledgeable about intervention programs. They received 300 program descriptions, and, in the end, selected 14 model programs. All 14 met stringent criteria. Each clearly specified an intervention goal for an emotional condition and provided a rationale for the intervention. Each also indicated when and how the program was implemented, and discussed recruitment issues. In addition, program objectives and evaluation, and how program transfer to other settings was dealt with, were described. Most of the programs, which were often implemented in schools, were oriented to children and adolescents, many of whom were poor and members of minority groups.

Despite this selectiveness, descriptions of these 14 programs present some concerns. At times, too little information is given about success/failure ratios. Also, details about statistical analyses and actual data are sometimes sparse. In addition, cost/benefits analyses are neglected. Occasionally, there also is no information about long-term effects that resulted from the prevention efforts. Thus, while intervention programs can work, even the best programs have conceptual and methodological limitations and typically encounter many practical impediments during implementation.

A similar perspective is presented by Dryfoos (1990) who, among other things, organizes the literature on program effectiveness for different categories of at-risk behavior of adolescents. In reading these chapters in her book one cannot escape from the realization that most efforts to prevent the onset of these risk behaviors end in failure. However, Dryfoos does not surrender to disillusion; instead, she suggests a number of common concepts for successful programs and strategies for preventing high-risk behavior.

ISSUES IN UTILIZING INTERPERSONAL RESOURCES

Examples of the use of interpersonal resources in stress interventions have been provided in a number of preceding chapters. There also is a fair amount of evidence from prospective studies indicating that social support serves as a protective factor, enhancing psychological and educational well-being and physical health (Gottlieb, 1987; House, Umberson, & Landis, 1988). However, evidence that naturally ocurring support is effective does not mean that the same can be expected of artificially induced support (i.e., social support *interventions*; Rook & Dooley, 1985). It also in not clear when, and under what conditions, intentionally provided support can overcome prior support deficiencies. The most basic problem is that the exact mechanisms by which supportive ties produce educational, psychological, and health-protective benefits are still largely unknown. Support programs have been applied indiscriminately to populations "at risk," without much thought about whether the treatment provided meets the specific needs of targeted individuals. Underspecified and indiscriminately applied intervention programs do not tend to generate meaningful information.

One way to improve support interventions is to recognize the social context within which support occurs. Supportive relationships are imbedded in social rules and structures that define the parameters within which these relationships occur (House et al., 1988). In addition, support interventions are most useful when they restore or enhance normal role functioning, and when they reinforce rather than bypass existing social structures. Thus, a more focused view of social support would seem to be required in stress interventions in schools. In addition, social support should be viewed as only one component of a multipronged stress program, rather than as a free-standing intervention. Other components might include those that contribute to the achievement of role competence, such as learning new skills, or being given the opportunity to display already learned behaviors. Support occurs naturally as individuals (e.g., students) engage in shared activities, are socially useful, provide for others, and demonstrate mastery of stressful life transitions. These reciprocal characteristics of normal social relationships are the elements that should be captured in stress interventions that emphasize social support in the schools.

LIMITATIONS OF INTERVENTION PROGRAMS DESIGNED TO STRENGTHEN INDIVIDUAL SKILLS AND COMPETENCES

There is an individualistic bias in education and psychology that is further reinforced by the notion of individual responsibility, which has always been a cherished and pervasive value in American society. It should come as no surprise, therefore, that federal grant money for prevention in the past decade has emphasized individual rather than social-level interventions, and that the bulk of the intervention literature concerns efforts to help individuals develop the skills needed to overcome environmental stressors, rather than dealing with deleterious social conditions directly. Advocates of individually oriented programs are implicitly accepting the assumptions that individuals are responsible for problem solutions, and that they can be trained to deal more effectively with impinging negative events.

One good example of this individually oriented approach is the teaching of social problem–solving skills in schools and other settings through the use of models developed by D'Zurilla and Goldfried (1971) and Spivak and Shure (1974). This type of intervention involves teaching the components of problem solving in a series of steps that include problem recognition and definition, the generation of alternative solutions, selecting the best alternative, and noting its degree of success so that self-correction becomes possible. Variations of this basic strategy have been used as approaches to intervention in a variety of contexts, with the expectation that the enhancement of problem-solving skills will positively influence adjustment by reducing the negative effects of environmental stress. Although the evidence is fairly clear that appropriate social problem–solving skills can be learned by a variety of individuals, including children and adolescents, it is less clear that these skills transfer to problem situations in schools, families, peer groups and other aspects of everyday life, and that general adjustment is improved when individuals practice problem-solving skills (Weissberg & Allen, 1986).

STRENGTHS AND WEAKNESSES OF INTERVENTIONS THAT FOCUS ON DIFFERENT ASPECTS OF THE STRESS PROCESS

Most intervention programs for children and adolescents are derived from adult-level theory and practice. There also has been little evaluation of the efficacy of such programs and not much research to support what should be included. Interventions have focused on the individual child or adolescent, on groups of children or adolescents, or on the families of children or adolescents. Three basic types of interventions are briefly reviewed below: ameliorating stressors, changing the individual's interpretations of stressors, and improving stress-coping strategies.

Changing the Stressors

Brenner (1984) suggested that school and other professionals help children and adolescents by assisting them to remove stressors. This requires that children and youth be helped to identify their own stressors, and evaluate the extent to which stressors can be changed. Interviews, self-report instruments, and diaries can be used to identify sources of stress. Unfortunately, many of the school-related, as well as family and neighborhood and developmentally based, stressors that children and adolescents experience are outside the control of children and adolescents, as well as school and other professionals. In such cases, children and adolescents could still be helped to change their perceptions of the stressors, or change the way that they deal with them (Ryan, 1988).

Changing Perceptions of Stressors

The ways that the brain organizes and interprets information about stressors predisposes children and adolescents to make either adaptive or maladaptive responses, so that there are potential benefits from interventions that focus on changing interpretations of stressors. Changing children's and adolescents' appraisal of stressors may employ individual counseling of a supportive type, although introspective counseling with children, and some adolescents, may exacerbate difficulties by reinforcing an already dysfunctional overconcern with the self (Brenner, 1984). Although it is generally agreed that children and adolescents should be assisted to reframe their perceptions of stressors from negative to positive, from hopeless to hopeful, or from destructive to growth producing, specific methods for accomplishing this have not been well identified.

Changing Coping Strategies

Coping strategies are learned and can be acquired, changed, or eliminated (Moos, 1976). Therefore, interventions in the schools that involve cognitive-behavioral or other strategies may be successful in preventing and treating stress symptoms. A child's or adolescent's repertoire of coping strategies should first be assessed by self-report, observation, or interview, then the child's or adolescent's perceived effectiveness of the strategies should be evaluated. This is an important second step because adults' perceptions of effectiveness or adequacy of coping strategies may be quite different from the perceptions of children and adolescents (Ryan, 1988).

As to the kinds of coping strategies that should be taught, some researchers believe that only strategies that focus on changing the stressor are adaptive (Yarcheski & Mahon, 1986), whereas other stress researchers (e.g., Lazarus & Folkman, 1984) assert that coping strategies that serve to distract from or ignore the stressor are sometimes appropriate when stressors cannot be changed. Lazarus and Folkman (1984) also point out that coping strategies used in anticipation of stressors are often different from those used during or after a stressful event. In a study of 8- to 12- year-olds, Ryan (1989) found that children most frequently used social support and isolating and avoiding strategies *before* a stressor, social support *during* a stressor, and avoidant and distracting strategies *after* a stressor.

Another note of caution is that too little is known about the validity of teaching children and adolescents new coping strategies, such as relaxation or imagery (Stanton, 1985). At least for younger children, it may be best to encourage use of strategies in their own repertoire that they have found to be successful, and discourage use of strategies that they report are ineffective, but which they use anyway. Creative coping-skills programs that are taught in small groups or classroom settings offer more promise, although the efficacy of this approach has not been fully validated. The contents of such programs typically consist of social competence skills, and self-awareness and stress-reduction techniques (Brenner, 1984; Humphrey & Humphrey, 1985; Medeiros, Porter, & Welch, 1983). More typical coping strategies that children themselves find useful should also be included in these programs, such as physical exercise, distracting behaviors, and cognitive strategies that involve thinking, reading, making drawings, and writing about the problem (Ryan, 1989).

PRECAUTIONS IN THE USE OF SOCIAL PROBLEM–SOLVING TRAINING

Positive evidence of the benefits of social problem–solving skills training in the schools comes from such studies as the one by Elias and his associates (Elias et al., 1986), who found that 1 year of interpersonal problem-solving training in elementary school led to a reduction in the rated severity of stressors children experience in the transition to middle school. It also appears that better results with social problem–solving skills training are obtained when training is started early, in the preschool years (Shure & Spivak, 1982), when programs are of adequate duration, and when program content is matched to the sociodemographic and ethnic characteristics of students (Gilchrist, Schinke, Trimble, & Cvetkovich, 1987; Schinke, Orlandi, Botvin, Gilchrist, & Trimble, 1988). In some programs, peer leaders tend to produce more consistent positive results than do teachers (Botvin & Tortu, 1988). This emphasizes the importance of the social milieu in which skill-acquisition programs are imbedded.

Proponents of social problem–solving approaches to intervention believe that a generic problem-solving strategy can be learned by children and adolescents that will be applicable across a wide variety of in-school and out-of-school situations. Children and adolescents can "learn how to learn" and create learning sets that can have a powerful influence on their behavior. But whether learning sets are utilized depends upon a number of factors (e.g., the similarity between training and generalization situations, the motivation and prior experience of the learner, and the potency of other competing responses).

It also can be argued that learning is likely to be most effective when it occurs in situation-specific contexts. As a case in point, social problem–solving approaches have been applied to a variety of child and adolescent problem situations with a fair degree of success. They have been an important component of programs to prevent child and adolescent substance abuse (Botvin & Tortu, 1988; Schinke & Gilchrist, 1985), programs to prevent teenage pregnancy (Gilchrist & Schinke, 1983), programs for children of divorce (Pedro-Carroll, Cowen, Hightower, & Guare, 1986), and programs to lower the incidence of teen suicide (Davis, Sandoval, & Wilson, 1988).

CAUTIONS IN MOBILIZING SOCIAL SUPPORT PROGRAMS

Programs aimed at marshalling, augmenting, or improving the informal support children and adolescents receive and provide have taken many forms, differing in their structure and content as a function of the developmental level and psychosocial needs of children and adolescents and the ecological niches they inhabit. Programs also differ with respect to the settings in which they take place, although the vast majority have occurred in the school and the home.

Gottlieb (1988) has edited a book in which a typology of support interventions is presented and then systematically applied. In the typology, support interventions are classified in terms of their focus on the individual, dyadic, group, social system, or community levels. At the dyadic level, the most widely known example is the Big Brothers/Sisters organization, a prototype of many other intergenerational support programs designed to improve the life chances of a variety of at-risk children and youth. Such programs offer diffuse support, and rarely prescribe content, the frequency and focus of interaction, or the settings in which contacts take place. They typically aim to compensate for a more general deficiency in adult attachments, and therefore concentrate on developing the kinds of support that are gained from such a close adult relationship. The relationship is the end in itself rather than a means of enlarging particular kinds of coping assistance.

To date, there has been no systematic research about how to match adults to children and adolescents in ways that optimize the likelihood of a relationship developing as a basis for the expression of support. However, as Pearlin (1989) has pointed out, the forms of support, its reciprocity, its stability, the connections between seeking support and getting it, its stability, and even whether or not it is welcomed, depend not on the recipient alone, but on the helper–recipient relationship. For example, when nonprofessional helping relationships are structured in a way that permits bidirectional expressions of support, they are more attractive. In addition, when the aid of support providers is seen to be voluntarily tendered rather than constrained by role obligations, they are liked more, and their support is more highly valued and accepted.

The most popular dyadic peer helping strategy has been to train adolescents as peer counselors, and a number of good examples of this approach are provided by Buck (1977) and McManus (1982). Many secondary schools have recruited and trained students to engage in personal and academic counseling with their peers. Peer counseling has also been widely implemented in substance abuse and teen parenting programs (e.g., Halpern & Covey, 1983). Generally, peer counseling programs are more likely to be successful if they provide opportunities for the expression of mutual rather than unidirectional aid, and if peer helpers are recruited on the basis of their abilities rather than their handicaps or deficiencies.

Support groups constitute another strategy that has been used to marshall help for children and adolescents, although primarily used with adolescent substance abusers, victims of domestic sexual abuse, and those involved in raising children at an early age. Typically, the groups are convened and led by professionals who combine skills in facilitating the process of mutual aid with expert knowledge about the stressors members face and productive ways of coping with them. The most detailed information about their process, structure, and outcomes has come from reports of groups created for children and adolescents whose parents have separated or divorced (e.g., Kalter, Schaefer, Lesowitz, Alpern, & Pickar, 1988; Pedro-Carroll et al., 1986).

When children and adolescents lack family support, it is likely that the support available to their parents is deficient as well, suggesting the need for stress interventions in the schools that are responsive to the needs of both students and parents. The absence of support is a risk factor, hampering family adjustment, as much as its presence can be a protective factor that facilitates adjustment. Children and adolescents are at risk of deficient parental support for many different reasons. Their parents may not be well enough themselves to meet their children's needs for support, as in the case of parents who suffer from major mental illnesses or alcoholism. Parents also may be preoccupied with their own personal problems, making them less available to their children or causing them to behave inappropriately with their children. For example, separation and divorce can entail not only the loss of support of one parent, but can result in parents making supportive demands of children and adolescents that are impossible for them to meet on the basis of their developmental maturation, a problem that is explored in depth by Elkind (1988, Chapter 2). Other stressful family contexts that call for support to parents and their children include the death of a parent or sibling (through illness, accidents, or suicide), chronic unemployment or repeated episodes of job loss, and serious or chronic illness occurring to the parent or child. These life events and chronic hardships collectively form an agenda for planning initiatives in the schools that augment *family* support.

The school, however, is an equally important primary socializing context for children and adolescents, and the school can be an important setting in which support for children and adolescents experiencing high levels of stress can be improved. For example, among the recommendations offered in the Carnegie Foundation's study of middle schools (Carnegie Council on Adolescent Development, 1989), the most prominent involve initiatives that counteract the impersonality of the school social environment. These recommendations include the creation of "houses" or "schools-within-schools," smaller learning environments that afford greater stability and familiarity among students and between them and teachers. A second recommendation that goes even farther toward dispelling the anonymity of the middle school is for teachers to collaborate with one another in teams, thereby gaining the support of their own peers. Each team of at least five teachers would become part of a larger "community of learning," composed of teachers and students who would remain intact for the duration of the middle school period. Third, recognizing the huge caseloads carried by school psychologists and guidance counselors, the report calls for the assignment of an adult advisor to each student (a teacher or other staff member) who would use his or her knowledge of development and principles of guidance to marshall school and community resources on behalf of the student. In this way, the credo that "Every student should be well known by at least one adult in the middle school" could be realized. Of course, there are aspects of this Carnegie vision of how to transform the social environment of the middle school that can be applied to other levels of schooling. In addition, aspects of this vision have aleady been implemented in many school districts, one good example being the work by Felner, Ginter, and Primavera (1982). In their intervention efforts, certain guidance and administrative duties were added to the homeroom teacher's role, including responsibility for maintaining contact with the students' families. In addition, at the structural level, they stabilized relations among the students by allowing the same set of students to attend all four core academic subjects together. Their evaluation of the effects of these efforts to generate greater peer and adult support revealed that students in the intervention, in comparison to a matched control group of students in another urban school, had significantly better academic records, developed more positive self-concepts, and viewed the school's social climate more favorably.

Schools can also host more broadly interpreted support interventions. Rutter (1987), for example, has pointed out and given examples of ways in which schools can enlarge opportunities for success in extracurricular activities, afford students equal access to positions of responsibility in school clubs, and involve them in tutoring other students. Such experiences can cultivate leadership skills and engender feelings of self-worth arising from the positive appraisals of others, and thus add to the availability of resources that protect students against the debilitative effects of stress.

Nevertheless, there are some needed cautions in applying research on the stress-related functions of social support to the development of stress interventions for children and adolescents. First, the school psychologists and other school professionals who plan such interventions must take into account the critical development and ecological differences affecting all aspects of the stress process in childhood and adolescence as contrasted with adult life. Second, they must take stock of the forms and meaning of social support among children and adolescents, recognizing that gender, age, socioeconomic, cultural, and ecological differences within these age groups have important effects on the ways support is construed and evaluated. Moreover, these demographic characteristics are bound to shape the types of support that are extended as much as they shape the reactions of these young recipients.

In addition, there are differences in the social role occupied by children, adolescents, and adults that expose them to different life stressors. As a final point for consideration, children and adolescents not only are likely to differ from adults in the coping resources they can marshall to regulate their emotional states and act on the stressors they encounter, but differences in cognitive, social, and emotional development of children and adolescents also are bound to affect what they deem stressful and how they respond to perceived threats.

VIEWING STRESS INTERVENTIONS AS COMPETENCE-BUILDING RATHER THAN PATHOLOGY-FIGHTING STRATEGIES

The mental health field has experienced much ferment and critical self-scrutiny over the past two decades. Because the field's emphases on understanding and repairing pathology are seen, increasingly, as self-limiting and insufficient to the magnitude of the problems that must be addressed, attention has turned to prevention and the development of competence as a bona fide conceptual alternative. One outstanding example of this approach is provided by Strayhorn (1988) who conceptualized child therapy as health building rather than pathology fighting. He stated the issue this way: "There are certain competencies that we want to see children and adolescents develop and certain methods of promoting those competencies. We can keep things straight more easily if we try to list those ends and means, and decide systematically which to adopt at which times" (p. v). In pursuit of this goal, Strayhorn's Table 2.1 (pp. 28-29) offers a concrete, detailed listing of 62 basic child and adolescent skills, grouped under 9 rational clusters. This comprehensive taxonomy of competences in childhood and adolescence establishes a clear, internally consistent framework for (1) defining therapeutic goals, and (2) directing attention to the conceptually grounded network of intervention methods.

A helpful companion table (Strayhorn, 1988, pp. 53-54) proposes a measurement framework that can be used to assess a child's or adolescent's current skill status, and to identify target skills around which to orient subsequent intervention efforts. Later, a taxonomy of methods is proposed that includes 9 clusters of behaviorally oriented "methods of influence" (e.g., goal setting, forming hierarchies, modeling, arranging behavioral contingencies, etc.), which together comprise a technique armamentarian for skill promotion. These techniques also are illustrated in rich detail. In addition, applications are cast in a developmental context, and Strayhorn shows how the goals of skill enhancement can profit from different methods and techniques at different age levels. The potentially facilitating role of the family in these interventions also is given special attention.

IN SEARCH OF A MODEL OF *INTENTIONAL* BEHAVIOR CHANGE

Numerous studies are cited in this and prior chapters that show that *some* children and adolescents can successfully change their stress-related problem behaviors with the help of professional intervention. Some of the cited studies also demonstrate that *some* children and adolescents can modify their stress-related problem behaviors without the benefit of formal intervention. Nevertheless, the puzzle of how children and adolescents *intentionally* change their behavior with or without professional assistance has not been well solved, and the need to concentrate more on the phenomenon of intentional change as opposed to change imposed by developmental forces or established by school, family, or societal authority has not been well recognized. A first step toward such understanding has recently occurred, however, in studies of self-initiated and professionally facilitated change of addictive behavior (Prochaska, DiClemente, & Norcross, 1992). Although this research was done primarily with young adults, one significant outcome has been a promising stages-and-processes model of intentional behavior change. In this research five *stages* have been identified (pp. 1103-1104):

a. *precontemplation*, unaware or underaware of the problem, with no intention to change behavior in the foreseeable future;

b. *contemplation*, aware that the problem exists, with serious thinking about it, but no commitment to take action;

c. *preparation*, intention to take action in near future to overcome the problem, with some past unsuccessful or partially successful actions taken in the near past;

    d. *action*, concerted actions taken to modify behavior, environ-
ment, or experiences to overcome the problem, although these
actions don't lead to consolidation of change;

    e. *maintenance*, efforts made to consolidate the gains attained, and
to prevent relapse.

According to these authors, a spiral pattern of change also is characteristic of people taking action to modify their problem behavior. For
example, successful self-changers usually make several action attempts
before they become long-term maintainers. Because relapse is the rule,
people often regress to an earlier stage and then recycle through the
remaining stages again. For this reason, change is not conceptualized as a
linear progression through the stages; instead, there is a spiral pattern of
change.

In developing their model, these authors also identified *processes of
change*, which they described as "covert and overt activities and experiences that individuals engage in when they attempt to modify problem
behavior" (p. 1107). Looked at in the context of stages of change, a
knowledge of such processes can enhance understanding of when and how
particular shifts in attitudes, intentions, and behavior occur. The authors
made the further point that processes of change are integrated with the
stages of change, so that "doing the right things (processes) at the right
time (stages)" (p. 1110) is essential to successful outcomes in both self-
change and professionally assisted change efforts.

As to some of the implications of their model for stress interventions
in the schools, it should be pointed out that most children and adolescents
who are experiencing debilitative stress are not in the action stage. Extrapolating from their data, it also would be reasonable to conclude that
the amount of progress during stress interventions would tend to be a
function of children's and adolescents' preintervention stages. To plan
stress interventions for children and adolescents without considering their
preintervention status would therefore be naive. In essence, there is likely
to be a mismatching of stage and intervention when stress intervention
programs don't take a stage model into account.

A second important implication for stress intervention programs is that
successful change will involve children and adolescents in a progression
through a series of stages, and that stress intervention programs must allow
most children and adolescents to recycle several times through the stages

in order to achieve long-term maintenance of the desired behavior changes. It also is important to realize that there appear to be similar stages and processes of change for both self-changers and professionally assisted changers, and that these stages and processes would seem to be relevant to the modification of a broad range of stress-related problem behaviors.

To sum up, one can argue that there are important commonalities in how children and adolescents intentionally modify their problem behavior, and that the most obvious and probable implication of the model proposed by these authors is that stress interventions that don't take account of the stage of a child's or adolescent's readiness for change, and that don't tailor interventions accordingly, are likely to achieve disappointing long-term results.

NEED FOR COLLEGIAL AND INTERACTIVE PROFESSIONAL ROLES IN STRESS INTERVENTION EFFORTS IN SCHOOLS

In recognition of the many problems associated with pull-out models of service delivery for students who are not succeeding in school, professionals who have traditionally supported such services, namely special educators and school psychologists, have been engaged in extensive debate over the fundamental patterns by which teachers obtain assistance for their problematic students. In recent years a strong preference has emerged for approaches to service delivery in which classroom teachers and support services staff engage jointly in problem solving and shared responsibility for helping students (especially students with handicaps) to succeed in the regular classroom. In this context, Zins et al. (1988) offered a reasoned, sensible, and practical guide to the introduction of collegial problem solving in the schools that stresses the need for an ecological, systems-oriented approach.

However, there can be inconsistencies in the way the operationalization of this role is carried out. To be successful, equal partnerships, parity, and mutual respect need to be genuinely advocated. Much concern also needs to be expressed for involving classroom teachers in every step of organizational planning. In addition, it needs to be understood that classroom teachers hold expertise in the areas of curriculum and instructional methods. At the same time, classroom teachers should not be viewed only as consumers of consultation services. For example, it should be realized that school psychologists and other specialists might seek out the expertise held by the classroom teacher for their own work in the schools, or that teachers could consult with other teachers.

Such problems exemplify the difficulties in making the transition from an expert model to a collegial, interactive model of problem solving in the schools. Specialists are socialized to their separate roles and it is difficult for them to achieve a genuine belief in mutual expertise among all school professionals, a point of considerable relevance to the development of stress interventions that involve classroom teachers in instrumental ways.

IMPORTANCE OF A MULTIDISCIPLINARY
AND ECOLOGICAL PERSPECTIVE:
AN EXEMPLARY MODEL

There is a burgeoning interest in educational, social, and psychological services to children and adolescents that is shared by professionals in schools and other community agencies who represent a variety of disciplines. In addition, special services work done in schools is increasingly done in cooperation with professionals in other settings, and this is work that also can generalize to those other settings. One good example of a stress-related intervention in the schools that has such a multidisciplinary orientation is the Improving Social Awareness-Social Problem Solving (ISA-SPS) project initiated and carried out by Elias and associates (see, especially, Elias & Clabby, 1989, 1991). Another strength of this project is that it approached the problem of transition to middle school, and related stress problems, from an ecological perspective. In addition to uncovering over 20 discrete stressors, ranging from remembering one's locker combination to resisting peer pressure to use alcohol or drugs, they found that there were two focal points for most of the students' difficulties: initial transition difficulties, centering around adapting to many new routines; and longitudinal difficulties, centering around peer pressure and acculturation into the social system of the middle school.

Based on an analysis of the problems from a child and systems perspective, a tripartite strategy for developing students' social competence was designed. The first component focused on the development of skills in self-control, group participation, and social awareness. It emphasized such things as the students' ability: to follow directions; to calm themselves when upset; to start and maintain a conversation without being provoked by others to lose self-control (or provoking others to do so); to give, receive, and obtain help; and to build trusting and caring friendships. The second strategy concerned the development of skill in social decision making and problem solving, and in this phase of the intervention students learned an eight-step affective and cognitive strategy to use when under stress, and when they faced problems for which they had to make choices or decisions. In fulfilling the third goal of the intervention, promoting skill acquisition and application in the environment, teachers and other school personnel and parents were trained in techniques that were used to elicit students' thoughts about decision making in social and academic situations and to cue and prompt students to use specific self-control and group participation skills.

Results of this intervention also have been evaluated. On a key measure that included 28 middle school stressors covering conflicts with authority and older students, academic pressure, peer relationships and peer pressure for substance abuse, and logistical hassles, significant differences occurred between students receiving the intervention and no-intervention controls (Elias, Gara, & Ubriaco, 1985). In additional analyses, there was evidence that students' levels of social decision-making and problem-solving skills mediated intervention outcomes (Elias et al., 1986).

As to generalizations of the intervention at other environmental levels, guidance contacts and disciplinary records showed that students used their social decision-making and problem-solving skills when prompted by the guidance counselor or school administrator, but their spontaneous use of these skills appeared to diminish over time. To overcome this problem, a middle school "survival skills" program was developed over a period of years that included an organizational and study skills component and an infusion of social decision making into the social studies curriculum. From the results of these further endeavors, it would appear to be necessary to complement a skills-focused intervention with supportive changes in the middle school environment if the stress of the transition process is to be minimized (Elias & Clabby, 1991).

Another, more general, finding was that efforts to obtain and maintain the support of parents, administrators, and school board members, and the teachers and students most closely involved in the work, were of utmost importance. The convergence of the interests and synergistic actions of multiple constituencies and systems is an implicit principle of all successful school intervention programs.

NECESSITY FOR DETAILED EXAMINATION OF LINES OF TRANSMISSION FROM DELIVERY OF AN INTERVENTION TO LONG-TERM EFFECTS

A reconceptualization of what it means to conduct a school intervention that is successful and enduring also is occurring in advances in school reform. It is fueled by the recognition that detailed examinations of the expected lines of transmission from delivery of an intervention to desired long-term effects need to be made. A good example of such an examination, in the context of establishing social competence promotion programs, has been provided by Weissberg, Caplan, and Sivo (1989). In articulating a new conceptual and operational approach for intervention work, they have provided descriptions of a number of key tasks in the development of successful and enduring interventions. These tasks, adapted from their chapter (Table 9.1, p. 266), are:

1. *program conceptualization*, which involves the use of existing theory, research, and intervention information at both person and environment levels to specify main program concepts, assumptions, and goals;

2. *program design*, in which potentially appropriate intervention materials and practices are identified and reviewed; then examined for developmental appropriateness and cultural relevance and modified as necessary; and then translated into explicit training materials and procedures and guidelines for implementation;

3. *program implementation*, where a pilot study is conducted and the intervention is adapted to recipients, implementers, and ecological realities; this being followed by a fine-tuning of implementer training and supervision procedures, the development of a system to ensure high-quality implementation, and the development of contacts at various school and other organizational levels to ensure ongoing support of the intervention and resources needed to carry it out;

4. *program evaluation*, which includes the selection of valid, viable approaches to measure the extent and quality of implementation, and changes in focal attitudes, knowledge, skills,

relationships, and mediating factors; and the design of an appropriate data-gathering and analysis system; and

5. *program diffusion*, that involves a conceptualization of how the program can be carried out elsewhere, perhaps with varying degrees of involvement by the program developers; the production of transportable materials and clear and specific training and replication guidelines; and a determination of procedures for minimal program evaluation in new sites.

Another good example of this type of comprehensive approach to school innovation is provided by Rosenfield (1992). She describes a program for developing school-based consultation teams that includes a design for organizational change consisting of three major stages — initiation, implementation, and institutionalization. She recognizes, among other important things, that innovative change in schools is a developmental process, and that program development activities must be integrated with efforts to change school culture and structures. The importance of evaluation at all stages of the innovation and change process also is emphasized.

CONCLUDING COMMENTS: STRESS RELIEF IN THE CONTEXT OF A PARADIGM SHIFT IN THE SCHOOLS

Stress relief for students and their teachers and parents will not just happen, of course; it will spring directly and indirectly from policy decisions that will be made in the schools and the larger society. Although the present often does shape the future, there is a paradigm shift occurring in the schools that can eventually reshape the school of the future in very dramatic ways. It makes sense, therefore, to devote these last words to a brief examination of what this paradigm shift might mean for the design and implementation of stress interventions in the schools.

The term "paradigm" provides a sense of the dramatic shifts that are beginning to occur in schools and schooling. Applied to school reform, a paradigm is more than just a model. It reflects the unstated and stated assumptions, the rules and regulations, and the "worldview" that is shaping the way we view schools and schooling.

Kuhn (1970), who studied how scientific revolutions occur, has helped us to understand the impact of paradigms. He recognized that a paradigm defines the problems to be explored and the rules to be followed. A paradigm also points to new ways to organize facts, and helps to set new directions. Kuhn further asserts that a paradigm is such a part of our premises and overarching view that we often are not aware of it. For this reason, when a paradigm begins to crumble, because it no longer helps to solve problems, we often are not aware of what is happening. The concept of paradigm thus helps to explain the shift in assumptions, understandings, and values now emerging in efforts to improve schools and schooling. A paradigmatic shift in schools and schooling also provides the framework for the design and implementation of stress interventions in the schools.

The move toward outcome-based education is a case in point. This paradigm shift has not been linear, but it is evident in many ways (Finn, 1990). School reform reports in the past decade have increasingly focused on poor achievement, lack of preparation for the world of work, and poor performance in international comparisons. Increasingly, accountability for educational outcomes has become the dominant theme. Emphasis on traditional test scores is a part of the new paradigm but in no way represents the extensiveness of the shift. For example, emphasis on site-management and flexibility in how outcomes are reached is part of the paradigm shift. In essence, there is the implication in this paradigm shift that it is no longer critical *to prescribe how* schools reach outcomes, but to determine *whether* they reach them.

It also is evident that outcome-based education is increasingly coming to mean a specific paradigm for transforming schools that focuses all instructional programs and operating structures around obtaining educational outcomes of significance (Spady, 1988; Spady & Marshall, 1991). Outcome-based education proponents ask what knowledge, skills, and orientation students will need in order to be prepared to live in the 21st century. The curriculum then is "designed down" from these outcomes so that programs are structured to equip all students to demonstrate mastery of the desired culminating outcomes.

This means that the question of the types of outcomes with which we are to be concerned is inherent in any discussion of outcome-based education. When outcomes are defined in terms of what is learned, the intended outcomes must also be set forth with care. Although school reform has mostly focused on achievement test scores, concern increasingly needs to be expressed about the lack of emphasis on social and affective outcomes, and for greater recognition of the complex interrelationships among cognitive, social, and affective processes and outcomes. Thus this emerging paradigm shift offers school psychologists and other professionals and community leaders a unique opportunity to make stress relief for students, teachers, and parents a key part of the outcome-based education provided by the school of the future.

REFERENCES

Abbott, D. A., & Meredith, W. H. (1986). Strength of parents with retarded children. *Family Relations, 35,* 371-375.

Ahrentzen, S., & Evans, G. W. (1984). Distraction, privacy, and classroom design. *Environment and Behavior, 16,* 437-454.

Aiello, J. R., Thompson, D. E., & Baum, A. (1985). Children, crowding, and control: Effects of environmental stress on social behavior. In J. F. Wohlwill & W. van Kliet (Eds.), *Habitats for children: The impacts of density* (pp. 97-124). Hillsdale, NJ: Erlbaum.

Aldwin, C. M., & Revenson, T. A. (1987). Does coping help? A reexamination of the relation between coping and mental health. *Journal of Personality and Social Psychology, 53,* 337-348.

Allen, D. A., & Hudd, S. S. (1987). Are we professionalizing parents?: Weighing the benefits and pitfalls. *Mental Retardation, 25,* 133-139.

Altemeier, D. A., O'Connor, S., Vietze, P. M., Sandler, H. M., & Sherrod, K. B. (1982). Antecedents of child abuse. *Journal of Pediatrics, 100,* 823-829.

Altman, L. K., & Rosenthal, E. (1990, February 18). Changes in medicine bring pain to healing profession. *New York Times,* p. A1.

American Association for the Advancement of Science. (1989). *Science for all Americans: A project 2061 report on literacy goals in science, mathematics, and technology.* Washington, DC: Author.

Anesko, J. R., & O'Leary, S. G. (1982). Effectiveness of brief parent training for the management of children's homework problems. *Child and Family Behavior Therapy, 4,* 112-122

Anesko, J. R., Schoiock, G., Ramirez, R., & Levine, F. M. (1987). The homework problems checklist: Assessing children's homework difficulties. *Behavioral Assessment, 9,* 179-185

Anesko, K. M., & Levine, F. M. (1987). *Winning the homework war.* New York: Simon and Schuster.

224   STRESS IN STUDENTS, TEACHERS, AND PARENTS

Anthony, E. J. (1978). From birth to breakdown: A prospective study of vulnerability. In E. J. Anthony, C. Koupernik, & C. Chiland (Eds.), *The child in his family: Vulnerable children* (pp. 273- 285). New York: Wiley.

Anthony, E. J., & Cohler, B. J. (Eds.). (1987). *The invulnerable child.* New York: Guilford Press.

Anthrop, J., & Allison, M.T. (1983). Role conflict and the high school female athlete. *Research Quarterly for Exercise and Sport, 54,* 104-111.

Arnold, L. E. (Ed.). (1990). *Childhood stress.* New York: Wiley.

Bak, J. J., & Siperstein, G. N. (1987). Perceived similarity as a factor affecting change in children's attitudes toward mentally retarded peers. *American Journal of Mental Deficiency, 91,* 524-531.

Baker, S. P., O'Neill, B., & Karph, R. S. (1984). *The injury fact book.* Lexington, MA: Lexington Books.

Baltes, P. B. (1987). Theoretical propositions of life-span developmental psychology: On the dynamics between growth and decline. *Developmental Psychology, 23,* 611-626.

Bancroft, B. A., & Lezotte, L. W. (1985). Growing use of effective schools model for school improvement. *Educational Leadership, 42,* 23-27.

Bandura, A. (1986). *Social foundations of thought and action: A social cognitive theory.* Englewood Cliffs, NJ: Prentice-Hall.

Banez, G. A., & Compas, B. E. (1990). Children's and parents' daily stressful events and psychological symptoms. *Journal of Abnormal Child Psychology, 18,* 591-605.

Barker, R. G. (1968). *Ecological psychology: Concepts and methods for studying the environment of human behavior.* Stanford, CA: Stanford University Press.

Barker, R. G., & Schoggen, P. (1973). *Qualities of community life: Methods of measuring environment and behavior applied to an American and English town.* San Francisco: Jossey-Bass.

Barnett, R. C., Biener, L., & Baruch, G. K. (Eds.). (1987). *Gender and stress.* New York: Free Press/MacMillan.

Baum, A., Fleming, R., & Singer, J. E. (1983). Coping with victimization by technological disaster. *Journal of Social Issues, 39,* 117-138.

Baum, A., & Singer, J. E. (Eds.). (1982). *Handbook of psychology and health: Issues in child health and adolescent health* (Vol. 2). Hillsdale, NJ: Erlbaum.

Bayh, B. (1979). Battered schools: Violence and vandalism in public education. *Viewpoints in Teaching and Learning, 5,* 1-17.

Becher, R. M. (1986). Parent involvement: A review of research and principles of successful practice. In L. G. Katz (Ed.), *Current topics in early childhood education* (Vol. VI, pp. 85-122). Norwood, NJ: Ablex.

Beck, C. L., & Gorgiulo, R. M. (1983). Burnout in teachers of retarded and nonretarded children. *Journal of Educational Research, 76,* 169-173.

Beckman, P. J., & Pokorni, J. L. (1988). A longitudinal study of families of preterm infants: Changes in stress and support over the first two years. *Journal of Special Education, 22,* 55-65.

Belle, D. (Ed.). (1989). *Children's social networks and social supports.* New York: Wiley.

Benedek, E. P. (1985). Children and psychic trauma: A brief review of contemporary thinking. In S. Eth & R. S. Pynoos (Eds.), *Post-Traumatic Stress Disorder in children* (pp. 1-16). Washington, DC: American Psychiatric Association.

Bergan, J. R., & Kratochwill, T. R. (1990). *Behavioral consultation and therapy.* New York: Plenum Press.

Berliner, D C. (1983). Developing conceptions of classroom environments: Some light on the T in classroom studies of ATI. *Educational Psychologist, 18,* 1-13.

Berry, G. L., & Chiappelli, F. (1985). The state of the economy and the psychosocial development of the school-age child. *Elementary School Guidance and Counseling, 19,* 300-306.

Berry, J. W. (1989). Psychology of acculturation. In J. Berman (Ed.), *Nebraska symposium on motivation* (Vol. 37, pp. 201-234). Lincoln: University of Nebraska Press.

Berry, J. W., & Kim, U. (1988). Acculturation and mental health. In P. Dasen, J. W. Berry, & N. Sartorius (Eds.), *Health and cross-cultural psychology: Towards application* (pp. 207-236). London: Sage.

Berry, J. W., Kim, U., Minde, T., & Mok, D. (1987). Comparative studies of acculturative stress. *International Migration Review, 21,* 491-511.

Bigelow, B. J., Lewko, J. H., & Salhani, L. (1989). Sport-involved children's friendship expectations. *Journal of Sport and Exercise Psychology, 11,* 152-160.

Billings, A. G., & Moos, R. H. (1981). The role of coping responses and social resources in attenuating the stress of life events. *Journal of Behavioral Medicine, 4,* 139-157.

Black, M. M., Molaison, V. A., & Small, M. W. (1990). Families caring for a young adult with mental retardation: Service needs and urgency of community living requests. *American Journal of Mental Retardation, 95,* 32-39.

Blase, J. J. (1986). A qualitative analysis of sources of teacher stress: Consequences for performance. *American Educational Research Journal, 23,* 13-40.

Bleuler, M. (1978). *The schizophrenic disorders: Long-term patient and family studies.* New Haven: Yale University Press.

Block, A. (1977). The battered teacher. *Today's Education, 66,* 58-62.

Blyth, D. A., Simmons, R. G., & Zakin, D. F. (1985). Satisfaction with body image for early adolescent females: The impact of puberty timing within different school environments. *Journal of Youth and Adolescence, 14,* 207-225.

Bond, L. A., & Compas, B. E. (1989). *Primary prevention and promotion in the schools.* Newbury Park, CA: Sage.

Bond, L. A., & Wagner, B. M. (Eds.). (1988). *Families in transition: Primary prevention programs that work.* Newbury Park, CA: Sage.

Botvin, G. J., & Tortu, S. (1988). Preventing adolescent substance abuse through life skills training. In R. H. Price, E. L. Cowen, R. P. Lorion, & J. Ramos-McKay (Eds.), *Fourteen ounces of prevention: A casebook for practitioners* (pp. 98-110). Washington, DC: American Psychological Association.

Boukydis, C. F. Z. (Ed.). (1987). *Research on support for parents and infants in the postnatal period.* Norwood, NJ: Ablex.
Boyer, E. L. (1988). *Report card on school reform.* Princeton, NJ: Carnegie Foundation for the Advancement of Teaching.
Boyer, E. L. (1991). *Ready to learn.* Princeton, NJ: Carnegie Foundation for the Advancement of Learning.
Bramson, R. M. (1981). *Coping with difficult people.* New York: Doubleday.
Brassard, M. R., Germain, R., & Hart, S. N. (1987). *Psychological maltreatment of children and youth.* New York: Pergamon Press.
Brenner, A. (1984). *Helping children cope with stress.* Lexington, MA: Lexington Books.
Brickman, P., Rabinowitz, V. C., Karuza, J. Jr., Coates, D., Cohen, E., & Kidder, L. (1982). Models of helping and coping. *American Psychologist, 37,* 368-384.
Brodbelt, S. (1978). The epidemic of school violence. *The Clearing House, 51,* 383-388.
Brodzinsky, D. M., Singer, L. M., & Braff, A. M. (1984). Children's understanding of adoption. *Child Development, 55,* 869-878.
Bronfenbrenner, U. (1979). Contexts of child rearing: Problems and prospects. *American Psychologist, 34,* 844-850.
Bronfenbrenner, U. (1986). Ecology of the family as a context for human development: Research perspectives. *Developmental Psychology, 22,* 723-742.
Brooks, A. E. (1989). *Children of fast-track parents.* New York: Viking.
Brooks-Gunn, J., & Furstenberg, F. F., Jr. (1989). Adolescent sexual behavior. *American Psychologist, 44,* 249-257.
Brooks-Gunn, J., & Ruble, D. N. (1983). The experience of menarche from a developmental perspective. In J. Brooks-Gunn & A. C. Peterson (Eds.), *Girls at puberty: Biological and psychosocial perspectives* (pp. 155-177). New York: Plenum Press.
Brooks-Gunn, J., Samelson, M., Warren, M. P., & Fox, R. (1986). Physical similarity of and disclosure of menarcheal status to friends: Effects of age and pubertal status. *Journal of Early Adolescence, 6,* 3-14.
Brooks-Gunn, J., & Warren, M. P. (1988). The psychological significance of secondary sexual characteristics in 9- to 11- year-old girls. *Child Development, 59,* 161-169.
Brooks-Gunn, J., & Zahaykevich, M. (1989). Parent-child relationships in early adolescence: A developmental perspective. In K. Kreppner & R. M Lerner (Eds.), *Family systems and life-span development* (pp. 223-246). Hillsdale, NJ: Erlbaum.
Brophy, J. E. (1983). Research on the self-fulfiling prophecy and teacher expectations. *Journal of Educational Psychology, 75,* 631-661.
Brown, D., Pryzwansky, W., & Schulte, A. (1990). *Psychological consultation* (2nd ed.). Needham Heights, MA: Allyn & Bacon.
Brown, J. D., & Lawton, M. (1986). Stress and well-being in adolescence: The moderating role of physical exercise. *Journal of Human Stress, 12,* 125-131.

Browne, A. B., & Finkelhor, D. (1986). Impact of child sexual abuse: A review of the research. *Psychological Bulletin, 99,* 66-77.

Browne, D. H. (1986). The role of stress in the commission of subsequent acts of child abuse and neglect. *Journal of Family Violence, 1,* 289-297.

Buck, M. R. (1977). Peer counseling in an urban high school setting. *Journal of School Psychology, 15,* 362-366.

Business Advisory Commission. (1985). *Reconnecting youth, the next state of reform: A report.* Denver, CO: Education Commission of the States.

Butterworth, G., & Bryant, P. (Eds.). (1990). *Causes of development: Interdisciplinary perspectives.* Hillsdale, NJ: Erlbaum.

Canter, L., & Hausner, C. (1987). *Homework without tears: A parent guide for motivating children to do homework and succeed in school.* New York: Harper and Row.

Caplan, N., Choy, M. H., & Whitmore, J. K. (1992). Indochinese refugee families and academic achievement. *Scientific American, 266,* 36-42.

Carnegie Council on Adolescent Development. (1989). *Turning points: Preparing America's youth for the 21st century.* New York: Carnegie Corporation of New York.

Carnegie Foundation for the Advancement of Teaching. (1988). *The condition of teaching: A state-by-state analysis, 1988.* Princeton, NJ: Author.

Carnegie Task Force on Teaching as a Profession. (1986). *A nation prepared: Teachers for the 21st century.* New York: Carnegie Foundation for the Advancement of Teaching.

Carriere, R. (1979). Peer violence forces kids out of school. *The American School Board Journal, 166,* 35-36.

Carter, L. F. (1984). The sustaining effects study of compensatory and elementary education. *Educational Researcher, 13,* 4-13.

Caruso, C. M., Gill, D. L., Dzewaltowski, D. A., & McElroy, M. A. (1990). Psychological and physiological changes in competitive state anxiety during noncompetition and competitive success and failure. *Journal of Sport and Exercise Psychology, 12,* 6-20.

Cauce, A. M., & Srebnik, D. S. (1989). Peer networks and social support: A focus for preventive efforts with youth. In L. Bond & B. Compas (Eds.), *Primary prevention and promotion in the schools, Primary prevention of psychopathology* (Vol. 12, pp. 235-254). Newbury Park, CA: Sage.

Cazden, C. B. (1988). *Classroom discourse: The language of teaching and learning.* Portsmouth, NH: Heinemann.

Chandler, L. A. (1985a). *Assessing stress in children.* New York: Praeger.

Chandler, L. A. (1985b). *Children under stress: Understanding emotional adjustment reactions* (2nd ed.). Springfield, IL: Charles C. Thomas.

Chandler, L. A., Million, M. E., & Shermis, M. D. (1985). The incidence of stressful events of elementary school-aged children. *American Journal of Community Psychology, 13,* 743-746.

Chandler, L. A., & Shermis, M. D. (1986). Behavioral responses to stress: Profile patterns of children. *Journal of Clinical Child Psychology, 15,* 317-323.

Cheatham, A. (1988). *Directory of school mediation and conflict resolution programs.* Amherst, MA: National Association of Mediation in Education.

Cherniss, C. (1980). *Professional burnout in human service organizations.* New York: Praeger.

Cherniss, C. (1985). Stress, burnout, and the special services provider. *Special Services in the Schools, 2,* 45-61.

Children's Defense Fund. (1986). *Preventing adolescent pregnancy: What schools can do.* Washington, DC: Author.

Cicchetti, D., & Schneider-Rosen, K. (1986). An organizational approach to childhood depression. In M. Rutter, C. E. Izard, & P. B. Read (Eds.), *Depression in young people* (pp. 71-134). New York: Guilford Press.

Clarke-Stewart, A. (1989). Infant day care: Maligned or malignant? *American Psychologist, 44,* 266-273.

Cloninger, C. R., & Gottesman, I. I. (1987). Genetic and environmental factors in antisocial behavior disorders. In S. Mednick, T. Moffit, & S. Stack (Eds.), *The causes of crime* (pp. 92-109). New York: Cambridge University Press.

Clune, W. H., & Witte, J. F. (Eds.). (1990). *Choice and control in American education.* Philadelphia: Falmer Press.

Cohen, L. H. (1988). *Life events and psychological functioning: Theoretical and methodological issues.* Newbury Park, CA: Sage.

Cohen, L. H., Burt, C. E., & Bjorck, J. (1987). Life stress and adjustment: Effects of life events experienced by young adolescents and their parents. *Developmental Psychology, 23,* 583-592.

Cohen, M., Adler, N., Beck, A., & Irwin, C. E. (1986). Parental reactions to the onset of adolescence. *Journal of Adolescent Health Care, 7,* 101-106.

Collins, A. (1991). The role of computer technology in restructuring schools. *Phi Delta Kappan, 73,* 28-36.

Colten, M. E., Gore, S., & Aseltine, J. (1991). The patterning of distress and disorder in a community sample of high school aged youth. In M. E. Colten & S. Gore (Eds.), *Adolescent stress: Causes and consequences* (pp. 157-180). New York: Aldine de Gruyter.

Comer, J. P. (1980). *School power.* New York: Free Press.

Comer, J. P. (1986). Parent participation in the schools. *Phi Delta Kappan, 67,* 442-446.

Commission on Work, Family, and Citizenship. (1988a). *Non-college youth in America.* Washington, DC: William T. Grant Foundation.

Commission on Work, Family, and Citizenship. (1988b). *The forgotten half: Pathways to success for America's youth and young families.* Washington, DC: William T. Grant Foundation.

Committee for Economic Development. (1985). *Investing in our children: Business and the public schools, a policy statement.* Washington, DC: Research and Policy Council.

Community Board Program. (1987). *Conflict resolution: A secondary school curriculum.* San Francisco, CA: The Community Board Program.

Compas, B. E. (1987a). Coping with stress during childhood and adolescence. *Psychological Bulletin, 101*, 393-403.

Compas, B. E. (1987b). Stress and life events during childhood and adolescence. *Clinical Psychology Review, 7*, 275-302.

Compas, B. E., Davis, G. E., & Forsythe, C. J. (1985). Characteristics of life events during adolescence. *American Journal of Community Psychology, 13*, 677-691.

Compas, B. E., Davis, G. E., Forsythe, C. J., & Wagner, B. M. (1987c). Assessment of major and daily stressful events during adolescence: The adolescent perceived events scale. *Journal of Consulting and Clinical Psychology, 55*, 534-541.

Compas, B. E., & Wagner, B. M. (1991). Psychosocial stress during adolescence: Intrapersonal and interpersonal processes. In M. E. Colten & S. Gore (Eds.), *Adolescent stress: Causes and consequences* (pp. 67-85). New York: Aldine de Gruyter.

Coner-Edwards, A. F., & Spurlock, J. (Eds.). (1988). *Black families in crisis: The middle class.* New York: Brunner/Mazel.

Conoley, J. C. (1987). Schools and families: Theoretical and practical bridges. *Professional School Psychology, 2*, 191-203.

Conrad, D., & Hedin, D. (1991). School-based community service: What we know from research and theory. *Phi Delta Kappan, 72*, 743-749.

Constable, J. F., & Russell, D. (1986). The effect of social support and the work environment on burnout among nurses. *Journal of Human Stress, 12*, 20-26.

Cooper, H. (1989). *Homework.* White Plains, NY: Longman.

Coyne, J. C., & Downey, G. (1991). Social factors and psychopathology: Stress, social support, and coping processes. *Annual Review of Psychology, 42*, 401-425.

Craig, S. E. (1992). The educational needs of children living with violence. *Phi Delta Kappan, 74*, 67-71.

Cremin, L. A. (1988). *American education: The metropolitan experience, 1876-1980.* New York: Harper and Row.

Crittenden, P. M. (1985). Social networks, quality of child rearing, and child development. *Child Development, 56*, 1299-1313.

Crnic, K. A., Friedrich, W. N., & Greenberg, M. T. (1983). Adaptation of families with mentally retarded children: A model of stress, coping, and family ecology. *American Journal of Mental Deficiency, 88*, 125-138.

Crockenberg, S., & McCluskey, K. (1986). Change in maternal behavior during the baby's first year of life. *Child Development, 57*, 746-753.

Csikszentmihalyi, M., & Larson, R. (1984). *Being adolescent: Conflict and growth in the teenage years.* New York: Basic Books.

Csikszentmihalyi, M., & Larson, R. (1987). Validity and reliability of the experience-sampling method. *The Journal of Nervous and Mental Disease, 175*, 526-536.

Cuban, L. (1989). The "at-risk" label and the problem of urban school reform. *Phi Delta Kappan, 70*, 780-794, 799-801.

Cullinan, D., & Epstein, M. H. (1984). Behavior problems of mentally retarded and nonretarded adolescent pupils. *School Psychology Review, 13,* 381-384.

Cunningham, W. G. (1983). Teacher burnout—solutions for the 1980's: A review of the literature. *The Urban Review, 15,* 37-51.

D'Amato, R. C., & Rothlisberg, B. A. (Eds.). (1992). *Psychological perspectives on intervention.* New York: Longman.

D'Arienzo, R. V., Moracco, J. C., & Krajewski, R. J. (1982). *Stress in teaching: A comparison of perceived occupational stress factors between special education and regular classroom teachers.* Washington, DC: University Press of America, Inc.

D'Zurilla, T. J., & Goldfried, M. R. (1971). Problem solving and behavior modification. *Journal of Abnormal Psychology, 78,* 107-126.

Damon, W., & Phelps, E. (1989). Strategic uses of peer learning in children's education. In T. J. Berndt & G. W. Ladd (Eds.), *Peer relationships in child development* (pp. 135-157). New York: Wiley.

Darling, R. B. (1991). Parent-professional interaction: The roots of misunderstanding. In M. Seligman (Ed.), *The family with a handicapped child* (pp 119-149). Needham Heights, MA: Allyn & Bacon.

Darling-Hammond, L., & Berry, B. (1988). *The evolution of teacher policy.* Santa Ana, CA: RAND Corporation.

Dauber, S. L., & Epstein, J. L. (1989). *Parent attitudes and practices of parent involvement in inner-city elementary and middle schools* (Report No. 33). Baltimore, MD: The Johns Hopkins University Center for Research on Elementary and Middle Schools.

Davies, D. (1991). Schools reaching out: Family, school, and community partnerships for student success. *Phi Delta Kappan, 72,* 376-382.

Davis, J. M., Sandoval, J. & Wilson, M. P. (1988). Strategies for the primary prevention of adolescent suicide. *School Psychology Review, 17,* 559-569.

Davis, L. L. (1986). The role of the teacher in preventing child sexual abuse. In M. Nelson & K. Clark (Eds.), *The educator's guide to preventing child sexual abuse* (pp. 87-92). Santa Cruz, CA: Network Publications.

Dembo, M. H., & Gibson, S. (1985). Teachers' sense of efficacy: An important factor in school improvement. *The Elementary School Journal, 86,* 172-184.

Divoky, D. (1988). The model minority goes to school. *Phi Delta Kappan, 70,* 219-222.

Dohrenwend, B. P., & Dohrenwend, B. S. (1974). Overview and prospects for research on stressful life events. In B. S. Dohrenwend & B. P. Dohrenwend (Eds.), *Stressful life events: Their nature and effects* (pp. 313-331). New York: Wiley.

Dooley, D., Catalano, R., & Serxner, S. (1987). Economic development and community mental health. In L. A. Jason, R. E. Hess, R. D. Felner, & J. N. Moritsugu (Eds.), *Prevention: Toward a multidisciplinary approach* (pp. 91-115). New York: Haworth.

Dornbusch, S. M., Mont-Reynaud, R., Ritter, P. L., Chen, Z., & Streinberg, L. (1991). Stressful events and their correlates among adolescents of diverse backgrounds. In M. E. Colten & S. Gore (Eds.), *Adolescent stress: Causes and consequences* (pp. 111-130). New York: Aldine de Gruyter.

Dryfoos, J. G. (1990). *Adolescents at risk: Prevalence and prevention.* New York: Oxford University Press.

Dubrow, N., & Garbarino, J. (1988). Living in the war zone: Mothers and young children in a housing project. *Child Welfare, 68,* 3- 20.

Dugan, T. F., & Coles, R. (1989). *The child in our times: Studies in the development of resilience.* New York: Brunner/Mazel.

Dunham, J. (1980). An exploratory comparative study of staff in English and German comprehensive schools. *Educational Review, 32,* 11-20.

Dunham, J. (1984). *Stress in teaching.* New York: Nichols.

Dunn, J., & Plomin, R. (1990). *Separate lives: Why siblings are so different.* New York: Basic Books.

Eaton, J. W. (1980). Stress in social work practice. In C. L. Cooper & J. Marshall (Eds.), *White collar and professional stress* (pp. 167-185). New York: Wiley.

Education Research Group. (1987). *Teen pregnancy: Impact on the schools.* Alexandria, VA: Capitol Publications.

Education Writers Association. (1989). *Wolves at the schoolhouse door.* Washington, DC: Education Writers Association.

Edwards, J. R. (1988). The determinants and consequences of coping with stress. In C. L.Cooper & R. Payne (Eds.), *Causes, coping, and consequences of stress at work* (pp. 233-263). New York: Wiley.

Eisner, E. (1988). The ecology of school improvement. *Educational Leadership, 45,* 24-29.

Elder, G. H., Jr. (1974). *Children of the Great Depression: Social change in life experience.* Chicago: University of Chicago Press.

Elias, M. J. (1989). Schools as a source of stress to children: An analysis of causal and ameliorative influences. *Journal of School Psychology, 27,* 393-407.

Elias, M. J. (1991). A multilevel action-research perspective on stress-related interventions. In M. E. Colten & S. Gore (Eds.), *Adolescent stress: Causes and consequences* (pp. 261-279). New York: Aldine de Gruyter.

Elias, M. J., & Clabby, J. F. (1989). *Social decision making skills: A curriculum guide for the elementary grades.* Rockville, MD: Aspen.

Elias, M. J., & Clabby, J. F. (1991). *School-based enhancement of children and adolescents' social problem solving skills.* San Francisco: Jossey-Bass.

Elias, M. J., Gara, M., & Ubriaco, M. (1985). Sources of stress and support in children's transition to middle school: An empirical analysis. *Journal of Clinical Child Psychology, 14,* 112-118.

Elias, M. J., Gara, M., Ubriaco, M., Rothbaum, P. A., Clabby, J. F., & Schuyler, T. (1986). The impact of a preventive social problem solving intervention on children's coping with middle school stressors. *American Journal of Community Psychology, 14,* 259-275.

Elkind, D. (1988). *The hurried child: Growing up too fast too soon* (Rev. ed.). Reading, MA: Addison-Wesley.

Epstein, J. L. (1983). Longitudinal effects of family-school-person interactions on student outcomes. In A. Kerckhoff (Ed.), *Research in sociology of education and socialization* (pp. 90- 130). Greenwich, CT: JAI Press.

Epstein, J. L. (1986). Parents' reactions to teacher practices of parent involvement. *The Elementary School Journal, 86,* 277-294.

Epstein, J. L. (1987). Toward a theory of family-school connections: Teacher practices and parent involvement. In K. Hurrelman, F. Kaufman, & F. Losel (Eds.), *Social intervention: Potential and constraints* (pp. 121-136). New York: Aldine de Gruyter.

Epstein, J. L. (1989). The selection of friends: Changes across the grades and in different school environments. In T. J. Berndt & G. W. Ladd (Eds.), *Peer relationships in child development* (pp. 158-187). New York: Wiley.

Epstein, J. L., & Becker, H. J. (1982). Teachers' reported practices of parent involvement: Problems and possibilities. *The Elementary School Journal, 83,* 103-113.

Epstein, Y. M. (1982). Crowding stress and human behavior. In G. W. Evans (Ed.), *Environmental stress* (pp. 133-148). Cambridge, UK: Cambridge University Press.

Erickson, M., & Upshur, C. C. (1989). Caretaking burden and social support: Comparison of mothers of infants with and without disabilities. *American Journal on Mental Retardation, 94,* 250-258.

Etzioni, D., & Pines, A. (1986). Sex and culture in burnout and coping among human service professionals: A social psychological perspective. *Journal of Cross-Cultural Psychology, 17,* 191-209.

Factor, D. C., Perry, A., & Freeman, N. (1990). Brief report: Stress, social support, and respite care in families with austistic children. *Journal of Autism and Developmental Disorders, 20,* 139-146.

Faller, K. C. (1984). Is the child victim of sexual abuse telling the truth? *Child Abuse and Neglect, 8,* 473-481.

Farber, B. A. (1984). Teacher burnout: Assumptions, myths, and issues. *Teachers College Record, 86,* 321-338.

Farber, B. A. (1991). *Crisis in education: Stress and burnout in the American teacher.* San Francisco: Jossey-Bass.

Farber, B. A., & Miller, J. (1981). Teacher burnout: A psychoeducational perspective. *Teachers College Record, 82,* 235-243.

Farran, D. C., Metzger, J., & Sparling, J. (1986). Immediate and continuing adaptation in parents of handicapped children. In J. J. Gallagher & P. M. Vietze (Eds.), *Families of handicapped persons: Research, programs, and policy issues* (pp. 143-166). Baltimore: Paul H. Brookes.

Felner, M. T., Primavera, J., & Cauce, A. M. (1981). The impact of school transitions: A focus for preventive efforts. *American Journal of Community Psychology, 10,* 277-290.

Felner, R. D., Ginter, M., & Primavera, J. (1982). Primary prevention during school transitions: Social support and environmental structure. *American Journal of Community Psychology, 10,* 277-290.

Felton, B. J., & Revenson, T. A. (1984). Coping with chronic illness: A study of illness controllability and the influence of coping strategies on psychological adjustment. *Journal of Consulting and Clinical Psychology, 52,* 343-353.

Feltz, D. L. (1988). Self-confidence and sports performance. In K. B. Pandolf (Ed.), *Exercise and sport science reviews* (Vol. 16, pp. 423-457). New York: Macmillan.

Feltz, D. L., & Albrecht, R. R. (1986). Psychological implications of competitive running. In M. R. Weiss & D. Gould (Eds.), *Sport for children and youth* (pp. 225-230). Champaign, IL: Human Kinetics.

Finkelhor, D. (1986). *A source book on child sexual abuse.* Beverly Hills, CA: Sage.

Finkelhor, D. (1987). The trauma of child sexual abuse: Two models. *Journal of Interpersonal Violence, 2,* 348-366.

Finn, C. E. (1990). The biggest reform of all. *Phi Delta Kappan, 71,* 584-592.

Fleming, R., Baum, A., & Singer, J. E. (1984). Toward an integrative approach to the study of stress. *Journal of Personality and Social Psychology, 46,* 939-949.

Flynt, S. W., & Wood, T. A. (1989). Stress and coping of mothers of children with moderate retardation. *American Journal on Mental Retardation, 94,* 278-283.

Folkman, S., & Lazarus, R. S. (1985). If it changes it must be a process: Study of emotion and coping during three stages of a college examination. *Journal of Personality and Social Psychology, 48,* 150-170.

Folkman, S., & Lazarus, R. S. (1988a). Coping as a mediator of emotion. *Journal of Personality and Social Psychology, 54,* 466- 475.

Folkman, S., & Lazarus, R. S. (1988b). The relation between coping and emotion: Implications for theory and research. *Social Science and Medicine, 26,* 309-317.

Ford, D. L. (1985). Facets of work support and employee work outcomes: An exploratory study. *Journal of Management, 11,* 5-20.

Forman, S. G. (Ed.). (1987). *School-based affective and social interventions.* New York: Haworth.

Forman, S. G., & Cecil, M. A. (1986). Teacher stress: Causes, effects, interventions. In T. R. Kratochwill (Ed.), *Advances in school psychology* (Vol. 5, pp. 203-229). Hillsdale, NJ: Erlbaum.

Forman, S. G., & O'Malley, P. (1984). School stress and anxiety interventions. *School Psychology Review, 13,* 162-170.

Foster, M., Berger, M., & McLean, M. (1981). Rethinking a good idea: A reassessment of parent involvement. *Topics in Early Childhood Special Education, 1,* 55-65.

Freud, A., & Burlingham, D. (1943). *War and children.* New York: Ernest Willard.

Frey, K. S., Fewell, R. R., & Vadasy, P. F. (1988). Parental adjustment and changes in child outcome among families of young handicapped children. *Topics in Early Childhood Special Education, 8,* 38-57.

Frey, K. S., Greenberg, M. T., & Fewell, R. R. (1989). Stress and coping among parents of handicapped chiildren: A multidimensional approach. *American Journal on Mental Retardation, 94,* 240-249.

Friedrich, W. N., & Friedrich, W. L. (1981). Psychosocial assets of parents of handicapped and nonhandicapped children. *American Journal of Mental Deficiency, 85,* 551-553.

Frymier, J. (1989). *A study of students at risk: Collaborating to do research.* Bloomington, IN: Phi Delta Kappa Educational Foundation.

Furham, A., & Bochner, S. (1986). *Culture shock: Psychological reactions to unfamiliar environments.* New York: Methuen.

Furstenberg, F. F., Jr., Brooks-Gunn, J., & Chase-Lansdale, L. (1989). Teenaged pregnancy and childbearing. *American Psychologist, 44,* 313-320.

Futcher, J. A. (1988). Chronic illness and family dynamics. *Pediatric Nursing, 14,* 381-385.

Gallagher, J. J. (1989). A new policy initiative: Infants and toddlers with handicapping conditions. *American Psychologist, 44,* 387-391.

Gamoran, A., & Berends, M. (1987). The effects of stratification in secondary schools: Synthesis of survey and ethnographic research. *Review of Educational Research, 57,* 415-435.

Gandra, P. (1982). Passing through the eye of the needle: High achieving Chicanas. *Hispanic Journal of Behavioral Sciences, 4,* 167-180.

Garbarino, J. (1988). Preventing childhood injury: Developmental and mental health issues. *American Journal of Orthopsychiatry, 58,* 25-45.

Garbarino, J., Kostelny, K., & Dubrow, N. (1991). What children can tell us about living in danger. *American Psychologist, 46,* 376-383.

Garmezy, N. (1981). Children under stress: Perspectives on antecedents and correlates of vulnerability and resistance to psychopathology. In A. I. Rabin, J. Aronoff, A. M. Barclay, & R. A. Zucker (Eds.), *Further explorations in personality* (pp. 196- 270). New York: Wiley.

Garmezy, N. (1983). Stressors in childhood. In N. Garmezy & M. Rutter (Eds.), *Stress, coping, and development in children* (pp. 43-84). New York: McGraw-Hill.

Garmezy, N., & Masten, A. M. (1986). Stress, competence, and resilience: Common frontiers for therapist and psychopathologist. *Behavior Therapy, 17,* 500-521.

Garmezy, N., & Masten, A. (1990). The adaptation of children to a stressful world: Mastery of fear. In L. E. Arnold (Ed.), *Childhood stress* (pp. 459-473). New York: Wiley.

Garmezy, N., Masten, A. M., & Tellegen, A. (1984). The study of stress and competence in children: A building block for developmental psychopathology. *Child Development, 55,* 97-111.

Garmezy, N., & Rutter, M. (Eds.). (1983). *Stress, coping, and development in children.* New York: McGraw-Hill.

Gass, K. A., & Chang, A. S. (1989). Appraisals of bereavement, coping, resources, and psychosocial health dysfunction in widows and widowers. *Nursing Research, 38,* 31-36.

Gelles, R. (1987). The family and its role in the abuse of children. *Psychiatric Annals, 17,* 229-232.

Gerber, P. J., Banbury, M. M., Miller, J. H., & Griffin, L. (1986). Special educators' perceptions of parental participation in the individual education plan process. *Psychology in the Schools, 23,* 158-163.

Gibbs, J. (1986). Assessment of depression in urban adolescent females: Implications for early intervention strategies. *American Journal of Social Psychiatry, 6,* 50-56.

Gibson, M. A. (1987). Punyabi immigrants in an American high school. In G. D. Spindler & L. S. Spindler (Eds.), *Interpretative ethnography of education: At home and abroad* (pp. 281-310). Hillsdale, NJ: Erlbaum.

Gilchrist, L. D., & Schinke, S. P. (1983). Coping with contraception: Cognitive and behavioral methods with adolescents. *Cognitive Theory and Research, 7,* 379-388.

Gilchrist, L. D., Schinke, S. P., Trimble, J. E., & Cvetkovich, G. T. (1987). Skill enhancement to prevent substance abuse among American Indian adolescents. *International Journal of Addiction, 22,* 869-879.

Gill, D. L., & Gross, J. B. (1979). The influence of group success-failure on selected intrapersonal variables. In K. M. Newell & G. C. Roberts (Eds.), *Psychology of motor behavior and sport* (pp. 61-71). Champaign, IL: Human Kinetics.

Gill, D. L., & Martens, R. (1977). The role of task type and success-failure in group competition. *Journal of Sport Psychology, 8,*160-177.

Glenn, H. S., & Nelson, J. (1988). *Raising self-reliant children in a self-indulgent world.* Rocklin, CA: Prima.

Glidden, L. M. (1989). *Parents for children, children for parents: The adoption alternative.* Washington, DC: American Association on Mental Retardation.

Gold, Y. (1985). The relationship of six personal and life history variables to standing on three dimensions of the Maslach Burnout Inventory in a sample of elementary and junior high school teachers. *Educational and Psychological Measurement, 45,* 377-387.

Goldberg, S., Morris, P., Simmons, R. J., Fowler, R. S., & Levison, H. (1990). Chronic illness in infancy and parenting stress: A comparison of three groups of parents. *Journal of Pediatric Psychology, 15,* 347-358.

Goldring, E. B. (1990). Principals' relationships with parents: The homogeneity versus the social class of the parent clientele. *The Urban Review, 22,* 1-15.

Goldstein, A. P., Apter, S. J., & Harootunian, B. (1984). *School violence.* Englewood Cliffs, NJ: Prentice-Hall.

Goodlad, J., & Oakes, J. (1988). We must offer equal access to knowledge. *Educational Leadership, 45,* 16-19.

Gordon, H. W., Corbin, E. D., & Lee, L. A. (1986). Changes in specialized cognitive function following changes in hormone levels. *Cortex, 22,* 399-415.

Gore, S. (1978). The effect of social support in moderating the health consequences of unemployment. *Journal of Health and Social Behavior, 19,* 157-165.

Gottesman, I. I., & Bertelson, A. (1989). Confirming unexpressed genotypes for schizophrenia. *Archives of General Psychiatry, 46,* 867-872.

Gottfredson, G. D., & Gottfredson, D. C. (1985). *Victimization in schools: Law, society, and policy* (Vol. 2). New York: Plenum Press.

Gottlieb, B. H. (1987). Using social support to protect and promote health. *Journal of Primary Prevention, 8,* 49-70.

Gottlieb, B. H. (Ed.). (1988). *Marshalling social support: Formats, processes and effects.* Newbury Park, CA: Sage.

Gould, D. (1982). Sport psychology in the 1980s: Status, direction, and challenge in youth sports research. *Journal of Sport Psychology, 4,* 203-218.

Gould, D., Horn, J., & Spreeman, J. (1983). Sources of stress in junior elite wrestlers. *Journal of Sport Psychology, 5,* 58-71.

Gowen, J. W., Johnson-Martin, N., Goldman, B. D., & Appelbaum, M. (1989). Feelings of depression and parenting competence of mothers of handicapped infants: A longitudinal study. *American Journal on Mental Retardation, 94,* 259-271.

Grannis, J. C. (1992). Students' stress, distress, and achievement in an urban intermediate school. *The Journal of Early Adolescence, 12,* 4-27.

Greendorfer, S. L. (1987). Gender bias in theoretical perspectives. *Psychology of Women Quarterly, 11,* 327-340.

Gunnar, M. R., & Thelen, E. (Eds.). (1989). *The Minnesota symposia on child psychology. Vol. 22: Systems and development.* Hillsdale, NJ: Erlbaum.

Hackfort, D., & Spielberger, C. D. (Eds.). (1989). *Anxiety in sports: An international perspective.* New York: Hemisphere.

Halpern, R., & Covey, L. (1983). Community support for adolescent parents and their children: The parent-to-parent program in Vermont. *Journal of Primary Prevention, 3,* 160-173.

Hanna, J. L. (1988). *Disruptive school behavior: Class, race, and culture.* New York: Holmes and Meier.

Hannah, M. E., & Midlarsky, E. (1985). Siblings of the handicapped: A literature review for school psychologists. *School Psychology Review, 14,* 510-520.

Harlan, J. P., & McDowell, C. P. (1981). Crime and disorder in the public schools. *Education Studies, 12,* 221-229.

Harris, L., and Associates (1988). *The Metropolitan Life survey of the American teacher.* New York: Metropolitan Life Insurance Company.

Harris, S. L., & Fong, P. L. (1985). Developmental disabilities: The family and the school. *School Psychology Review, 14,* 162-165.

Harris, V. S., & McHale, S. M. (1989). Family life problems, daily caregiving activities, and the psychological well-being of mothers of mentally retarded children. *American Journal on Mental Retardation, 94,* 231-239.

Hart, D., & Rechif, M. (1986). *Mind movers: Creative homework assignments, Grades 3-6.* Reading, MA: Addison-Wesley.

Harter, S. (1989). Causes, correlates, and the functional role of global self-worth: A life-span prespective. In J. H. Killigan & R. Sternberg (Eds.), *Perceptions of competence and incompetence across the life-span* (pp. 67-98). New Haven, CT: Yale University Press.

Hartup, W. W. (1983). Peer relations. In E. M. Hetherington (Ed.), *Handbook of child psychology. Vol. 4: Socialization, personality, and social development* (pp. 103-196). New York: Wiley.

Hartup, W. W. (1989). Social relationships and their developmental significance. *American Psychologist, 44,* 120-126.

Heft, H. (1985). High residential density and perceptual-cognitive development: An examination of the effects of crowding in the home. In J. F. Wohlwill & W. van Kliet (Eds.), *Habitats for children: The impacts of density* (pp. 39-76). Hillsdale, NJ: Erlbaum.

Helson, H. (1948). Adaptation-level as a basis for a quantitative theory of frames of reference. *Psychological Review, 55,* 297-313.

Hendren, R. L. (1990). Stress in adolescence. In L. E. Arnold (Ed.), *Childhood stress* (pp. 247-264). New York: Wiley.

Hepburn, J. R., & Monti, D J. (1979). Victimization, fear of crime, and adaptive reponses among high school students. In W. H. Parsonage (Ed.), *Perspectives on victimology* (pp. 121-132). Beverly Hills, CA: Sage.

Hess, G. A., Jr., & Greer, J. L. (1987). *Bending the twig: The elementary years and dropout rates in the Chicago Public Schools.* Chicago: Report of the Chicago Panel on Public School Policy and Finance.

Hetherington, E. M., Cox, M., & Cox, R. (1982). Effects of divorce on parents and children. In M. E. Lamb (Ed.), *Nontraditional families: Parenting and child development* (pp. 223-288). Hillsdale, NJ: Erlbaum.

Hewlett, S. (1991). *When the bough breaks: The cost of neglecting our children.* New York: Basic Books.

Higgins, E. T., & Parsons, J. E. (1983). Social cognition and the social life of the child: Stages as subcultures. In E. T. Higgins, D. Ruble, & W. Hartup (Eds.), *Social cognition and social development: A sociocultural perspective* (pp. 15-62). New York: Cambridge University Press.

Hill, K. D. (1986). Legal conflicts in special education: How competing paradigms in the Education for All Handicapped Children Act create litigation. *University of Detroit Law Review, 64,* 129-167.

Hill, J. P. (1988). Adapting to menarche: Familial control and conflict. In M. R. Gunnar & W. A. Collins (Eds.), *Development during the transition to adolescence: Minnesota symposia on child psychology* (Vol. 21, pp. 43-77). Hillsdale, NJ: Erlbaum.

Hirsch, B. J., & Rapkin, B. D. (1987). The transition to junior high school: A longitudinal study of self-esteem, psychological symptomatology, school life, and social support. *Child Development, 58,* 1235-1243.

Hodgkinson, H. (1991). Reform versus reality. *Phi Delta Kappan, 73,* 9-16.

Hoffman, M. A., Ushpiz, V., & Levy-Shiff, R. (1988). Social support and self-esteem in adolescence. *Journal of Youth and Adolescence, 17,* 307-316.

Holland, A. J., Hall, A., Murray, R., Russell, G. F. M., & Crisp, A. H. (1984). Anorexia nervosa: A study of 34 twins and one set of triplets. *British Journal of Psychiatry, 145,* 414-419.

Hollon, S. D., & Beck, A. T. (1979). Cognitive therapy in depression, In P. C. Kendall & S. D. Hollon (Eds.), *Cognitive behavioral interventions: Theory, research, and procedures* (pp. 153-203). New York: Academic Press.

Hollon, S. D., & Beck, A. T. (1986). Cognitive and cognitive-behavior therapies. In C. L. Garfield & A. E. Bergin (Eds.), *Handbook of psychotherapy and behavior change: An empirical analysis* (3rd ed.) (pp. 443-482). New York: Wiley.

Holroyd, J. (1987). *Questionnaire on resources and stress for families with chronically ill or handicapped members.* Brandon, VT: Clinical Psychology Publishing.

Holtzman, W. H. (Ed.). (1992). *The school of the future.* Austin, TX: Hogg Foundation for Mental Health and the American Psychological Association.

Hoover-Dempsey, K. V., & Brissie, J. S. (1987). Parent involvement: Contributions of teacher efficacy, school socioeconomic status, and other school characteristics. *American Educational Research Journal, 24,* 417-435.

Horne, M. (1983). Attitudes of elementary classroom teachers toward mainstreaming. *Exceptional Child, 30,* 93-98.

House, J. S. (1981). *Work stress and social support.* Reading, MA: Addison-Wesley.

House, J. S., Umberson, D., & Landis, K. R. (1988). Structures and processes of social support. *Annual Review of Sociology, 14,* 293-318.

Houston, H. (1989). Restructuring secondary schools. In A. Lieberman (Ed.). *Building a professional culture in schools* (pp. 109-128). New York: Teachers College Press.

Huebner, E. S. (1992). Burnout among school psychologists: An exploratory investigation into its nature, extent, and correlates. *School Psychology Quarterly, 7,* 129-136.

Humphrey, J. H., & Humphrey, J. N. (1985). *Controlling stress in children.* Springfield, IL: C. C. Thomas.

Hunt, D. E. (1987). *Beginning with ourselves: In practive, theory, and human affairs.* Cambridge, MA: Brookline Books.

Hurrelmann, K., & Losel, F. (Eds.). (1990). *Health hazards in adolescence.* Berlin: Walter de Gruyter.

Hutton, J. B., Roberts, T. G., Walker, J., & Zuniga, J. (1987). Ratings of severity of life events by ninth-grade students. *Psychology in the Schools, 24,* 63-68.

Imahori, T. T., & Lanigan, M. L. (1989). Relational model of intercultural communication competence. *International Journal of Intercultural Relations, 13,* 269-286.

Jaeger, R. M. (1992). World class standards, choice, and privatization: Weak measurement serving presumptive policy. *Phi Delta Kappan, 74,* 118-128.

Johnson, J. E. (1986). *Stressful life events in children and adolescents.* Beverly Hills, CA: Sage.

Johnson, T. C. (1992). *Sexualized children and children who molest.* Walnut Creek, CA: Launch Press.

Jones, J. G., & Hardy, L. (Eds.). (1990). *Stress and performance in sports.* New York: Wiley.

Kagan, J. (1982). *The nature of the child.* New York: Basic Books.

Kagan, J. (1983). Stress and coping in early development. In N. Garmezy & M. Rutter (Eds.), *Stress, coping, and development in children* (pp. 191-216). New York: McGraw-Hill.

Kalker, P. (1984). Teacher stress and burnout: Causes and coping strategies. *Contemporary Education, 56,* 16-19.

Kalter, N., Schaefer, M., Lesowitz, M., Alpern, D., & Pickar, J. (1988). School-based support groups for children of divorce. In B. H. Gottlieb (Ed.), *Marshal-*

ling social support: Formats, processes, and effects (pp. 165-186). Newbury Park, CA: Sage.

Kamerman, S. B. (1980). *Parenting in an unresponsive society.* New York: Free Press.

Karasek, R., & Theorell, T. (1990). *Healthy work: Stress, productivity, and the reconstruction of working life.* New York: Basic Books.

Kazak, A. E. (1986). Families with physically handicapped children: Social ecology and family systems. *Family Process, 25,* 265-281.

Kazak, A. E. (1987). Families with disabled children: Stress and social networks in three samples. *Journal of Abnormal Child Psychology, 15,* 137-146.

Kazak, A. E., & Marvin, R. S. (1984). Differences, difficulties and adaptation: Stress and social networks in families with a handicapped child. *Family Relations, 33,* 67-77.

Kearns, D. T., & Doyle, D. P. (1988). *Winning the brain race.* San Francisco: Institute for Contemporary Studies.

Keith, T. Z. (1987). Children and homework. In A. Thomas & J. Grimes (Eds.), *Children's needs: Psychological perspectives* (pp. 275-282). Washington, DC: National Association of School Psychologists.

Kellam, S. G., Ensminger, M. T., & Turner, R. J. (1977). Family structure and the mental health of children. *Archives of General Psychiatry, 34,* 1012-1022.

Kendler, K. S., Heath, A., Martin, N. G., & Eaves, L. J. (1987). Symptoms of anxiety and symptoms of depression: Same genes, different environments? *Archives of General Psychiatry, 44,* 451-457.

Kennedy, M. M., Birman, B. F., & Demaline, R. (1986). *The effectiveness of Chapter 1 services.* Washington, DC: Office of Educational Research and Improvement, U. S. Department of Education.

Kennedy, M. M., Jung, R. K., & Orland, M. E. (1986). *Poverty, achievement, and the distribution of compensatory education services.* Washington, DC: Office of Educational Research and Improvement, U. S. Department of Education.

Kessler, R. C., & Cleary, P. D. (1980). Social class and prolonged distress. *American Sociological Review, 45,* 463-478.

Kessler, R. C., House, J. S., & Turner, J. B. (1987). Unemployment and health in a community sample. *Journal of Health and Social Behavior, 28,* 51-59.

Kessler, R. C., & Neighbors, H. W. (1986). A new perspective on the relationships among race, social class, and psychological distress. *Journal of Health and Social Behavior, 27,* 107-115.

Kilberg, R. R., Nathan, P. E., & Thoreson, R. W. (Eds.). (1986). *Professionals in distress: Issues, syndromes, and solutions in psychology.* Washington, DC: American Psychological Association.

Kirk, W., & Walter, G. (1981). Teacher support groups serve to minimize burnout: Principles for organizing. *Education, 102,* 147-150.

Kirsch, I. S., & Jungeblut, A. (1986). *Literacy: Profiles of America's young adults.* Princeton, NJ: National Assessment of Educational Progress.

Kirst, M. W. (1991). Improving children's services: Overcoming barriers, creating opportunities. *Phi Delta Kappan, 72,* 615-618.

Kohn, M. L. (1977). *Class and conformity* (2nd ed.). Chicago: University of Chicago Press.

Kozol, J. (1991). *Savage inequalities.* New York: Crown/Random House.

Kratochwill, T. R., & Bergan, J. R. (1990). *Behavioral consultation in applied settings: An individual guide.* New York: Plenum Press.

Kremer-Hagon, L., & Kurtz, P. (1985). The relation of personal and environmental variables to teacher burnout. *Teaching and Teacher Education, 1,* 243-249.

Kroth, R. L. (1987). Mixed or missed messages between parents and professionals. *Volta Review, 89,* 1-10.

Kruger, L. J. (Ed.). (1990). *Promoting success with at-risk students: Emerging perspectives and practical approaches.* New York: Haworth.

Kuepper, J. E. (1987). *Homework helpers: A guide for parents offering assistance.* Minneapolis, MN: Educational Media.

Kuhn, T. S. (1970). *The structure of scientific revolutions* (2nd ed.). Chicago: University of Chicago Press.

Kyriacou, C. (1980). Coping actions and organizational stress among school teachers. *Research in Education, 24,* 57-61.

Kyriacou, C. (1987). Teacher stress and burnout: An international review. *Educational Researcher, 29,* 146-152.

Kyriacou, C. (1989). The nature and prevalence of teacher stress. In M. Cole & S. Walker (Eds.), *Teaching and stress* (pp. 27-34). Philadelphia: Open University Press.

Kyriacou, C., & Sutcliffe, J. (1978a). A model of teacher stress. *Educational Studies, 4,* 1-6.

Kyriacou, C., & Sutcliffe, J. (1978b). Teacher stress: Prevalence, sources, and symptoms. *British Journal of Educational Psychology, 48,* 159-167.

Ladd, G. W., & Mize, J. (1983). A cognitive-social learning model of social-skill training. *Psychological Review, 90,* 127-157.

Lancaster, J. B., & Hamberg, B. A. (Eds.). (1986). *School-age pregnancy and parenthood: Biosocial dimensions.* New York: Aldine de Gruyter.

Larson, R., & Asmussen, L. (1991). Anger, worry, and hurt in early adolescence: An enlarging world of negative emotions. In M. E. Colten & S. Gore (Eds.), *Adolescent stress: Causes and consequences* (pp. 21-41). New York: Aldine de Gruyter.

Larson, R., & Lampman-Petraitis, C. (1989). Daily emotional stress as reported by children and adolescents. *Child Development, 60,* 1250-1260.

Larson, R., Raffaelli, M., Richards, M. H., Ham, M., & Jewell, L. (1990). The ecology of depression in early adolescence. *Journal of Abnormal Psychology, 99,* 92-102.

Lazarowitz, R., Baird, J. H., Hertz-Lazarowitz, R., & Jenkins, J. (1985). The effects of modified jigsaw on achievement, classroom social climate, and self-esteem in high-school science classes. In R. Slavin, S. Sharan, R. Hertz-Lazarowitz, C. Webb, & R. Schmuck (Eds.), *Learning to cooperate, cooperating to learn* (pp. 231- 248). New York: Plenum.

Lazarus, R. S. (1991a). Cognition and motivation in emotion. *American Psychologist, 46,* 352-367.

Lazarus, R. S. (1991b). Progress on a cognitive-motivational-relational theory of emotion. *American Psychologist, 46,* 352-367.

Lazarus, R. S., & Folkman, S. (1984). *Stress, appraisal and coping.* New York: Springer.

Lerner, J. V., Baker, N., & Lerner, R. M. (1985). A person-context goodness of fit model of adjustment. In P. C. Kendall (Ed.), *Advances in cognitive-behavioral research and therapy* (Vol. 4, pp. 111-136). New York: Academic Press.

Lerner, R. M. (1986). *Concepts and theories of human development* (2nd ed.). New York: Random House.

Lewin, K. (1951). *Field theory in social science.* Chicago: University of Chicago Press.

Lewis, C. E., Siegel, J. M., & Lewis, M. A. (1984). Feeling bad: Exploring sources of distress among pre-adolescent children. *American Journal of Public Health, 74,* 117-122.

Leyser, Y. (1985). Parent involvement in school: A survey of parents of handicapped children. *Contemporary Education, 57,* 38-43.

Lightfoot, S. L. (1987). On excellence and goodness. *Harvard Educational Review, 57,* 202-205.

Litt, M. D., & Turk, D. S. (1985). Sources of stress and dissatisfaction in experienced high school teachers. *Journal of Educational Research, 78,* 178-185.

Livson, N., & Peskin, H. (1980). Perspectives on adolescence from longitudinal research. in J. Adelson (Ed.), *Handbook of adolescent psychology* (pp. 47-98). New York: Wiley.

Lobato, D. (1983). Siblings of handicapped children: A review. *Journal of Autism and Developmental Disorders, 13,* 347-364.

Lockheed, M. E., & Harris, A. M. (1984). Cross-sex collaborative learning in elementary classrooms. *American Educational Research Journal, 21,* 275-294.

London, P. (1987). Character education and clinical intervention: A paradigm shift for U. S. schools. *Phi Delta Kappan, 68,* 667-673.

Long, B. C., & Gessaroli, M. E. (1989). The relationship between perceived stress and coping effectiveness: Gender and marital differences. *Alberta Journal of Education Research, 35,* 308-324.

Long, J. V. F., & Vaillant, G. E. (1989). Escape from the underclass. In T. F. Dugan & R. Coles (Eds.), *The child in our times: Studies in the development of resiliency* (pp. 200-213). New York: Brunner/Mazel.

Longo, D. C., & Bond, L. (1984). Families of the handicapped child: Research and practice. *Family Relations, 33,* 57-65.

Lowenbraun, S., Madge, S., & Affleck, J. (1990). Parental satisfaction with integrated class placements of special education and general education students. *Remedial and Special Education, 11,* 37-40.

Luftig, R. L. (1988). Assessment of the perceived school loneliness and isolation of mentally retarded and nonretarded students. *American Journal of Mental Deficiency, 5,* 472-475.

Lutz, C. A. (1988). *Unnatural emotions: Everyday sentiments on a Micronesian atoll and their challenge to Western theory.* Chicago: The University of Chicago Press.

Lyon, S. R., & Lyon, G. A. (1991). Collaboration with families of persons with severe disabilities. In M. Seligman (Ed.), *The family with a handicapped child* (2nd ed.) (pp. 237-268). Needham Heights, MA: Allyn and Bacon.

Maccoby, E. E. (1988). Gender as a social category. *Developmental Psychology, 24,* 755-765.

Macmillan, D. L., & Turnbull, A. P. (1983). Parent involvement in special education: Respecting individual preferences. *Education and Training of the Mentally Retarded, 18,* 4-9.

Madden, N. A., Slavin, R. E., Karweit, N. L., Dolan, L., & Wasik, B. A. (1991). Success for all. *Phi Delta Kappan, 72,* 593-599.

Magnusson, D., Strattin, R., & Allen, V. L. (1985). Biological maturation and social development: A longitudinal study of some adjustment processes from mid-adolescence to adulthood. *Journal of Youth and Adolescence, 14,* 267-283.

Makinen, R., & Kinnunen, U. (1986). Teacher stress over a school year. *Scandanavian Journal of Education Research, 30,* 55-70.

Marcelissen, F. H. G., Winnubst, J. A. M., Buunk, B., & Wolff, C. J. (1988). Social support and occupational stress: A causal analysis. *Social Science and Medicine, 26,* 365-373.

Margolick, D. (1990, March 9). At the bar. *New York Times,* p. B6.

Margolis, H., Shapiro, A., & Brown, G. (1987). Resolving conflicts with parents of handicapped children. *The Urban Review, 19,* 209-221.

Martens, R. (1988). Youth sport in the USA. In F. L. Small, R. A. Magill, & M. J. Ash (Eds.), *Children in sport* (3rd ed.) (pp. 17-23). Champaign, IL: Human Kinetics.

Martens, R., & Gill, D L. (1976). State anxiety among successful and unsuccessful competitors who differ in competitive trait anxiety. *Research Quarterly, 47,* 698-708.

Martens, R., Vealey, R. S., & Burton, D. (1990). *Competitive anxiety in sport.* Champaign, IL: Human Kinetics.

Martin, A. D., & Hetrick, E. S. (1988). The stigmatization of the gay and lesbian adolescent. *Journal of Homosexuality, 15,* 163-183.

Martin, J. M., & Gill, D. L. (1991). The relationship among competitive orientation, sport-confidence, self-esteem, anxiety, and performance. *Journal of Sport & Exercise Psychology, 13,* 149-159.

Mary, N. L. (1990). Reactions of black, hispanic and white mothers to having a child with handicaps. *Mental Retardation, 28,* 1-5.

Matteo, S. (1988). The effects of gender-schematic processing on decisions about sex-inappropriate behavior. *Sex Roles, 18,* 41-58.

Matteson, M. T. (1987). Individual-organizational relationships: Implications for preventing job stress and burnout. In J. C. Quick, R. S. Bhagat, J. E. Dalton, & J. D. Quick (Eds.), *Work stress: Health care systems in the workplace* (pp. 156-170). New York: Praeger.

Matteson, M. T., & Ivancevich, J. M. (1982). *Managing job stress and health.* New York: Free Press.

May, R. (1983). Anxiety and stress. In H. Selye (Ed.), *Selye's guide to stress research* (Vol. 2 pp. 134-145). New York: Scientific and Academic Editions.

Mazur, P. J., & Lynch, M. D. (1989). Differential impact of administrative, organizational, and personality factors on teacher burnout. *Teaching and Teacher Education, 5,* 337-353.

McAdoo, H. (1986). Strategies used by black single mothers against stress. In M. Simms & J. Malveaux (Eds.), *Slipping through the cracks: The status of black women* (pp. 153-166). New Brunswick, NJ: Transaction Books.

McBride, A. B. (1990). Mental health effects of women's multiple roles. *American Psychologist, 45,* 381-384.

McCrae, R. R. (1984). Situational determinants of coping responses: Loss, threat, and challenge. *Journal of Personality and Social Psychology, 46,* 919-928.

McCubbin, H. I., Patterson, J. M., & Wilson, L. R. (1987). Family inventory of life events and changes. In H. M. McCubbin & A. I. Thompson (Eds.), *Family assessment inventories for research and practice* (pp. 69-87). Madison, WI: University of Wisconsin- Madison.

McCubbin, M. A. (1988). Family stress, resources, and family types: Chronic illness in children. *Family Relations, 37,* 203-210.

McCubbin, M. A., & McCubbin, H. I. (1989). Theoretical orientations to family stress and coping. In C. R. Figley (Ed.), *Treating stress in families* (pp. 3-43). New York: Brunner/Mazel.

McDermott, J. (1980). High anxiety: Fear of crime in secondary schools. *Contemporary Education, 5,* 18-23.

McDermott, J. (1983). Crime in the schools and in the community: Offenders, victims, and fearful youth. *Crime and Delinquency, 29,* 270-282.

McGrew, K. C., Gilman, C. J., & Johnson, S. (1992). A review of scales to assess family needs. *Journal of Psychoeducational Assessment, 10,* 4-25.

McGuffin, P., Katz, R., & Bebbington, P. E. (1988a). The Camberwell Collaborative Depression Study. II. Investigation of family members. *British Journal of Psychiatry, 152,* 766-774.

McGuffin, P., Katz, R., & Bebbington, P. E. (1988b). The Camberwell Collaborative Depression Study. III. Depression and adversity in the relatives of depressed probands. *British Journal of Psychiatry, 152,* 775-782.

McKinney, B., & Peterson, R. A. (1987). Predictors of stress in parents of developmentally disabled children. *Journal of Pediatric Psychology, 12,* 133-150.

McManus, J. L. (1982). Comprehensive psychological services at the secondary level utilizing student paraprofessionals. *Journal of School Psychology, 20,* 280-298.

McNett, S. C. (1987). Social support, threat, and coping responses and effectiveness in the functionally disabled. *Nursing Research, 36,* 98-103.

McRoy, R. G., Grotevant, H. D., & Zurcher, L. A. (1988). *Emotional disturbance in adopted adolescents: Origins and development.* New York: Praeger.

Medeiros, D. C., Porter, B. J., & Welch, I. D. (1983). *Children under stress.* Englewood Cliffs, NJ: Prentice-Hall.

Meichenbaum, D. (1985). *Stress inoculation training*. Oxford, England: Pergamon Press.

Melton, G. B., & Limber, S. (1989). Psychologists' involvement in cases of child maltreatment: Limits of role and expertise. *American Psychologist, 44,* 1225-1233.

Menaghan, E. (1982). Measuring coping effectiveness: A panel analysis of marital problems and coping efforts. *Journal of Health and Social Behavior, 23,* 220-234.

Mensch, B. S., & Kandel, D. B. (1988). Dropping out of high school and drug involvement. *Sociology of Education, 61,* 95-113.

Meyers, C. C., & Blacher, J. (1987). Parents' perceptions of schooling for severely handicapped children: Home and family variables. *Exceptional Children, 53,* 441-449.

Meyers, D. E., Milne, A. M., Baker, K., & Ginsberg, K. (1987). Student discipline and high school performance. *Sociology of Education, 60,* 18-33.

Miller, W. H., & Keirn, W. C. (1978). Personality measurement in parents of retarded and emotionally disturbed children: A replication. *Journal of Clinical Psychology, 34,* 686-690.

Mills, R. C., Dunham, R. G., & Alpert, G. P. (1988). Working with high-risk youth in prevention and early intervention programs: Toward a comprehensive model. *Adolescence, 23,* 643-660.

Minnes, P. M. (1988). Family resources and stress associated with having a mentally retarded child. *American Journal on Mental Retardation, 93,* 184-192.

Minuchin, P., & Shapiro, E. (1983). The school as a context for social development. In E. M. Hetherington (Ed.), *Handbook of child psychology. Vol. 4: Socialization, personality, and social development* (pp. 197-294). New York: Wiley.

Mirowsky, J., & Ross, C. E. (1980). Minority status, ethnic culture, and distress: A comparison of Blacks, Whites, Mexicans, and Mexican Americans. *American Journal of Sociology, 86,* 479-495.

Mitchell, R. E., Cronkite, R. C., & Moos, R. H. (1983). Stress, coping, and depression among married couples. *Journal of Abnormal Psychology, 92,* 433-448.

Moos, R. (1976). *Human adaptation: Coping with life crises.* Lexington, MA: D. C. Heath.

Moos, R. H., & Billings, A. G. (1982). Conceptualizing and measuring coping resources and processes. In L. Goldberger & S. Breznitz (Eds.), *Handbook of stress: Theoretical and clinical aspects* (pp. 212-230). New York: Free Press.

Moracco, J. C., & McFadden, H. (1982). The counselor's role in reducing teacher stress. *The Personnel and Guidance Journal, 60,* 549-552.

Morine-Dershimer, G. (1983). Instructional strategy and the "creation" of classroom status. *American Educational Research Journal, 20,* 45-66.

Mullens, J. B. (1986). The relationship between child abuse and handicapping conditions. *Journal of School Health, 56,* 134-136.

Mullens, J. B. (1987). Authentic voices from parents of exceptional children. *Family Relations, 36,* 30-33.

Murphy, L., & Moriarty, A. (1976). *Vulnerability, coping and growth from infancy to adolescence.* New Haven, CT: Yale University Press.

Mussen, P. H. (Ed.). (1970). *Carmichael's manual of child psychology* (3rd ed.). New York: Wiley.

Myers, H. F., & King, L. (1983). Mental health issues in the development of black American children. In G. Powell, J. Yamamoto, A. Romero, & A. Morales (Eds.), *The psychosocial development of minority group children* (pp. 275-306). New York: Brunner/Mazel.

National Association of State Boards of Education. (1989). *Joining forces.* Washington, DC: Author.

National Commission on Excellence in Education. (1983). *A nation at risk: The imperative for educational reform.* Washington, DC: U. S. Department of Education.

National Committee for Prevention of Child Abuse. (1988, August). *NCPCA memorandum: Study of the national incidence and prevalence of child abuse and neglect.* Chicago, IL: Author.

National Governors' Association (Committee on Human Resources, Center for Policy Research) and Council of State Governments. (1987). *Focus on the first sixty months, The next steps: A guide to implementation.* Washington, DC: Author.

National Institute of Education, U. S. Department of Health, Education, and Welfare. (1978). *Violent schools - Safe schools: The safe school study report to Congress.* Washington, DC : U. S. Government Printing Office.

National Research Council. (1987). *Risking the future: Adolescent sexuality, pregnancy, and child-bearing.* Washington, DC: National Academy Press.

Needle, R. H., Griffin, T., & Svendsen, R. (1981). Occupational stress: Coping and health problems of teachers. *The Journal of School Health, 51,* 175-181.

Neff, J. (1985). Race and vulnerability to stress: An examination of differential vulnerability. *Journal of Personality and Social Psychology, 49,* 481-491.

Nelson, J. (1987). *Positive discipline.* New York: Ballantine.

Newberger, E. H., Newberger, C. M., & Hampton, R. L. (1983). Child abuse: The current theory base and future research needs. *Journal of the American Academy of Child and Adolescent Psychiatry, 22,* 262-268.

Newcomb, M. D., Huba, G. J., & Bentler, P. M. (1981). A multi-dimensional assessment of life events among adolescents. Derivation and correlates. *Journal of Health and Social Behavior, 22,* 400-415.

Nezu, A. M., & Ronan, G. F. (1985). Life stress, current problems, problem solving, and depressive symptoms: An integrative model. *Journal of Consulting and Clinical Psychology, 53,* 695-697.

Nicoll, D. (1982). Organizational declines as an OD issue. *Group and Organization Studies, 7,* 165-178.

Nihira, W. H., Mink, I. T., & Meyers, C. E. (1985). Home environment and development of slow-learning adolescents: Reciprocal relations. *Developmental Psychology, 21,* 784-794.

Nottelmann, E. D., Susman, E. J., Inoff-Germain, G., Cutler, G. B., Loriaux, D. L., & Chrousos, G. P. (1987). Developmental processes in early adolescence: Relationships between adolescent adjustment problems and chronological age, pubertal stage, and puberty-related serum hormone levels. *Journal of Pediatrics, 110,* 473-480.

O'Grady, D., & Metz, J. R. (1987). Resilience in children at high risk for psychological disorder. *Journal of Pediatric Psychology, 12,* 3-23.

Oakes, J. (1985). *Keeping track: How schools structure inequality.* New Haven, CT: Yale University Press.

Oakes, J., & Lipton, M. (1992). Detracking schools: Early lessons from the field. *Phi Delta Kappan, 73,* 448-454.

Olson, L., & Rodman, B. (1988, June 22). In the urban crucible. *Education Week,* pp. 27-33.

Orbach, I. (1988). *Children who don't want to live.* San Francisco: Jossey-Bass.

Otto, W. (1985). Homework: A meta-analysis. *Journal of Reading Research, 5,* 764-766.

Paikoff, R. L., & Collins, W. A. (Eds.). (1991). *New directions for child development.* San Francisco: Jossey-Bass.

Paine, W. S. (1981). The burnout phenomenon. *Vocational Education, 56,* 30-33.

Palfrey, J. S., Walker, D. K., Butler, J. A., & Singer, J. D. (1989). Patterns of response in families of chronically disabled children: An assessment in five metropolitan school districts. *American Journal of Orthopsychiatry, 59,* 94-104.

Parkay, F. W., Greenwood, G., Olejnik, S., & Proller, N. (1988). A study of the relationships among teacher efficacy, locus of control, and stress. *Journal of Research and Development in Education, 21,* 13-22.

Paschal, R. A., Weinstein, T., & Walberg, H. J. (1984). The effects of homework on learning: A quantitative synthesis. *Journal of Educational Research, 78,* 97-104.

Passer, M. W. (1982). Children in sport: Participation motives and psychological motives. *Quest, 33,* 231-244.

Payzant, T. W. (1992). New beginnings in San Diego: Developing a strategy for interagency collaboration. *Phi Delta Kappan, 74,* 139-146.

Pearlin, L. (1989). The sociological study of stress. *Journal of Health and Social Behavior, 30,* 241-256.

Pearlin, L., & Johnson, J. (1977). Marital status, life-strains, and depression. *American Sociological Review, 42,* 704-715.

Pearlin, L. I., & Schooler, C. (1978). The structure of coping. *Journal of Health and Social Behavior, 22,* 337-356.

Pedro-Carroll, J. L., Cowen, E. L., Hightower, A. D., & Guare, J. C. (1986). Preventive intervention with latency-aged children of divorce: A replication study. *American Journal of Community Psychology, 14,* 277-290.

Peters, D. L., & Kontos, S. (Eds.). (1987). *Continuity and discontinuity of experience in child care.* Norwood, NJ: Ablex.

Peterson, A. C. (1985). Pubertal development as a cause of disturbance: Myths, realities, and unanswered questions. *Genetic, Social and General Psychology Monographs, 111,* 205-232.

Peterson, L. (1988). Preventing the leading killer of children: The role of the school psychologist in injury prevention. *School Psychology Review, 17,* 593-600.

Peterson, P. (1984). Effects of moderator variables in reducing stress outcome in mothers of children with handicaps. *Journal of Psychosomatic Research, 28,* 337-344.

Phillips, B. N. (1978). *School stress and anxiety: Theory, research and intervention.* New York: Human Sciences Press.

Phillips, B. N. (1990). *School psychology at a turning point: Ensuring a bright future for the profession.* San Francisco: Jossey-Bass.

Phillips, B. N., & Lee, M. (1980). The changing role of the American teacher: Current and future sources of stress. In C. L. Cooper & J. Marshall (Eds.), *White collar and professional stress* (pp. 93-111). New York: Wiley.

Phillips, B. N., Pitcher, G. D., Worsham, M. E., & Miller, S. C. (1980). Test anxiety and the school environment. In I. G. Sarason (Ed.), *Test anxiety: Theory, research, and applications* (pp. 327-346). Hillsdale, NJ: Erlbaum.

Piccigallo, P. R. (1989). Renovating urban schools is fundamental to improving them. *Phi Delta Kappan, 70,* 402-406.

Plomin, R. (1988). The nature and nurture of cognitive abilities. In R. Sternberg (Ed.), *Advances in the psychology of intelligence* (pp. 1-33). Hillsdale, NJ: Erlbaum.

Plomin, R. (1990). *Nature and nurture.* Pacific Grove, CA: Brooks/Cole.

Plomin, R., & Daniels, D. (1987). Why are children in the same family so different from each other? *Behavior and Brain Science, 10,* 1-16.

Plomin, R., Nitz, K., & Rowe, D. C. (1990). Behavioral genetics and aggressive behavior in childhood. In M. Lewis & S. M. Miller (Eds.), *Handbook of developmental psychopathology* (pp. 119- 133). New York: Plenum.

Pogrow, S. (1992). What to do about Chapter 1: An alternative view from the street. *Phi Delta Kappan, 73,* 624-630.

Powell, D. R. (1991). How schools support families: Critical policy tensions. *The Elementary School Journal, 91,* 307.

Price, R. H., Cowen, E. L., Lorion, R. P., & Ramos-McKay, J. (1988). *Fourteen ounces of prevention: A casebook for practitioners.* Washington, DC: American Psychological Association.

Prochaska, J. O., DiClemente, C. C., & Norcross, J. C. (1992). In search of how people change: Applications to addictive behavior. *American Psychologist, 47,* 1102-1114.

Pryor-Brown, L., Cowen, E. L., Hightower, A. D., & Lotyczewski, B. S. (1986). Demographic differences among children in judging and experiencing specific stressful life events. *The Journal of Special Education, 20,* 339-345.

Pryor-Brown, L., Powell, J., & Earls, F. (1989). Stressful life events in black adolescent females. *Journal of Adolescent Research, 4,* 140-151.

Pynoos, R., & Nader, K. (1988). Psychological first aid and treatment approach to children exposed to community violence: Research implications. *Journal of Traumatic Stress, 1,* 445-473.

Quine, L., & Pahl, J. (1985). Examining the causes of stress in families with severely mentally handicapped children. *British Journal of Social Work, 15,* 501-517.

Rainey, D. W., Conklin, W. E., & Rainey, K. W. (1987). Competitive trait anxiety among male and female junior high school athletes. *International Journal of School Psychology, 18,* 171-179.

Ralph, J. H. (1989). Improving education for the disadvantaged: Do we know whom to help? *Phi Delta Kappan, 70,* 395-401.

Ralph, J. H., & Salganik, L. (1988). Dropouts, school performance, and standards: What is the causal link? *Youth Policy, 10,* 21-24.

Raywid, M. A. (1989). *The case for public schools of choice.* Bloomington, IN: Phi Delta Kappa Educational Foundation.

Reese, H. W., & Overton, W. F. (1970). Models of development and theories of development. In L. R. Goulet & P. B. Baltes (Eds.), *Life-span developmental psychology: Research and theory* (pp. 115-145). San Diego, CA: Academic Press.

Remafedi, G. (1987). Male homosexuality: The adolescent's perspective. *Pediatrics, 79,* 321-330.

Richards, M. H., Casper, R., & Larson, R. (1990). Weight and eating concerns among pre- and young adolescent boys and girls. *Journal of Adolescent Health, 11,* 203-209.

Riegel, K. F. (1975). Toward a dialectical theory of development. *Human Development, 18,* 50-64.

Riordan, C. (1990). *Girls and boys in school: Together or separate?* New York: Teachers College Press.

Rizzo, T. A. (1989). *Friendship development among children in school.* Norwood, NJ: Ablex.

Roberts, G. C. (1986). The perception of stress: A potential source and its development. In M. R. Weiss & D. Gould (Eds.), *Sport for children and youths* (pp. 119-126). Champaign, IL: Human Kinetics.

Rodrigue, J. R., Morgan, S. B., & Geffken, G. (1990). Families of autistic children: Psychological functioning of mothers. *Journal of Clinical Child Psychology, 19,* 371-379.

Rolf, J., Masten, A. S., Cicchetti, D., Neuchterlein, K. H., & Weintraub, S. (Eds.). (1990). *Risk and protective factors in the development of psychopathology.* Cambridge: Cambridge University Press.

Rook, K., & Dooley, D. (1985). Applying social support research: Theoretical problems and future directions. *Journal of Social Issues, 41,* 5-28.

Rose, S. D., & Edleson, J. L. (1987). *Working with children and adolescents in groups: A multimethod approach.* San Francisco: Jossey-Bass.

Roseman, I. J. (1984). Cognitive determinants of emotion: A structural theory. In P. Shaver (Ed.), *Review of personality and social psychology: Emotions, relationships, and health* (pp. 11-36). Beverly Hills, CA: Sage.

Rosenfield, S. (1992). Developing school-based consultation teams: A design for organizational change. *School Psychology Quarterly, 7,* 27-46.

Rosnow, R., & Georgoudi, M. (1986). *Contextualism and understanding in behavioral research.* New York: Praeger.

Ross, C. E., & Mirowsky, J. (1988). Child care and emotional adjustment to wives' employment. *Journal of Health and Social Behavior, 29,* 127-138.

Rotheram-Borus, M. J., Rosario, M., & Koopman, C. (1991). Minority youths at high risk: Gay males and runaways. In M. E. Colten & S. Gore (Eds.), *Adolescent stress: Causes and consequences* (pp. 181-200). New York: Aldine de Gruyter.

Rowley, S. (1987). Psychological effects of intensive training in young athletes. *Journal of Child Psychology and Psychiatry, 28,* 371-377.

Russell, D. W., Altmaier, E., & Velzen, D. V. (1987). Job-related stress, social support, and burnout among classroom teachers. *Journal of Applied Psychology, 72,* 269-274.

Rutter, M. (1983a). School effects on pupil progress: Research findings and policy implications. *Child Development, 54,* 1-29.

Rutter, M. (1983b). Stress, coping, and development: Some issues and some questions. *Journal of Child Psychology and Psychiatry, 22,* 323-356.

Rutter, M. (1987). Psychosocial resilience and protective mechanisms. *American Journal of Orthopsychiatry, 57,* 316-331.

Rutter, M., & Garmezy, N. (1983). Developmental psychopathology. In E. M. Hetherington (Ed.), *Socialization, personality and social development* (pp. 775-911). New York: Wiley.

Rutter, M., Maughan, B., Mortimore, P., Ouston, J., & Smith, A. (1979). *Fifteen thousand hours: Secondary schools and their effects on children.* Cambridge: Harvard University Press.

Ryan, N. M. (1988). The stress-coping process in school-age children: Gaps in the knowledge needed for health promotion. *Advances in Nursing Science, 11,* 1-12.

Ryan, N. M. (1989). Identification of children's coping strategies from the school-ager's perspective. *Research in Nursing and Health, 12,* 111-112.

Saegert, S. (1981). Environment and children's mental health: Residential density and low income children. In A. Baum & J. E. Singer (Eds.), *Handbook of psychology and health* (Vol. 2, pp. 247-271). Hillsdale, NJ: Erlbaum.

Sarason, S. B. (1982). *The culture of the school and the problem of change* (2nd ed.). Boston: Allyn & Bacon.

Sarason, S. B. (1990). *The predictable failure of educational reform: Can we change course before it's too late?* San Francisco: Jossey-Bass.

Sarason, S. B., & Klaber, M. (1985). The school as a social situation. *Annual Review of Psychology, 36,* 115-140.

Satterfield, J. H., Hoppe, C. M., & Schell, A. M. (1982). A prospective study of delinquency in 110 adolescent boys with attention deficit disorder and 88 normal adolescent boys. *American Journal of Psychiatry, 139,* 795-798.

Scanlan, T. K. (1977). The effect of success-failure on the perception of threat in a competitive situation. *Research Quarterly, 48,* 144-153.

Scanlan, T. K., & Passer, M. W. (1978a). Anxiety-inducing factors in competitive youth sports. In F. L. Small & R. E. Smith (Eds.), *Psychological perspectives in youth sports* (pp. 107-122). Washington, DC: Hemisphere.

Scanlan, T. K., & Passer, M. W. (1978b). Factors related to competitive stress among male youth sport participants. *Medicine and Science in Sports, 10,* 103-108.

Scanlan, T. K., & Passer, M. W. (1979). Sources of competitive stress in young female athletes. *Journal of Sport Psychology, 1,* 151-159.

Scarr, S. (1992). Developmental theories for the 1990s: Development and individual differences. *Child Development, 63,* 1-19.

Scarr, S., & McCartney, K. (1983). How people make their own environments: A theory of genotype–environment effects. *Child Development, 54,* 424-435.

Scarr, S., Phillips, D., & McCartney, K. (1989). Working mothers and their families. *American Psychologist, 44,* 1402-1409.

Scheffer, M. W. (1987). *Policing from the schoolhouse: Police-school liaison and resource officers programs: A case study.* Springfield, IL: Charles C. Thomas.

Scheier, M. F., & Carver, C. S. (1992). Effects of optimism on psychological and physical well-being: Theoretical overview and empirical update. *Cognitive Therapy and Research, 16,* 201-228.

Scheinfeld, D. (1983). Family relationship and school achievement among boys of lower-income urban black families. *American Journal of Orthopsychiatry, 53,* 127-143.

Scherer, J. E., & Stimson, J. (1984). Is school violence a serious concern? *School Administrator, 41,* 19-20.

Scherer, K. R. (1984). *Emotion as a multicomponent process: A model and some cross-cultural data* (pp. 37-63). Beverly Hills, CA: Sage.

Schinke, S. P., & Gilchrist, L. D. (1985). Preventing substance abuse with children and adolescents. *Journal of Consulting and Clinical Psychology, 53,* 596-602.

Schinke, S. P., Orlandi, M. A., Botvin, G. J., Gilchrist, L. D., & Trimble, J. E. (1988). Preventing substance abuse among American Indian adolescents: A bicultural competence skills approach. *Journal of Counseling Psychology, 35,* 87-90.

Schinke, S. P., Schilling, R. F., Barth, R. P., Gilchrist, L.D. & Maxwell, J. S. (1986). Stress-management intervention to prevent family violence. *Journal of Family Violence, 1,* 13-26.

Schinke, S. P., Schilling, R. F., Palleja, J., & Zayas, L. H. (1987). Prevention research among ethnic-racial minority group adolescents. *The Behavior Therapist, 10,* 151-155.

Schneider, S. G., Farberow, N. L., & Kruks, G. N. (1989). Suicidal behavior in adolescent and young adult gay men. *Suicide and Life-Threatening Behavior, 19,* 381-394.

Schoggen, P. (1989). *Behavior settings: A revision and extension of Roger G. Barker's "Ecological Psychology."* Stanford, CA: Stanford University Press.

Schorr, L. (1988). *Within our reach.* New York: Doubleday.

Sears, S. J., & Navin, S. L. (1983). Stressors in school counseling. *Education, 103,* 333-337.

Seeley, D. S. (1989). A new paradigm for parent involvement. *Educational Leadership, 47,* 21-23.

Seifer, R., & Sameroff, A. J. (1987). Multiple determinants of risk and invulnerability. In E. J. Anthony & B. J. Cohen (Eds.), *The invulnerable child* (pp. 51-69). New York: Guilford Press.

Seligman, M. (1991). Family systems and beyond: Conceptual issues. In M. Seligman (Ed.), *The family with the handicapped child.* (pp. 27-53). Needham Heights, MA: Allyn & Bacon.

Seligman, M., & Darling, R. B. (1989). *Ordinary families, special children: A systems approach to childhood disability.* New York: Guilford Press.

Selye, H. (1980). The stress concept today. In I. L. Kutash, L. B. Schlesinger, and Associates (Eds.), *Handbook on stress and anxiety* (pp. 127-143). San Francisco: Jossey-Bass.

Shermis, M. D., Rudin, D., & Chandler, L. A. (1992). An extension of the norms for the Stress Response Scale for Children. *Journal of Psychoeducational Assessment, 10,* 65-75.

Showers, J., & Johnson, C. F. (1984). Students' knowledge of child health and development: Effects on approaches to discipline. *Journal of School Health, 54,* 122-125.

Shure, M. B., & Spivak, G. (1982). Interpersonal problem-solving in young children: A cognitive approach to prevention. *American Journal of Community Psychology, 10,* 341-356.

Silva, J. M., III, & Weinberg, R. S. (Eds.). (1984). *Psychological foundations of sport.* Champaign, IL: Human Kinetics.

Silverberg, S. B., & Steinberg, L. (1987). Adolescent autonomy, parent–adolescent conflict, and parental well-being. *Journal of Youth and Adolescence, 16,* 293-312.

Simmons, R. G., & Blyth, D. A. (1987). *Moving into adolescence: The impact of pubertal change and school context.* New York: Aldine de Gruyter.

Simmons, R. G., Burgeson, R., & Reef, M. J. (1988). Cumulative change at entry to adolescence. In M. Gunnar & W. A. Collins (Eds.), *Development during transition to adolescence: Minnesota symposia on child psychology* (Vol. 21, pp. 123-150). Hillsdale, NJ: Erlbaum.

Simon, J. A., & Martens, R. (1979). Children's anxiety in sport and nonsport evaluative activities. *Journal of Sport Psychology, 1,* 160-169.

Siperstein, G. N., & Bak, J. J. (1989). Social relationships of adolescents with moderate mental retardation. *Mental Retardation, 27,* 5-10.

Siperstein, G. N., & Goding, M. J. (1985). Teachers' behavior toward LD and non-LD children: A strategy for change. *Journal of Learning Disabilities, 18,* 139-144.

Slavin, R. E. (1987). Developmental and motivational perspectives on cooperative learning: A reconciliation. *Child Development, 58,* 1161-1167.

Slavin, R. E. (1990a). Ability grouping and student achievement in secondary schools. *Review of Educational Research, 60,* 417-499.

Slavin, R. E. (1990b). *Cooperative learning: Theory, research, and practice.* Englewood Cliffs, NJ: Prentice-Hall.

Slavin, R. E. (1991). Chapter 1: A vision for the next quarter century. *Phi Delta Kappan, 72,* 586-592.

Sloman, L., & Konstantareas, M. M. (1990). Why families of children with biological deficits require a systems approach. *Family Process, 29,* 417-429.

Smalley, S. L., Asarnow, R. F., & Spence, M. A. (1988). Autism and genetics: A decade of research. *Archives of General Psychiatry, 45,* 953-961.

Smetana, J. G. (1988). Concepts of self and social convention: Adolescents' and parents' reasoning about hypothetical and actual family conflicts. In M. Gunnar & W. A. Collins (Eds.), *Development during transition to adolescence: Minnesota symposia on child psychology* (Vol. 21, pp. 79-122). Hillsdale, NJ: Erlbaum.

Smetana, J. G. (1989). Adolescents' and parents' conceptions of parental authority. *Child Development, 59,* 321-335.

Smith, M. L. (1991). Put to the test: The effects of external testing on teachers. *Educational Researcher, 20,* 8-11.

Spady, W. G. (1988). Organizing for results: The basis of authentic restructuring. *Educational Leadership, 46,* 4-8.

Spady, W. G., & Marshall, K. J. (1991). Beyond traditional outcome-based education. *Educational Leadership, 49,* 67-72.

Spivak, G., & Shure, M B. (1974). *Social adjustment of young children.* San Francisco: Jossey-Bass.

Stanton, H. E. (1985). The reduction of children's school-related stress. *Australian Psychologist, 20,* 171-193.

Staples, R. (1978). The black family revisited. In R. Staples (Ed.), *The black family: Essay and studies* (pp. 13-18). Belmont, CA: Wadsworth.

Stein, R. C. (1983). Hispanic parents' perspectives and participation in their children's special education program: Comparisons by program and race. *Learning Disability Quarterly, 6,* 432-439.

Steinberg, L., & Silverberg, S. B. (1986). The vicissitudes of autonomy in early adolescence. *Child Development, 57,* 1-10.

Stevens, J. J., & Pfost, K. S. (1983). A problem-solving approach to staff burnout in rehabilitation settings. *Rehabilitation Counseling Bulletin, 27,* 101-107.

Stevenson, D. L., & Baker, D. (1987). The family-school relation and the child's school performance. *Child Development, 58,* 1348-1357.

Straus, M. A. (1980). Stress and physical child abuse. *Child Abuse and Neglect, 4,* 75-88.

Straus, M. A., Gelles, R. J., & Steinmetz, S. K. (1980). *Behind closed doors: Violence in American families.* New York: Doubleday.

Strayhorn, J. M. (1988). *The competent child: An approach to psychotherapy and preventive mental health.* New York: Guilford Press.

Suarez-Orozco, M. M. (1989). *Central American refugees and U. S. high schools: A psychosocial study of motivation and achievement.* Stanford, CA: Stanford University Press.

Suelzle, M., & Keenan, V. (1981). Changes in family support networks over the life cycle of mentally retarded persons. *American Journal of Mental Deficiency, 86,* 267-274.

Suls, J., & Fletcher, B. (1985). The relative efficacy of avoidant and non-avoidant coping strategies: A meta-analysis. *Health Psychology, 4,* 249-288.

Sze, W., & Lamar, B. (1981). Causes of child abuse: A reexamination. *Health and Social Work, 6,* 19-25.

Task Force on Education for Economic Growth. (1984). *Action for excellence: A comprehensive plan to improve our nation's schools.* Denver, CO: Education Commission of the States.

Task Force on Education of Young Adolescents. (1989). *Turning points: Preparing American youth for the 21st century.* Washington, DC: Carnegie Council on Adolescent Development.

Tellenback, S., Brenner, S., & Lofgren, H. (1983). Teacher stress: Exploratory model building. *Journal of Occupational Psychology, 56,* 19-33.

Terr, L. (1988). What happens to early memories of trauma: A study of 20 children under age 5 at the time of documented traumatic events. *Journal of the American Academy of Child Psychiatry, 27,* 96-104.

Tharinger, D. J., Krivacska, J. J., Laye-McDonough, M., Jamison, L., Vincent, G. G., & Hedlund, A. D. (1988). Prevention of child sexual abuse: An analysis of issues, educational programs, and research findings. *School Psychology Review, 17,* 614-634.

Thomas, A., & Chess, S. (1984). Genesis and evolution of behavior disorders: From infancy to early adult life. *American Journal of Psychiatry, 141,* 1-9.

Tienari, P., Lahti, I., Sorri, A., Naarala, M., Moring, J., & Wahlberg, K. (1989). The Finnish Adoptive Family Study of Schizophrenia: Possible joint effects of genetic vulnerability and family environment. *British Journal of Psychiatry, 155* (Suppl. 5), 29-32.

Truch, S. (1980). *Teacher burnout and what to do about it.* Novato, CA: Academic Therapy Publications.

Trute, B., & Hauch, C. (1988). Building on family strength: A study of families with positive adjustment to the birth of a developmentally disabled child. *Journal of Marital and Family Therapy, 14,* 185-193.

Tung, R. L., & Koch, J. L. (1980). School administrators: Sources of stress and ways of coping with it. In C. L. Cooper & J. Marshall (Eds.), *White collar and professional stress* (pp. 63-91). New York: Wiley.

Turk, D. C., Meeks, S., & Turk, L. M. (1982). Factors contributing to teacher stress: Implications for research, prevention, and remediation. *Behavioral Counseling Quarterly, 2,* 3-25.

Turnbull, A. P. (1983). Parental participation in the IEP process. In J. S. Mulick & S. M. Pueschel (Eds.), *Parent-professional partnerships in developmental disabilities services* (pp. 107-124). Cambridge, MA: Academic Guild.

Turnbull, A. P., & Leonard, J. (1981). Parent involvement in special education: Emerging advocacy roles. *School Psychology Review, 10,* 37-44.

Turnbull, A. P., & Turnbull, H. R. (1986). *Families, professionals, and exceptionalities: A special partnership.* Columbus, OH: Merrill.

U. S. Congress, House of Representatives, Committee on the Judiciary Subcommittee on Crime. (1991). *Gun-Free School Zones Act of 1990: Hearing before the Subcommittee on Crime of the Committee on the Judiciary* (September 6, 1990). Washington, DC: U. S. Government Printing Office.

Udry, J. R., Billy, J. O. G., Morris, N. M., Groff, T. R., & Madhwa, R. A. (1985). Serum androgenic hormones motivate sexual behavior in adolescent boys. *Fertility and Sterility, 43,* 90-94.

Waggoner, K., & Wilgosh, L. (1990). Concerns of families of children with learning disabilities. *Journal of Learning Disabilities, 23,* 97-98, 113.

Walker, C. E., Bonner, B. L., & Kaufman, K. L. (1988). *The physically and sexually abused child: Evaluation and treatment.* New York: Pergamon Press.

Wallerstein, J. S. (1983). Children of divorce: Stress and developmental tasks. In N. Garmezy & M. Rutter (Eds.), *Stress, coping, and development in children* (pp. 265-302). New York: McGraw-Hill.

Wallerstein, J. S. (1987). Children of divorce: Report of a 10-year follow-up of early latency-age children. *American Journal of Orthopsychiatry, 57,* 199-211.

Wallerstein, J., & Blakeslee, S. (1989). *Second chances: Men, women and children a decade after divorce.* San Francisco: Ticknor & Fields.

Wallerstein, J. S., & Kelly, J. (1980). *Surviving the breakup: How children and parents cope with divorce.* New York: Basic Books.

Walsh, W. M., & Giblin, N. J. (1988). *Family counseling in school settings.* Springfield, IL: Charles C. Thomas.

Wayment, H. A., & Zetlin, A. (1989). Coping responses of adolescents with and without mild learning handicaps. *Mental Retardation, 27,* 311-316.

Weade, R.. & Evertson, C. E. (1988). The construction of lessons in effective and less effective classrooms. *Teaching and Teacher Education, 4,* 189-213.

Webb, N. M., & Kenderski, C. M. (1984). Student interaction and learning in small-group and whole-class settings. In P. L. Peterson, L. C. Wilkinson, & M. Halliman (Eds.), *The social context of instruction* (pp. 153-170). New York: Academic Press.

Weber, G., & Parker, T. (1981). A study of family and professional views of factors affecting family adaptaion to a disabled child. In N. Stinnett, J. DeFrain, K. King, P. Knaub, & G. Rowe (Eds.), *Family strengths 3: Roots of well-being* (pp. 379-393). Omaha: University of Nebraska Press.

Weber, J., & Stoneman, Z. (1986). Parental participation in program planning for mentally retarded children: An empirical investigation. *Applied Research in Mental Retardation, 7,* 359- 369.

Weinberg, R. S., & Genuchi, M. (1980). Relationships between competitive trait anxiety, state anxiety, and golf performance: A field study. *Journal of Sport Psychology, 2,* 148-154.

Weintraub, M., & Wolf, B. (1983). Effects of stress and social supports on mother-child interactions in single- and two-parent families. *Child Development, 54,* 1297-1311.

Weiss, R. S. (1974). The provisions of social relations. In Z. Rubin (Ed.), *Doing unto others* (pp. 17-26). Englewood Cliffs, NJ: Prentice-Hall.

Weissberg, R., & Allen, J. P. (1986). Promoting children's adaptive skills and interpersonal behavior. In B. A. Edelstein & L. Michelson (Eds.), *Handbook of prevention* (pp. 153-175). New York: Plenum.

Weissberg, R., Caplan, M., & Sivo, P. (1989). A new conceptual framework for establishing school-based social competence promotion programs. In L. Bond & B. Compas (Eds.), *Primary prevention and promotion in the schools* (pp. 255-296). Newbury Park, CA: Sage.

Werner, E. E. (1989). High risk children in young adulthood: A longitudinal study from birth to age 32. *American Journal of Orthopsychiatry, 59,* 72-78.

Werner, E. E., & Smith, R. S. (1982). *Vulnerable but invincible: A longitudinal study of resilient children and youth.* New York: McGraw-Hill.

Widom, C. S. (1989). The cycle of violence. *Science, 244,* 160-166.

Wiegerink, R., Hocutt, A., Posante-Loro, R., & Bristol, M. (1980). Parent involvement in early education programs for handicapped children. In J. J. Gallagher (Ed.), *New directions for exceptional children: Ecology of exceptional children* (pp. 67-85). San Francisco: Jossey-Bass.

Wikler, L., Haack, J., & Intagliata, J. (1984). Bearing the burden alone?: Helping divorced mothers with children with developmental disabilities. In J. C. Hanson & E. I. Coopersmith (Eds.), *Families with handicapped members* (pp. 44-62). Rockville, MD: Aspen Systems.

Wills, T. A. (1985). Supportive functions of interpersonal relationships. In S. Cohen & S. L. Syme (Eds.), *Social support and health* (pp. 61-82). Orlando, FL: Academic Press.

Wilson, H. (1974). Parenting in poverty. *British Journal of Social Work, 4,* 241-254.

Wilton, K., & Renaut, J. (1986). Stress levels in families with intellectually handicapped preschool children and families with nonhandicapped preschool children. Topics in Early Childhood Special Education, 1, 11-19.

Winnick, B. M. (1987). Congress, Smith v. Robinson, and the myth of attorney representation in special education hearings: Is attorney representation desirable? *Syracuse Law Review, 37,* 1161-1187.

Wise, A. E. (1979). *Legislated learning: The bureaucratization of the American classroom.* Berkeley, CA: University of California Press.

Wise, P. S. (1985). School psychologists' ranking of stressful events. *Journal of School Psychology, 23,* 31-41.

Witt, J. C., Miller, C. D., McIntyre, R. M., & Smith, D. (1984). Effects of variables on parental perceptions of staffings. *Exceptional Children, 51,* 27-32.

Woody, R. H., Yeager, M., & Woody, J. D. (1990). Appropriate education for handicapped children: Introducing family therapy to school-based decision making. *American Journal of Family Therapy, 18,* 189-196.

Wynne, L. C., Jones, J. E., & Al-Khayyal, M. (1982). Healthy family communications patterns: Observations in families "at risk" for psychopathology. In F. Walsh (Ed.), *Normal family processes* (pp. 142-167). New York: Guilford Press.

Yao, E. L. (1985). Adjustment needs of Asian immigrant children. *Elementary School Guidance and Counseling Journal, 19,* 222-228.

Yao, E. L. (1987). Asian immigrant students — Unique problems that hamper learning. *NAASP Bulletin, 70,* 82-88.

Yarcheski, A., & Mahon, N. E. (1986). Perceived stress and symptom patterns in early adolescents: The role of mediating variables. *Research in Nursing and Health, 9,* 289-297.

Zaharna, R. S. (1992). Self-shock: The double-binding challenge of identity. *International Journal of Intercultural Relations, 13,* 501-525.

Zins, J. E., Curtis, M. J., Graden, J. L., & Ponti, C. R. (1988). *Helping students succeed in the regular classroom: A guide for developing intervention assistance programs.* San Francisco: Jossey-Bass.

AUTHOR INDEX

A

Abbott, D. A., 152
Adler, N., 99
Affleck, J., 142
Ahrentzen, S., 83
Aiello, J. R., 83
Albrecht, R. R., 89
Aldwin, C. M., 195, 196
Allen, D. A., 105, 142, 145, 205
Allison, M. T., 90
Alpern, D., 209
Alpert, G. P., 14
Altemeier, D. A., 149
Altmaier, E., 198
Altman, L. K., 186
Al-Khayyal, M., 176
Anesko, J. R., 84, 85
Anthony, E. J., 169, 177
Anthrop, J., 90
Appelbaum, M., 139
Apter, S. J., 156
Arnold, L. E., 172
Asarnow, R. F., 179
Aseltine, J., 100
Asmussen, L., 102

B

Baird, J. H., 79
Bak, J. J., 115, 118
Baker, S. P., 19, 47, 49, 155
Baltes, P. B., 93
Banbury, M. M., 143
Bancroft, B. A., 8
Bandura, A., 43, 190
Banez, G. A., 32
Barker, R. G., 47, 75, 76
Barnett, R. C., 191
Barth, R. P., 152
Baruch, G. K., 191
Baum, A., 37, 83, 87, 195
Bayh, B., 158
Bebbington, P. E., 178
Becher, R. M., 86
Beck, C. L., 57, 58, 99, 188
Becker, H. J., 69, 70
Beckman, P. J., 134, 139
Belle, D., 48
Benedek, E. P., 50
Bentler, P. M., 100
Berends, M., 78
Bergan, J. R., 64

Berger, M., 143
Berliner, D. C., 79
Berry, G. L., 50
Berry, B., 7
Berry, J. W., 118, 119
Bertelsen, A., 179
Biener, L., 191
Bigelow, B. J., 87
Billings, A. G., 42, 198
Billy, J. O. G., 98
Birman, B. F., 18
Bjorck, J., 102
Blacher, J., 136, 142
Black, M. M., 135
Blakeslee, S., 162
Blase, J. J., 188
Bleuler, M., 167, 168
Block, A., 156
Blyth, D. A., 48, 49, 105, 107
Bochner, S., 121
Bond, L. A., 63, 64, 132
Bonner, B. L., 148
Botvin, G. J., 207, 208
Boukydis, C. F. Z., 152
Boyer, E. L., 4, 7, 185
Braff, A. M., 139
Bramson, R. M., 67
Brassard, M. R., 148
Brenner, A., 186, 205, 206, 207
Brickman, P., 56
Brissie, J. S., 68, 69
Bristol, M., 145
Brodbelt, S., 158
Bronfenbrenner, U., 47, 76, 77, 84
Brooks, A. E., 126, 127
Brooks-Gunn, J., 104, 105, 106, 126
Brophy, J. E., 115
Brown, D., 64
Brown, G., 68
Brown, J. D., 87
Browne, D. H., 147, 148, 149, 150, 151
Bryant, P., 94
Buck, M. R., 209
Burgeson, R., 105
Burlingham, D., 162

Burt, C. E., 102
Burton, D., 87
Butler, J. A., 132
Butterworth, G., 94
Buunk, B., 198

C

Cannon, W., 37
Canter, L., 85
Caplan, N., 122, 218
Carriere, R., 158
Carter, L. F., 18
Caruso, C. M., 89
Carver, C. S., 119
Casper, R., 102
Catalano, R., 35
Cauce, A. M., 115, 202
Cazden, C. B., 79
Cecil, M. A., 187
Chandler, L. A., 30, 62, 63
Chang, A. S., 195
Chase-Landsdale, L., 126
Cheatham, A., 159
Chen, Z., 31
Cherniss, C., 40, 196
Chess, S., 61
Chiappelli, F., 50
Choy, M. H., 122
Cicchetti, D., 94, 95, 168
Clabby, J. F., 216, 217
Clarke-Stewart, A., 191
Cleary, P. D., 112
Cloninger, C. R., 179
Clune, W. H., 8
Cohen, L. H., 34, 102
Cohen, M., 99
Cohler, B. J., 177
Coles, R., 171, 172
Collins, A., 8, 107
Colten, M. E., 100
Comer, J. P., 3, 9, 68
Compas, B. E., 32, 33, 47, 48, 60, 62, 64, 95, 100
Coner-Edwards, A. F., 121, 122

Conklin, W. E., 90
Conoley, J. C., 68
Conrad, D., 8
Constable, J. F., 199
Cooper, H. 84
Corbin, E. D., 98
Covey, L., 209
Cowen, E. L., 50, 202, 208
Cox, M., 176
Cox, R., 176
Coyne, J. C., 178
Craig, S. E., 154
Cremin, L. A., 2
Crisp, A. H., 179
Crittenden, P. M., 48
Crnic, K. A., 116
Crockenberg, S., 48
Cronkite, R. C., 195
Csikszentmihalyi, M., 48, 102
Cuban, L., 78
Cullinan, D., 114
Cunningham, W. G., 194
Curtis, M. J., 154
Cvetkovich, G. T., 207

D

Damon, W., 49
Daniels, D., 180
Darling, R. B., 133, 134, 135, 136, 137
Darling-Hammond, L., 7
Dauber, S. L., 69, 70
Davies, D., 70
Davis, G. E., 32, 100
Davis, D., 153
Davis, J. M., 208
Demaline, R., 18
Dembo, M. H., 190
DiClemente, C. C., 213
Divoky, D., 122
Dohrenwend, B. P., 112
Dohrenwend, B. S., 112
Dolan, L., 8
Dooley, D., 35, 203
Dornbusch, S. M., 31, 33, 111,

112, 113
Downey, G., 178
Doyle, D. P., 8
Dryfoos, J. G., 203
Dubrow, N., 162, 163
Dugan, T. F., 171, 172
Dunham, J., 14, 40, 186, 194
Dunn, J., 97, 181
Dzewaltowski, D. A., 89
D'Amato, R. C., 57, 64
D'Arienzo, R. V., 40
D'Zurilla, T. J., 205

E

Earls, F., 113
Eaton, J. W., 186
Eaves, L. J., 179
Edleson, J. L., 64
Edwards, J. R., 41, 42
Eisner, E., 11
Elder, G. H., Jr., 24
Elias, M. J., 25, 27, 202, 207, 216, 217
Elkind, D., 25, 26, 31, 210
Ensminger, M. T., 176
Epstein, J. L., 49, 68, 69, 70, 82
Epstein, M. H., 114
Erickson, M., 138, 139
Etzioni, D., 195
Evans, G. W., 83
Evertson, C. E., 79

F

Factor, D. C., 138
Faller, K. C., 151
Farber, B. A., 40, 185, 186, 187, 188, 194, 196
Farberow, N. L., 124
Farran, D. C., 139
Felner, M. T., 115
Felner, R. D., 211
Felton, B. J., 195
Feltz, D. L., 89
Fewell, R. R., 135

Finkelhor, D., 147, 148, 149, 151, 153
Finn, C. E., 8, 220
Fleming, R., 37, 38, 195
Fletcher, B., 41
Flynt, S. W., 133, 134, 136
Folkman, S., 24, 38, 39, 40, 41, 42, 43,
    44, 51, 59, 118, 119, 186, 195,
    196, 207
Fong, P. L., 132
Ford, D. L., 198
Forman, S. G., 11, 27, 64, 187
Forsythe, C. J., 32, 100
Foster, M., 143
Fowler, R. S., 132
Fox, R., 105
Freeman, N., 138
Freud, A., 162
Frey, K. S., 135, 138
Friedrich, W. L., 116, 132
Friedrich, W. N., 116, 132
Frymier, J., 20, 22
Furham, A., 121
Furstenberg, F. F., Jr., 126
Futcher, J. A., 152

G

Gallagher, J. J., 141
Gamoran, A., 78
Gandra, P., 176
Gara, M., 217
Garbarino, J., 154, 155, 162, 163
Garmezy, N., 24, 111, 116, 169, 170,
    171, 172, 173, 174, 175, 176,
    177, 179
Gass, K. A., 195
Geffkin, G., 132
Gelles, R., 147, 148
Genuchi, M., 89
Georgoudi, M., 94
Gerber, P. J., 143
Germain, R., 148
Gessaroli, M. E., 195
Gibbs, J., 111
Giblin, N. J., 63

Gibson, M. A., 120, 190
Gilchrist, L. D., 152, 207, 208
Gill, D. L., 89, 90
Gilman, C. J., 34
Ginsberg, K., 19
Ginter, M., 211
Glenn, H. S., 15
Glidden, L. M., 139, 140
Goding, M. J., 115
Gold, Y., 188
Goldberg, S., 132
Goldfried, M. R., 205
Goldman, B. D., 139
Goldring, E. B., 68, 69
Goldstein, A. P., 156, 158, 161
Goodlad, J., 11
Gordon, H. W., 98
Gore, S., 100, 198
Gorgiulo, R. M., 188
Gottesman, I. I., 179
Gottfredson, D. C., 160
Gottfredson, G. D., 160
Gottlieb, B. H., 203, 208
Gould, D., 87, 88, 89, 90
Gowen, J. W., 139
Graden, J. L., 154
Grannis, J. C., 32
Greenberg, M. T., 116, 135
Greendorfer, S. L., 90
Greenwood, G., 188
Greer, J. L., 21
Griffin, L., 143, 194
Groff, T. R., 98
Gross, J. B., 89
Grotevant, H. D., 139
Guare, J. C., 208
Gunnar, M. R., 48

H

Haack, J., 132
Hackfort, D., 87
Hall, A., 179
Halpern, R., 209
Ham, M., 102

Hamberg, B. A., 125
Hampton, R. L., 153
Hanna, J. L., 80, 81, 82
Hannah, M. E., 133
Hardy, L., 87, 88
Harlan, J. P., 157
Harootunian, B., 156
Harris, A. M., 79
Harris, L., 185
Harris, S. L., 132
Harris, V. S., 139
Hart, D., 85, 148
Harter, S., 15
Hartup, W. W., 48, 105, 118
Hauch, C., 133, 138
Hausner, C., 85
Heath, A., 179
Hedin, D., 8
Heft, H., 83
Helson, H., 65
Hendren, R. L., 61, 95
Hepburn, J. R., 158
Hertz-Lazarowitz, R., 79
Hess, G. A., Jr., 21
Hetherington, E. M., 176
Hetrick, E. S., 124
Hewlett, S., 4
Higgins, E. T., 48
Hightower, A. D., 50, 208
Hill, J. P., 106
Hill, K. D., 140
Hirsch, B. J., 49
Hocutt, A., 145
Hodgkinson, H., 4
Hoffman, M. A., 48
Holland, A. J., 179
Hollon, S. D., 57, 58
Holroyd, J., 140
Holtzman, W. H., 4
Hoover-Dempsey, K. V., 68, 69
Hoppe, C. M., 179
Horn, J., 89
Horne, M., 115
House, J. S., 35, 198, 199, 203, 204
Houston, H., 8

Huba, G. J., 100
Hudd, S. S., 142, 145
Huebner, E. S., 186
Humphrey, J. H., 207
Humphrey, J. N., 207
Hunt, D. E., 197
Hurrelmann, K., 162
Hutton, J. B., 30

I

Imahori, T. T., 121
Intagliata, J., 132
Irwin, C. E., 99
Ivancevich, J. M., 38

J

Jaeger, R. M., 4
Jenkins, J., 79
Jewell, L., 102
Johnson, C. F., 151
Johnson, J., 112
Johnson, J. E., 95
Johnson, S., 34
Johnson, T. C., 148, 149, 150, 153
Johnson-Mattin, N., 139
Jones, J. G., 87, 88, 176
Jung, R. K., 19
Jungeblut, A., 22

K

Kagan, J., 111, 151
Kalker, P., 194
Kalter, N., 209
Kamerman, S. B., 192
Kandel, D. B., 19
Karasek, R., 194
Karph, R. S., 155
Karweit, N. L., 8
Katz, R., 178
Kaufman, K. L., 148
Kazak, A. E., 132, 133, 134, 135, 136, 137, 138, 139

Kearns, D. T., 8
Keenan, V., 136
Keirn, W. C., 116
Keith, T. Z., 84
Kellam, S. G., 176
Kelly, J., 176
Kenderski, C. M., 79
Kendler, K. S., 179
Kennedy, M. M., 18, 19
Kessler, R. C., 35, 112
Kilberg, R. R., 186
Kim, U., 118, 119
King, L., 111
Kinnunen, U., 188
Kirk, W., 198
Kirsch, I. S., 22
Kirst, M. W., 72
Klaber, M., 202
Koch, J. L., 186
Kohn, M. L., 99
Konstantareas, M. M., 134
Kontos, S., 192
Koopman, C., 123
Kostelny, K., 163
Kozol, J., 4
Krajewski, R. J., 40
Kratochwill, T. R., 64
Kremer-Hagon, L., 188
Kroth, R. L., 144
Kruger, L. J., 64
Kruks, G. N., 124
Kubler-Ross, E., 41
Kuepper, J. E., 85
Kuhn, T. S., 220
Kurtz, P., 188
Kyriacou, C., 186, 187, 196

L

Ladd, G. W., 67
Lamar, B., 149
Lampman-Petraitis, C., 101
Lancaster, J. B., 125
Landis, K. R., 203
Lanigan, M. L ., 121

Larson, R., 48, 101, 102
Lawton, M., 87
Lazarowitz, R., 79
Lazarus, R. S., 24, 38, 39, 40, 41, 42,
    43, 44, 45, 51, 59, 118, 119, 186,
    187, 195, 196, 207
Lee, L. A., 39, 98, 186, 187, 188, 194
Leonard, J., 141
Lerner, J. V., 47
Lerner, R. M., 47, 93
Lesowitz, M., 209
Levine, F. M., 85
Levison, H., 132
Levy-Shiff, R., 48
Lewin, K., 47, 197
Lewis, C. E., 113
Lewis, M. A., 113
Lewko, J. H., 87
Leyser, Y., 142
Lezotte, L. W., 8
Lightfoot, S. L., 25
Limber, S., 151
Lipton, M., 78
Litt, M. D., 188, 196
Livson, N., 99
Lobato, D., 133
Lockheed, M. E., 79
Lofgren, H., 186
Lotyczewski, B. S., 50
London, P., 11
Long, B. C., 195
Long, J. V. F., 172
Longo, D. C., 132
Lorion, R. P., 202
Losel, F., 162
Lowenbraun, S., 142
Luftig, R. L., 117
Lutz, C. A., 101
Lynch, M. D., 188
Lyon, G. A., 134
Lyon, S. R., 134

M

Maccoby, E. E., 49, 95

Madden, N. A., 8
Madge, S., 142
Madhwa, R. A., 98
Magnusson, D., 105
Mahon, N. E., 206
Makinen, R., 188
Marcelissen, F. H. G., 198
Margolick, D., 186
Margolis, H., 68, 143, 144
Marshall, J., 220
Martens, R., 87, 88, 89, 90
Martin, A. D., 90, 124, 179
Marvin, R. S., 132, 133, 137
Mary, N. L., 134
Masten, A. S., 24, 168, 170, 171, 172
Mateo, S., 90
Matteson, M. T., 38, 39, 40
Maughan, B., 173
Maxwell, J. S., 152
May, R., 39
Mazur, P. J., 188
McAdoo, H., 112
McBride, A. B., 192
McCartney, K., 49, 192
McCluskey, K., 48
McCrae, R. R., 196
McCubbin, H. I., 34, 134, 137
McCubbin, M. A., 137
McDermott, J., 158, 159
McDowell, C. P., 157
McElroy, M. A., 89
McFadden, H., 186, 187, 198
McGrew, K. C., 34
McGuffin, P., 178
McHale, S. M., 132, 139
McIntyre, R. M., 142
McKinney, B., 135
McLean, M., 143
McManus, J. L., 209
McNett, S. C., 198
McRoy, R. G., 139
Medeiros, D. C., 207
Meeks, S., 188
Meichenbaum, D., 64
Melton, G. B., 151

Menaghan, E., 195
Mensch, B. S., 19
Meredith, W. H., 152
Metz, J. R., 118
Metzger, J., 139
Meyers, D. E., 19, 116, 136, 142
Midlarsky, E., 133
Miller, W. H., 79, 115, 142, 143, 186, 194
Million, M. E., 30
Mills, R. C., 14, 15
Milne, A. M., 19
Minde, T., 118
Mink, I. T., 116
Minnes, P. M., 135, 139
Minuchin, P., 48
Mirowsky, J., 113, 192
Mitchell, R. E., 195
Mize, J., 67
Mok, D., 118
Molaison, V. A., 135
Monti, D. J., 158
Mont-Reynaud, R., 31
Moos, R., 206
Moos, R. H., 42, 195, 198
Moracco, J. C., 40, 186, 187, 198
Morgan, S. B., 132
Moriarity, A., 51, 168, 174, 176
Morine-Dershimer, G., 79
Morris, P., 98, 132
Mortimore, P., 173
Mullens, J. B., 131, 150
Murphy, L., 51, 168, 174, 176
Murray, R., 179
Mussen, P. H., 93
Myers, H. F., 111

N

Nader, K., 162
Nathan, P. E., 186
Navin, S. L., 25
Needle, R. H., 194, 196
Neff, J., 112
Neighbors, H. W., 112

Nelson, J., 15
Neuchterlein, K. H., 168
Newberger, C. M., 153
Newberger, E. H., 153
Newcomb, M. D., 100, 113
Nezu, A. M., 195
Nicoll, D., 190
Nihira, W. H., 116
Nitz, K., 181
Norcross, J. C., 213
Nottelmann, E. D., 98

O

Oakes, J., 8, 11, 78
Olejnik, S., 188
Olson, L., 185
Orbach, I., 161
Orland, M. E., 19
Orlandi, M. A., 207
Otto, W., 84
Ousten, J., 173
Overton, W. F., 93
O'Connor, S., 149
O'Grady, D., 118
O'Leary, S. G., 84
O'Malley, P., 11, 27
O'Neill, B., 155

P

Pahl, J., 134, 135
Paikoff, R. L., 107
Paine, W. S., 198
Palfrey, J. S., 132, 133, 134, 142
Palleja, J., 124
Parkay, F. W., 188, 196
Parker, T., 139
Parsons, J. E., 48
Paschal, R. A., 84
Passer, M. W., 89, 91
Patterson, J. M., 34
Payzant, T. W., 3
Pearlin, L., 42, 112, 209
Pedro-Carroll, J. L., 208, 209

Perkin, F., 99
Perry, A., 138
Peters, D. L., 192
Peterson, A. C., 98, 99
Peterson, P., 137
Peterson, L., 155
Peterson, R. A., 135
Pfost, K. S., 196
Phelps, E., 49
Phillips, B. N., 3, 27, 28, 39, 78, 186,
    187, 188, 192, 194
Piccigallo, P. R., 7
Pickar, J., 209
Pines, A., 195
Pitcher, G. D., 78
Plomin, R., 97, 180, 181
Pogrow, S., 19
Pokorni, J. L., 134, 139
Ponti, C. R., 154
Porter, B. J., 207
Posantel-Loro, R., 145
Powell, D. R., 70, 113
Price, R. H., 202
Primavera, J., 115, 211
Prochaska, J. O., 213
Proller, N., 188
Pryor-Brown, L., 50, 113
Pryzwansky, W., 64
Pynoos, R. S., 162

Q

Quine, L., 134, 135

R

Raffaelli, M., 102
Rainey, D. W., 90
Rainey, K. W., 90
Ralph, J. H., 19, 21
Ramirez, R., 85
Ramos-McKay, J., 202
Rapkin, B. D., 49
Raywid, M. A., 8
Rechif, M., 85

Reef, M. J., 105
Reese, H. W., 93
Remafedi, G., 124
Renaut, J., 132
Revenson, T. A., 195, 196
Richards, M. H., 102
Riegel, K. F., 93
Riordan, C., 80
Ritter, P. L., 31
Rizzo, T. A., 79
Roberts, T. G., 30, 90
Rodman, B., 185
Rodrigue, J. R., 132
Rolf, J., 168, 172
Ronan, G. F., 195
Rook, K., 203
Rosario, M., 123
Rose, S. D., 64
Roseman, I. J., 101
Rosenfield, S., 219
Rosenthal, E., 186
Rosnow, R., 94
Ross, C. E., 113, 192
Rotheram-Borus, M. J., 123
Rothlisberg, B. A., 57, 64
Rowe, D. C., 180
Rowley, S., 90
Ruble, D. N., 106
Rudin, D., 30
Russell, D. W., 179, 198, 199
Rutter, M., 11, 25, 111, 169, 170, 173, 174, 175, 176, 177, 179, 211
Ryan, N. M., 206, 207

S

Saegert, S., 83
Salganik, L., 21
Salhani, L., 87
Samelson, M., 105
Sameroff, A. J., 111, 169
Sandler, H. M., 149
Sandoval, J., 208
Sarason, S. B., 15, 68, 202
Satterfield, J. H., 179

Scanlon, T. K., 89
Scarr, S., 49, 97, 192
Schaefer, M., 209
Scheffer, M. W., 160
Scheier, M. F., 119
Scheinfeld, D., 163
Schell, A. M., 179
Scherer, J. E., 156
Scherer, K. R., 101
Schilling, R. F., 124, 152
Schinke, S. P., 124, 152, 207, 208
Schneider, S. G., 124
Schneider-Rosen, K., 94, 95
Schoggen, P., 75, 76
Schoiock, G., 85
Schooler, C., 42
Schorr, L., 72
Schulte, A., 64
Sears, S. J., 25
Seeley, D. S., 70
Seifer, R., 111, 169
Seligman, M., 133, 134, 135, 136, 137
Selye, H., 37, 38
Serxner, S., 35
Shapiro, A., 48, 68
Shermis, M. D., 30
Sherrod, K. B., 149
Showers, J., 151
Shure, M. B., 205, 207
Siegel, J. M., 113
Silva, J. M., III, 86
Silverberg, S. B., 99, 103
Simmons, R. G., 48, 49, 105, 107, 132
Simon, J. A., 88
Singer, J. E., 37, 87, 132, 139, 195
Siperstein, G. N., 115, 118
Sivo, P., 218
Slavin, R. E., 8, 19, 49, 78, 79
Sloman, L., 134
Small, M. W., 135
Smalley, S. L., 179
Smetana, J. G., 106
Smith, M. L., 142, 168, 169, 170, 172, 173, 174, 175, 177, 189
Spady, W. G., 220

Sparling, J., 139
Spence, M. A., 179
Spielberger, C. D., 87
Spivak, G., 205, 207
Spreeman, J., 89
Spurlock, J., 121, 122
Srebnik, D. S., 202
Stanton, H. E., 207
Staples, R., 121
Stein, R. C., 142
Steinberg, L., 31, 99, 103
Steinmetz, S. K., 147
Stevens, J. J., 196
Stevenson, D. L., 49
Stimson, J., 156
Stoneman, Z., 142
Strattin, R., 105
Straus, M. A., 147, 148, 150
Strayhorn, J. M., 212
Suarez-Orozco, M. M., 119
Suelzle, M., 136
Suls, J., 41
Sutcliffe, J., 186, 187
Svendsen, R., 194
Sze, W., 149

T

Tellegen, A., 171, 172
Tellenback, S., 186, 187
Tharinger, D. J., 153
Thelen, E., 48
Theorell, T., 194
Thomas, A., 61
Thompson, D. E., 83
Thoreson, R. W., 186
Tienari, P., 179
Tortu, S., 208
Trimble, J. E., 207
Truch, S., 194
Trute, B., 133, 138
Tung, R. L., 186
Turk, D. C., 188, 196
Turk, L. M., 188
Turnbull, A. P., 135, 139, 141, 142,
143, 144
Turnbull, H. R., 135, 139, 142, 143,
144
Turner, R. J., 35, 176

U

Ubriaco, M., 217
Udry, J. R., 98
Umberson, D., 203
Upshur, C. C., 138, 139
Ushpiz, V., 48

V

Vadasy, P. F., 135
Vaillant, G. E., 172
Vealey, R. S., 87
Veltzen, D. V., 198
Vietze, P. M., 149

W

Waggoner, K., 143
Wagner, B. M., 32, 63, 95
Walberg, H. J., 84
Walker, C. E., 30, 132, 148
Wallerstein, J. S., 116, 162, 176
Walsh, W. M., 63
Walter, G., 198
Warren, M. P., 104, 105
Wasik, B. A., 8
Wayment, H. A., 114, 116, 117, 118
Weade, R., 79
Webb, N. M., 79
Weber, G., 139
Weber, J., 142
Weinberg, R. S., 86, 89
Weinstein, T., 84
Weintraub, M., 112, 168
Weiss, R. S., 199
Weissberg, R., 205, 218
Welch, I. D., 207
Werner, E. E., 168, 169, 170, 172, 173,
174, 175, 177

Whitmore, J. K., 122
Widom, C. S., 148
Wiegerink, R., 145
Wikler, L., 132, 137
Wilgosh, L., 143
Wills, T. A., 198
Wilson, H., 34, 175, 208
Wilton, K., 132
Winnick, B. M., 140
Winnubst, J. A. M., 198
Wise, A. E., 7
Wise, P. S., 186
Witt, J. C., 142, 143
Witte, J. F., 8
Wolf, B., 112
Wolff, C. J., 198
Wood, T. A., 133, 134, 136
Woody, J. D., 141
Woody, R. H., 141
Worsham, M. E., 78

Wynne, L. C., 176

Y

Yao, E. L., 122
Yarcheski, A., 206
Yeager, M., 141

Z

Zaharna, R. S., 121
Zahaykevich, M., 106
Zakin, D. F., 105
Zayas, L. H., 124
Zetlin, A., 114, 116, 117, 118
Zins, J. E., 154, 215
Zuniga, J., 30
Zurcher, L. A., 139

SUBJECT INDEX

A

Accidents, as form of violence and source of stress, 154-155
Acculturative stress
  appropriate intervention, 121
  moderating variables, 121
  nature of and significance for school achievement, 118-121
Adaptation vs. optimization, 56
Adaptational outcomes, nature of and special considerations, 45-52
African-American middle-class families, special stresses, 121-122
Age-graded classrooms, stressors in, 77-79
American values, relation to views of coping, 51-52
Anxiety and burnout vs. stress, 39-40
Appraisal, in relation to stress and coping, 24
Appraisals, threat vs. challenge, 118
Approaches to the amelioration of teacher stress, 196-199
Asian-American families, special stresses, 122-123
Assaults on teachers, as source of stress, 156
Assessment of stress of
  molar environmental events, 34-35
  parents and families, 34
  students, 30-33
  teachers and other professionals, 185-186
At-risk students
  identification of, 19-23
  problems in identification, 22-23
  stressors as at-risk factors, 23-24

B

Basic approaches to stress, 37-38
Behavioral-genetic analyses, of individual differences in stress and coping, 181

C

Chandler's diagnostic-intervention model, 62-63
Child abuse
  as cause of stress, 148-149
  correlates and consequences, 148

Cognitive appraisal processes, in relation to stress and coping, 42-43
Collegial and interactive professional relationships, role in planning stress intervention, 215-216
Community social services systems, problems and implications for stress intervention, 71-72
Competence-building vs. pathology-fighting intervention approaches, 212-213
Competitive youth sports, situational and personal factors contributing to stress, 88-90
Coping
    and emotion, 44-45
    as adjustment, 40-41
    as mastery of environment, 51-52
    Lazarus' theory, 42-44
    methods and strategies, 40-42, 60-61
    stages, 41
    taxonomies, 41-42
Coping strategies, of teachers, 195-196
Coping styles, of handicapped children and adolescents, 117
Coupling, in study of stress in relation to study of behavior settings, 75-77
Culture, as both cause and moderator of stress, 113
"Culture of detracking," role in reforming age-graded classrooms, 78

D

Daily experiences, effects on negative emotions, 102-104
Dangerous neighborhoods
    as sources of stress, 161-162
    implications for long-term development and school intervention, 162-164
Defense mechanisms, as attempts to

manage stress, 60-61
Demographic factors, as influences on stress, 111-113
Desegregated schools, stressors in, 80-82
Designing interventions, from a shared vs. nonshared environment perspective, 97-98
Developmental contextual framework, in study of developmental aspects of stress, 94-95
Developmental ecology, as perspective on stress, 75-77
Developmental stages and tasks, source of core stress problems, 94-95
Developmental trajectories, 96
Diverse approaches to stress prevention and intervention, some examples and related issues and problems, 201-215

E

"Educational malls," designing schools as hubs for human service delivery, 72-73
Ethnic-specific sources of stress, 113
Extra-curricular activities, stressors in competitive youth sports, 86-91

F

Families with handicapped children and adolescents
    early intervention programs, 136
    role of social support, 137-139
Family stress, sources of stress in families with handicapped children and adolescents, 131-136
Family support centers in schools, 50-51
Focusing interventions on only one aspect of the stress process, strengths and weaknesses,

205-207
Functions of coping, 52

G

Gay youth, special stresses,
123-124
Gender, as factor in differences in
stress, 113
General intervention knowledge and
skills, 63-65
"Goodness of fit" between school
environment and developmental
needs, as source of stress,
107-108
"Goodness of fit" paradigm, 47
Guided participation, an apprentice
model of stress intervention,
183

H

Helson's adaptation level theory, role
of baseline conditions in stress,
65
Hollon and Beck intervention classification system, 57-58
Homework, school-family stress and
related intervention programs,
84-86

I

Impact of adopted handicapped children on stress in families,
139-140
Intentional behavior change, a model
of stress intervention,
213-215
Interrelatedness of interventions for
stress and for emotional problems, 65
Intervention programs, general low
quality, 202-203
Interventions designed to strengthen

only individual skills and competencies, limitations of, 204-205

L

Life events, effects on mental health
and school achievement problems,
100-107, 122-124, 174-175
Life events, importance in assessment
of stress, 31-35

M

Mastery and competence, in relation to
stress, 24-25
Mastery of environment, as coping
ideal, 51-52
Microintervention vs. macrointerven-
tion, 66-68
Minisettings in classrooms, as differentiated sources of stress, 78-79
Mobilizing social support programs,
some of the problems,
208-212
Models of helping and coping, nature
of student rsponsibility for the
problem and solution, 50-57
Models of the relationship between
stress and protective factors,
171
Motivation, as component of theories
of stress and emotion, 44-45
Multidisciplinary-ecological approaches to stress intervention, an
exemplary model, 216-217
Multiple general approaches to stress
intervention, 63-68

N

Niche-picking, and the study of stress,
49
Nonshared family environment influences on stress, 97-98

O

Overprivileged children and adolescents, special stresses and related school interventions, 126-128

P

Paradigm
nature of, 219-220
outcome-based education, 220-221
Parent involvement in schools, factors affecting it, 68-71
Parent involvement in special education, stress related to, 140-145
Parental stress, as cause of child abuse, 150-151
Parents who abuse their children, predispositional factors, 148-149
Partnerships between schools and social service agencies, role in stress intervention programs, 71-73
Peer stress of handicapped students, 116-117
Person-environment interaction and coping process, implications for intervention, 59-60
Physical and sexual abuse of children and adolescents,
prevention and intervention efforts, 152-154
stress related to, 147-148
Physically dense environments, stressors in, 82-84
Premises, philosophical views, and a transactional perspective on stress intervention, 55-57, 59-60
Psychopathologies in children and adolescents
implications for stress prevention and intervention, 182-184
importance of nonshared

environmental influences, 180-181
role of stressful events and genetic factors, 178-179
Puberty
and disruptive effects of school transitions, 49
special stresses associated with, 98-100

R

Reciprocal influence, role in planning stress interventions, 60
Resource for dealing with stress in handicapped students, 117-118
Role of coping styles, in stress and stress interventions, 60-62

S

School behavior settings, viewed from a developmental ecological perspective, 75-77
School failure, alternate ways to frame the problem, 5
School-family relationships
in stress intervention, 68-71
shift in how they are conceptualized, 70-71
School reform
national commissions and study groups reports, 5-7
nature of past school reform, 7-9
role of stress-related problems in future school reform, 10-14
school reform and optimal student development, 14-15
shift to an outcome-based education paradigm, 220-221
School stress of handicapped students, 114-115
Schools, purpose of

narrowed vision, 2-3
views that ask more, 3-4
Self-efficacy, Bandura's theory, 43, 190
Social problem solving training, limitations, 207-208
Social support,
  and stress in handicapped children and adolescents, 118
  buffering effects 137-138
  in families with handicapped children, 137-139
  role of professionals in, 139
Stress
  and emotion, 44-45
  basic approaches and definitions, 37-39
  Lazarus' theory, 42-44
Stress associated with being identified as an abused child or adolescent, 151-152
Stress, a dynamic entity, 62-63
Stress, general sources, 45-47
Stress "inoculation," 184
Stress interventions in the schools, some general considerations, 55-73
Stress problems of children of "fast-track" parents, and compensating school intervention strategies, 127-128
Stress problems of handicapped children and adolescents, in schools and families and with peers, 113-117
Stress resilience, positive impact of teachers, 177
Stressful impact of handicapped children and adolescents on their families, 131-133
Stressfulness of the transition to adolescence, 104-107
Student-environment optimization, 56
Symptoms of stress, general, 13

T

Targeting students with stress-related problems for special services
  school-related stressors, 25-30
  stress as a risk factor, 17-25
Teacher stress
  consequences of, 194-195
  meaning of, 186-187
  sources of, 187-193
Teenage mothers, special stresses, 124-126
Teenage pregnancy, prevention as highest priority, 125-126
Transaction and process in stress, implications for intervention, 56-60

U

Unemployment and poverty of parents, impact on stress of school-aged children and adolescents, 50-51
Utilizing interpersonal resources in stress intervention, issues in, 203-204

V

Violence in schools
  nature of, 155-157
  prevention and intervention efforts, 159-161
  stress related to, 157-159
"Vulnerable but invincible" children and adolescents
  competence, invulnerability, resiliency, and protective factors, 168-171
  guided participation and other

intervention strategies,
182-184
past neglect by researchers,
167-168
role of the school, 176-177
social and family influence on,
171-176
Vulnerability, intraindividual
and interindividual factors,
59-60

W

Working within constraints of institutional "regularities," 201-202

Y

Young adolescents and children, as
child molesters, 149